BISON
BOOKS

W9-APM-635

Moving Out

A Nebraska Woman's Life

Polly Spence

Edited and with an afterword by
Karl Spence Richardson

University of Nebraska Press
Lincoln and London

Illustrations are courtesy of Karl Spence Richardson.
© 2002 by the Board of Regents of the University of Nebraska
All rights reserved
Manufactured in the United States of America
♾
Library of Congress Cataloging-in-Publication Data
Spence, Polly, 1914–1998
Moving out : a Nebraska woman's life / Polly Spence ;
edited and with an afterword by Karl Spence Richardson.
   p. cm.—(Women in the West)
ISBN 0-8032-9297-X (pbk. : alk. paper)
1. Spence, Polly, 1814–1998.   2. Working class women—Nebraska—Biography.   3. Rural women—
Nebraska—Biography.   4. Country life—Nebraska.   5. Nebraska—Social life and customs.
6. Nebraska—Biography.   I. Richardson, Karl Spence.
II. Title.   III. Series.
CT275.S6226 A3 2002
978.2'033'092—dc21
2002003119

Contents

Illustrations

Acknowledgments

I wish to express my sincere thanks to the University of Nebraska Press, whose staff has been very helpful. Elizabeth Gratch, the copyeditor for the manuscript, edited it with sympathy and professionalism. Dr. Larry Skogen, a historian I met when I taught Japanese at the Air Force Academy, became a friend. His editing suggestions and encouragement have been invaluable. *Nebraskaland* magazine and its editor at the time, Don Cunningham, kindly gave permission to publish material that previously had been published there. Finally, my wife, Sharon, has put in many hours improving my editing, suggesting changes, and supporting the project.

Moving Out

CHAPTER ONE

In the early day, as Nebraskans say, disaster came in many forms to the pioneer woman. There were the hailstorms and the hunger, the grasshopper plagues and the fear of Indians, and drought, disease, and death.

Even before telephone lines were strung on fence posts, word somehow got around, and people reached out to one another with help and comfort. The easiest catastrophes to handle were those that required action, immediate and almost instinctive. When grasshoppers swarmed overhead in a great black cloud, everyone grabbed a shovel or a gunnysack and ran out and beat and flailed at the insects until they could beat and flail no more. It didn't kill enough grasshoppers to make a difference, but the effort eased the anger and the pain. What was left behind were the stories of fields laid bare in thirty minutes, of fence posts and hoe handles eaten away so thin that they broke at the first strain.

Drought was harder to bear. There's no excitement—no awe of nature's magnificent malevolence—only day following hot, glassy day. Hope would grow each afternoon as clouds built up in the west but then withered and wasted away like the crop as the thunder rumbled farther and farther away. A few drops of rain—no more—spattered in the dust.

But the calamity that killed more women than any of these—killed them through suicide or madness—was loneliness. Nebraska's Mari Sandoz wrote that it was the loneliness and the wind that broke so many women in pioneer days. She wrote of the kind of loneliness that comes from having no neighbors nearby and from living weeks and sometimes months without seeing anyone but the husband and the children. But automobiles and roads and telephones wiped out that kind of isolation long ago, even in ranch country, and still people die of loneliness, there and everywhere. Men and women die all around us, and the death certificates say acute alcoholism, or coronary occlusion, or internal injuries sustained in an accident. They never say loneliness. They never mention the ghastliest death of all—the death that is the leaking away of life without love or warmth or closeness to another human being.

It's the kind of death that comes not because people choose to die, but because they choose not to live. It's being somehow tied to someone after the sense of warmth and closeness is gone. It's sitting before the TV every evening, five feet from someone you've loved, reading a bit, working the puzzle a bit, even watching the picture a bit, falling asleep and getting a crick in the neck, and wanting to go to bed but postponing it because it might mean the loveless coupling you've come to loathe. It's the kind of loneliness that brought me, at age fifty-six, to make the final break, to leave home and husband and everything familiar.

I don't know when the loneliness started. It was always there, as long as I can remember. It's only been during the last few years, since I've been living alone, that loneliness hasn't set the flavor and texture of my life. There were many years when it was held at bay—the first years of marriage, the years when the children were little, the years after the boys were grown and gone and I'd left, meaning to stay, but coming back—coming back and finding it there waiting for me, always waiting.

CHAPTER TWO

Almost as soon as Levi and I got married, in 1929, I got fat, the surest indicator there is that things are not well with me. My weight went up and down but mostly up. I've lost enough weight in my life to equal a half-dozen good-sized women.

And I began to have migraine headaches. I had a dream too, a hideous dream of walking along a sort of scaffolding in an immense, loftlike building, scared to death of falling. I'd wake up in a cold sweat.

The uneasiness may have started from a message my mother gave me early in my life. She loved me, I know that, but in our daily personal contacts she couldn't stand me. I remember her saying, many times, "When you were born you were just what we wanted . . . ," and she never finished the sentence; she just shook her head. She didn't have to finish it. I knew what she meant: "and just see how you turned out."

There was so much antipathy between us that I never knew whether my views came from independent thinking or from an automatic reflex to counter whatever her opinion happened to be. If she said black, I'd say white. Still, I wanted her approval, and I never got it, not until she was feeble from Parkinson's disease; then she said approving things to me and about me, and it scared me half to death. I missed the rigidity I'd grown used to, the high moral tone. I didn't know how to handle my mother's approval, which to me was a sure sign she was over the hill.

Being my mother's daughter wasn't easy. I suppose it wasn't easy being her son either, but it was difficult in a different way.

My brothers, simply by coming up in the big lottery with gonads, had something going for them which women—in my day at least—had to struggle for and still may never achieve: a sense of identity. The lack of identity wasn't imposed on me by my mother; it was just there, for me, for her, for every female. It's one of those givens so deep in the fiber of human society—so vast, so constraining—that nobody can separate it out. We don't even know it's there. There wasn't a beginning—at least anything I can pinpoint—to my feeling that I lacked a real identity. It may be that there's no end.

Mother reinforced the lack, of course, every time she said, "Don't you see, what you do reflects on me?" I sneered openly at her bland assumption that I might want to please her by meeting her standards. Yet even my acts of defiance were designed to get her notice, if only the martyrish disappointment I despised. If I hadn't cared, I wouldn't have bothered. I ended up defining myself by her frustration and anger. It was all I could get from her without caving in to what she wanted me to be.

I wish I were as sure of anything as my mother was of almost everything. She knew precisely how people should behave, and the idea that she might be in error no more crossed her mind than the possibility that the sun would rise in the west. It never occurred to her that children had feelings, and, if someone had told her that they do, she would have found the assumption behind the question, as well as the question itself, intolerably impertinent.

I used to lie in bed and bite the sheet in rage, wishing my mother dead and in hell. I despised her intellectually and felt vastly superior to her. I sneered openly at the poetry of Edgar A. Guest, the compositions of Carrie Jacobs Bond, and the politics of William Jennings Bryan, all idols of Mother's, and got slapped across the mouth for my pains. I derided the photograph, a fad of the time, in which Mother had posed as Madonna. She held her baby—my older brother Loris—with a filmy white scarf enfolding both of them. I jeered at a pillow cover she'd made of net and stuffed with my dad's crumpled love letters and chuckled as I showed it to my friends. I was appalled when she said with a laugh, as she did from time to time, that her opinions on politics depended on what she'd read last. I'd absorbed my dad's preoccupation with politics like a sponge.

Yet there were things I admired about my mother, even then. And in retrospect they seem even more remarkable.

There was always room in her house for the younger sister of a friend of mine, plagued and harassed by her irascible, unreasonable father, to stay as long as she liked. Company was always welcome, for meals or a bed. A good meal would be whipped up in no time from what had seemed a barren cupboard. It never was bare, though; we always had plenty to eat, and my friends and I were always free to make ghastly messes in the kitchen—candy or cookies or whatever we pleased.

Tramps came to our door and asked for food, and Mother readily gave it to them. A pretense was made that the chicken house would be cleaned or wood split, and often enough after the food was eaten the boy or man would vanish, but the next tramp would never be turned away hungry. It was vain for other, thriftier housewives to say, "Those no-goods have your house marked. Don't you know they carry a piece of chalk and leave a signal for the next no-account who wants a free meal?" When people were in need, my mother gave freely and gladly. The woman who was so rigid and self-righteous with her own children was never judgmental when someone asked for help.

There was no idea too far-fetched for my mother to seize and put into practice in raising us, so long as it was touted as being about character building. God only knows where some of her ideas came from. I was grown with babies of my own before Mother told me that when I was a baby she'd bathe me in the sink, and at the end she'd take a pitcher of ice water, made ready for the purpose, and pour it over my head. She'd heard somewhere that doing so built character.

"You'd just gasp and gasp!" she said, laughing.

The hatred that existed between my mother and me must have been vital to both of us because so long as my mother lived and had her wits, neither of us ever allowed it to flag. It's a strange and bitter thing to cherish, and yet we cherished it and fed it. In the last few years I've said, once or twice, that I no longer hate my mother because she's no longer important to me, but that's not true. It's the hatred that's no longer important. For my mother not to be important to me would be a denial of all I am and all that brought me to it. My mother carried me for nine months; I'll carry her all my life.

CHAPTER THREE

My rebellions may have seemed all too visible on the surface, but their roots were deep. I fought and shrieked and howled against the things I was made to do, yet in the end I did them. One of my mother's long suits was making me apologize to people. This, she was convinced, was an act of character building. Often I was forced to apologize to somebody I loathed and despised, and sometimes it was for something I hadn't done. Yet I did it. I went, livid with suppressed rage, to people who had lied about me, and I apologized for doing what I had not done.

When I was about seven, Mother gave me a pamphlet intended to explain how babies were born, and she tenderly told me that we were going to have a Dear Little Baby in the spring. At that very moment, she said, she was carrying that Dear Little Baby near her heart. The pamphlet was a "new approach" to the questions children asked and was intended, of course, to forestall the awkward ones. In my case it raised several that hadn't occurred to me before. There were a good many words, and some diagrams, about the way the bee behaves with the blossom; there was a rather clinical discussion, no diagrams, about human sexual equipment, which concluded with the statement that the penis is introduced into the vagina and thus the seed is planted.

"Introduced? How do you do that?" I wondered. This obfuscatory passage led me to wonder if the whole proceeding was rather more formal than I might have supposed from the bumpings and rustlings I had heard from my parents' room as I snuggled in bed. I asked Mother about it, and she told me that all these things would become clear to me as I grew up. In the meantime we had our secret: the Dear Little Baby who would be born in the spring. I was to discuss it with no one.

The gestation period in the human animal is so long and tedious that I forgot all about the Dear Little Baby until months later, when one day I came home from school and learned that Mrs. Bush, an old woman living down the street, had told somebody, who had told Mother, that she had overheard me telling my friends that we were going to have a baby.

"I did not," I said. "I haven't told anybody, not even Erma. Old Lady Bush is a liar," I said. "I did not, did not, did not."

It was useless. Although my mother knew I did not lie, I had to go to old Mrs. Bush and apologize. My cheeks burning and my guts seething with rage, I apologized for doing what I had not done. I then went home and into my parents' room, where I took the cotton lace curtains in my two hands and ripped them apart in scores of places. As they hung at the windows, it was hardly noticeable, but later Mother said, with surprise, "Why, these curtains have gone all to pieces. The sun must have rotted them."

Mother not only believed in organized good works, she organized and performed them. If the dinner dishes were on the table unwashed when I got home from school, and they usually were, I knew she was playing the piano for a funeral or a club meeting. I thought longingly of the Fruhling house, where Pauline, Erma's mother, always washed the dishes promptly after every meal and made the beds as soon as everyone had left in the morning and where, when Erma and I got there after school, everything was orderly and all the window shades were drawn to precisely the same level.

Mother started playing the piano for church and for every public and club function in town and the surrounding area while she was a student at the Franklin Academy. The academy was a small Congregational Church preparatory school with a superior music department, where Mother took piano lessons from Professor Aller. She loved playing piano, never said no, and didn't expect nor was ever offered payment.

Mother had little raw musical talent; she never did figure out what jazz was. Still, she studied hard and learned well. She had wanted to be a music teacher ever since she could remember. When she enrolled at the Franklin Academy, she had already taught piano lessons for three years, and people knew she was competent. Being a student at the academy only enhanced her reputation, and she ended up teaching piano all of her life.

Nothing was more natural to me than the sound of somebody laboring over scales or sonatinas or struggling with "Simple Aveu" or "Turkish Dance." There were occasional recitals at which each student had to play a piece; most of them performed well. Mother's only failures as a piano teacher were her own children. We all sang and read music, and the boys played instruments, but none of us played the piano. My sessions with Mother were so painful for both of us that she sent me to learn from a woman I liked but I failed to learn to play from her too.

Mother was a Camp Fire Girls guardian, a member of the Ladies Circle of the Congregational Church, of the Daughters of the American Revolution (DAR), and a charter member of Chapter BG, PEO. The meaning of the abbreviation PEO was never divulged to nonmembers. I was given to understand that the women who were lucky enough to have been invited to become PEOs realized that this honor had been bestowed upon them because of their worthiness. They were ladylike before being invited, and, if anything, more ladylike afterwards. They wore small star-shaped gold pins inscribed *PEO* on their bosoms; they held meetings cloaked in inviolable secrecy, and they awarded sufficiently ladylike high school girls scholarships to a small women's college in Missouri which they sponsored. They referred to themselves as "the sacred sisterhood," a phrase I found irresistibly funny. The ladies, however, were deadly serious about it, as I discovered when I was about eleven.

Mother and one of her sister PEOs were talking and didn't hear me come in from school. They were discussing Lois Cyr's having been "blackballed." That was a word I didn't know, and when the woman left I asked Mother about it. First she rebuked me for asking questions about something sacrosanct. Then, when I persisted in demanding to know what *blackballed* meant, Mother told me that someone, no one knew who, had voted in the club's secret ballot against inviting Lois to become a PEO.

"But why?" I shouted, outraged that anyone should consider Lois not good enough for anything. "Why? Why? Why?" Lois was one of the nicest people I knew. She was never too busy to talk to a kid, and she had once rowed Erma Fruhling and me out to a little island in the river at dawn to watch birds and other wild things, and we'd cooked breakfast over a campfire and talked.

The Cyrs were notably intellectual, and all the Cyr children had graduated from college. Mr. and Mrs. Cyr were deacon and deaconess in our church. The family was considered "odd," but I didn't know why. Lois was in her thirties and had not married, but I didn't see why that made her family odd.

I didn't get an answer to my why. Mother told me in her loftiest tone, which I loathed, that doubtless one of the PEO ladies had her own good reason.

"But how will Lois feel when she finds out she's been turned down?" I wailed.

"Oh, she'll never be told," Mother said. "No one will ever mention it."

"She'll have to have an answer, won't she?" I asked.

"Oh no," Mother said. "She'll never know her name came up."

I was stunned. "You mean, she didn't ask to be a PEO and you voted on her and turned her down anyway?"

"*I* didn't turn her down," Mother said firmly. "Someone else did and for a good reason, I'm sure. And now we'll talk about something good to eat."

This was my mother's stock reply when she didn't want to talk about something: That's enough now; we'll talk about something else. Let's talk about something good to eat. This was almost more infuriating than the back of the hand I frequently got across the face, and the only recourse I had was to fantasize about the torture I'd inflict on her if I could and about my plans to run away.

I'm an old woman now, but when I think of those women's effrontery I still shudder. A gaggle of overfed provincial housewives took the name of a decent, intelligent woman they all knew and discussed her with a view to her worthiness to be one of them. An unidentified somebody decided she wouldn't do. No reason was given, and nobody protested. No doubt they drank their tea and ate their cake and went home feeling complacent.

Along with her membership in the PEO, Mother gravitated naturally to being a Camp Fire Girl guardian. This was a "good work" that contributed to character building in girls. She began when she was a young married woman with a group of girls not many years younger than she was.

The Camp Fire Girls idea was a strange mishmash of notions about the American Indian. The girls and their guardians affected long braids and robes made of heavy khaki cloth, which were supposed to resemble Indian robes. As the girls committed certain deeds considered to be worthy, they were awarded wooden beads of various colors and shapes as tokens of achievement. Those who were really earnest about improving themselves acquired great numbers of these honor beads, which they sewed to their robes or wore in strings around their necks.

There was a summer camp for Camp Fire Girls on the Blue River, and groups from Nebraska and Iowa gathered there for a week or two in July and engaged in supervised boating and swimming and crafts. They stayed in cabins and tents and ate in a communal dining room. Each evening everyone gathered for a "council," with a real campfire, inspirational talks by counselors, and singing.

I was taken to these camps from the time I was four or five, and I tagged along after the girls, swimming when they swam, boating when they boated, and messing around with paste and birch bark in crafts class. The campers wore voluminous black sateen bloomers fastened well below the knee, black lisle stockings, and high-topped canvas basketball shoes. I thought some of them, like Hallie Campbell, were beautiful and dashing, with their hair in ratted buns over their ears and their talk of boys. Others, like Madge Morris and Nellie Townsend, were my friends, and I was comfortable with them.

As I got on toward the magic age (eleven, I think), it became plain that I was going to be a Camp Fire Girl. I'd been in on meetings and activities for as long as I could remember, and it was old stuff to me. I made a few feints at wriggling out of it, but they were useless. "Of course," said Mother, "you will be a Camp Fire Girl." It would reflect on her if I did not.

I became a Camp Fire Girl but not a good one. I earned very few beads, and, when I got my khaki Indian robe, I said, "I'm not going to wear that baggy thing; it looks like a gunnysack." I took it to the sewing machine, made curving seams at both sides, and cut off the excess material.

CHAPTER FOUR

My Dad was love, warmth, joy, and comfort. He was an intense, high-spirited, deeply romantic man. In a studio photograph taken about 1907, he was a slim, handsome young dude in a Panama suit. His eyes were blazing blue, his hair raven black, shiny, and abundant. Black curly hair grew on his hands and arms; it grew on his legs and back and chest, a fine pelt we saw only in the summertime when we went swimming.

Some psychologists say every little girl is in love with her father. I haven't been a little girl for decades, and I'm still in love with mine. I knew my mother loved me; it's one's duty to love one's child, and Mother never shirked her duty. But, besides loving me, Dad also thought I was great; I could see it in his bright blue eyes. His love was never tempered with "Yes, but—." He punished me, sometimes severely, but he never humiliated me.

Dad was not only warm; he was impulsive, generous, improvident, idealistic, and impressionable. He was never circumspect; he had no lukewarm opinions. Anything he cared about he cared about a lot. And he cared about me.

Being Irish came from both of my parents; being proud of it came from Dad. Both my parents' families had emigrated from County Cork, Dad's a generation earlier than Mother's. Dad was delighted with everything imaginative and poetic and absurd in the Irish; he sang Irish songs and told Irish stories he'd heard from his mother. A green pennant appliquéd in silk and embroidered with a harp and "ERIN GO BRAGH" hung in our living room. I was incredulous at learning that employment notices in the great eastern cities in the nineteenth and early twentieth centuries had often included the line "NO IRISH NEED APPLY."

The Dohers, my mother's family, were just as Irish as the Spences, the McBrides, and the Cullens; they just didn't feel the same way about it. The *ty* was dropped from *Doherty* upon the family's arrival in America, and to this day my relatives who bear the name insist that it be pronounced *Doo-er*, not *Doe-er*. The name change could hardly have been Michael Doher's idea; by the time he came to Franklin County, Nebraska, he was a raffish old man with a big thirst and a second wife who smoked a clay pipe, hardly a refined fellow. It must have come from his first wife, my great-grandmother, who may also have something to do with my mother's determination to be genteel.

Michael Doherty brought his family to Nebraska Territory in 1857, ten years before statehood was achieved. On the death of his first wife, he moved the children—Bridget, Steve, and Sarah—to Franklin County to live on land he had homesteaded. Bridget married Henderson Murray; Sarah, Gus Peake; and Steve married Idyl Mae Gillette. Steve and Idyl, called Ida, were my grandparents.

By the time he married, Steve had a farm and was part owner, with Gee Townsend, of a hardware store. But, as the nine children—Roy, Sarah (my mother, called Sadie), Tom, Mabel, Paul, Carolyn, Louise, Margaret, and Esther—came along at two-year intervals, he took to waking everybody up during the night shouting that they were eating him out of house and home and would all land in the poorhouse. He'd demand that his wife tell him how he was to pay the bill for food and shoes at Austin's store. The family had enough to eat and enough to wear. Indeed, the Dohers were thought to be rather prosperous; thus, Steve's midnight outbursts were considered recreational rather than reflecting real worry. Nevertheless, Grandmother wept, the children wept, and all but Mabel, who was her father's favorite and wasn't frightened by him, hated his guts.

Sadie, the eldest girl and the strongest of all the children, felt a special loathing for him; as her mother swelled and gave birth to each new baby, Sadie assumed the care of the next youngest child. She wiped noses and behinds, she fed and comforted the children, and she washed dishes and clothes. Each time their mother was brought to bed, the children were packed off to Aunt Sarah's. Each time their father came to get them, he would say triumphantly, "Bet you don't know what we've got at home!" Each time my mother silently cursed him.

Tom, the third child, helped my mother as soon as he was old enough. Tom was a loving child; he wanted everybody to be happy, and he tried not to run afoul of his father. He loved to surprise his mother with a newly scrubbed kitchen floor, a pan of potatoes peeled for supper, and a wood box full of firewood and kindling ready for morning.

"Mama didn't have an easy time," Uncle Tom told me. "Sadie tried to do everything for all of us because Mama felt poorly a lot of the time. Mama was nervous, and it didn't help any when old Granddad Mike would come to our place of a Saturday afternoon and want to take me to town with him. I was his favorite 'boyo,' but Mama knew he liked to have a drink or two with the old men, and she knew there might be a runaway by the horses, because old Mike didn't pay attention to what he was doing."

He smiled, remembering old times. "I liked the excitement when the horses r'ared up and ran away, but Mama was afraid the old man wouldn't look after me. Still, she didn't know how to refuse him. And, sure enough, old Mike would get a little boisterous, and when he'd take me home he'd say, 'Tommy, me boyo, I think we'd better throw our hats in first. I'm in danger of yer ma tearin' me to pieces because of the time of the day it is, and me just bringin' ye home.'"

"And he'd do it!" Uncle Tom said. "We'd throw our hats into the house when we got there and laugh like crazy when Mama came and broke into tears and hugged me. I didn't care. I liked old Mike." He sat there thinking of that disreputable old grandfather and of his mother and his sister.

"Sadie was the steady one," he said. "She worked hard and tried to make things easier for Mama. By the time we were all in school there were a lot of lunches to fix. Sadie'd go out and catch two or three chickens, yank their heads off, and get them fried before time to go to school."

I'd seen my mother kill a chicken. No fooling around with a hatchet; she simply put her foot on the chicken's head and yanked its feet up, leaving its head on the ground. And I knew she could scald one, pick the feathers off, singe the carcass, and have it washed and cut up while I was still thinking about doing it.

"She didn't have much time to play," Uncle Tom said. "But we lived next door to the Whites, and she and Ruby managed to have some fun. They got up a circus one time," he said, smiling. "They rigged up a trapeze in the corncrib to practice their act on, and they set me as sentry. They didn't want the big boys to see their bloomers; I was so little I didn't count."

I was thirty-five by the time Uncle Tom told me about the half-brother he'd met for the first time when he was already grown. I found it rather touching that he thought at last I was old enough to know about his father's bastard son. In fact, I'd known about him from my mother; it was one of the many things she hated her father for.

"Dad asked me to drive him to Ayer," said Uncle Tom. "Said there was a hardware store there he was interested in. I was already out of medical school, already going with Fern Meadows. When we got in the store there was this fellow a few years older than me, and when I looked at him I thought I was looking at my dad. Dad introduced me to him, and we talked a while. My head was in a whirl; I don't know what I said." Uncle Tom shrugged. "I knew that Fern's parents, the Meadows, had taken a boy to raise, but he was gone from home by the time I was courting Fern, and

I knew nothing about him. That day I found out that this was the boy. I never did figure out why Dad wanted me to meet him. What worried him was what the Meadows would do when they found out he was my half-brother." He shook his head. "I was already getting serious about Fern—I sweat blood till I found out they wouldn't hold it against me. Funny," he said, "Dad never said a word about him, and I was too shocked to ask him anything. By the time I pulled myself together, it seemed too awkward to ask questions."

In that family there were many questions that couldn't be asked, comments that couldn't be made, and conditions that couldn't be noticed. Mother told me one of them. She was nearly sixteen, and once again the familiar sickness gripped her mother. Her mother stumbled into the kitchen with red, swollen eyes, and once again her daughter longed to comfort her.

"I know what's the matter with you," Sadie said. "I know, all right."

Her mother turned on her. "What do you mean?" she demanded. "What are you talking about?"

"You're going to have another baby," Sadie said."

Her mother sobbed. "Don't you talk to me like that! Don't you ever talk to me like that! What kind of daughter would talk to her mother that way?"

Sadie started teaching piano when she was eleven. She'd learned to play on Aunt Sarah's reed organ as soon as she could balance herself on the stool. Uncle Gus taught her to "chord" so she could accompany him as he played his fiddle. When her father got a piano in the hardware and furniture store, she played that; he encouraged it, and he paid for lessons from Mrs. Marshall.

Sadie began to teach other children almost at once. Steve saw that this was good business. Some of the parents might buy pianos, and indeed some did.

At fourteen Sadie enrolled in Franklin Academy. The summer after her first term, she persuaded her father to let her use a horse and buggy to drive out into the country to teach children in homes where there was a piano. For the use of the piano she taught the family's children for free; others came to her from the neighborhood, and many a mother, bringing the eldest for instruction, brought along the younger children too, well scrubbed and under orders to sit quietly nearby and absorb all they could. It was a well-established custom; Sadie knew she'd get them later, at thirty-five cents each. The following summers she branched out—to Campbell, where she stayed with a French family; to Hildreth, to stay with the Frank Lantzes; and to Upland, to stay with the Petersons, and there she met Karl Spence.

Karl Spence fell in love with Sadie Doher at once, and he courted her furiously. Since the age of fourteen, he'd been the editor, publisher, and printer of the *Upland Eagle*. His uncle Ernest Spence had taught him the printer's trade and set him up as the newspaper's publisher in order to get the Franklin County legal notices.

Karl simply had to see this lovely girl he'd fallen in love with; he borrowed his uncle's Overland automobile and drove to Franklin every weekend. The towns were eighteen miles apart; Karl drove the distance in an hour and boasted about it. Steve Doher announced that no daughter of his was going to go out with a young fool who would risk his daughter's neck driving at such speeds; he forbade her from seeing him.

They were married in February 1908, three weeks after Karl's nineteenth birthday and two days before Sadie's twentieth. It was bad enough to marry a man eleven months younger, Sadie thought; it would look better—more genteel—for them to be the same age, if only for two days.

Sadie had learned to do her hair in a Gibson girl pompadour. The wedding dress had been planned for her May graduation from the academy. The shirtwaist dress was of sheerest white silk, with scores of pin tucks, and there was a blue camisole to show through. By May winter underwear would have been laid aside; this was February, however, and it had turned suddenly cold—too cold, Grandmother said on the day of the wedding, to think of wearing short-sleeved summer underwear under Sadie's graduation dress.

"Those sleeves are full," she told Sadie. "They'll cover up the underwear. Nobody's going to notice."

"Notice!" Sadie shrieked. "Nobody's going to notice that I'm lumpy?"

"Lumpy or not," said Grandmother, "You're not going to risk pneumonia changing from winter to summer underwear in February!" The battle raged on for half the afternoon, until Tom, ever the peacemaker, said, "Mama, Sadie doesn't want to get pneumonia; she just wants to look nice for her wedding and the photographs. How would it be if she'd just wear the summer union suit for the ceremony and the pictures and then go upstairs and change?"

This compromise was finally accepted. Time was running out.

"Now Sis," said Tom, "you'd better go wash your face and put a cold compress on your eyes for a while. Karl doesn't want you to look like you've been crying, and people might think you don't want to get married."

They boarded the evening train for Lincoln. At Blue Hill they changed to a Pullman car, with a lower berth reserved. There were three days at the state capital, a room at the Lincoln Hotel, Nebraska's newest and finest, and meals in the dining room. Neither of them had ever known such luxury and elegance.

During the months of courtship Karl had started the *Franklin County News* in competition with the *Sentinel;* he was full of optimism about what a really good newspaper could do for the town. He was sure that once he got it well under way subscriptions and advertising would pour in; the newspaper was sure to be a moneymaker.

He'd found a little acreage near the edge of town and made a down payment. The home they'd make there would give them the best of both worlds: a quiet country refuge, within easy walking distance of the shop, the church, and the academy, where most cultural and musical events took place. True, the house was pretty old and dilapidated, but they could fix it up for the short term, and before long they'd build a new one.

He'd already bought a heifer; when it calved there'd be an abundance of milk, butter, and cheese. If it dropped a bull calf, they'd feed him to beef size; if it was a heifer, it would be an addition to their herd, and later they would have its calves to sell. They'd get a few chickens, say a hundred, and several hogs. They'd plant a garden, and in April they'd plant fruit trees and berry bushes. During the summer Karl would dig out the fallen root cellar, where they'd put the home-canned and dried foods they'd have by fall. What few things they couldn't produce they'd get in barter for advertising from the grocer, the hardware store, and the drug store. Later in the new house there'd be a piano so Sadie could teach at home; for now she could use Mamie Humphrey's piano.

It was delightful being married. As a surprise, Karl presented his bride with a box of finest woven visiting cards elegantly engraved, "Mrs. Karl Loris Spence." The Karl Loris Spences were in demand in the community; Sadie played for every occasion at the Congregational Church and the academy and for weddings and funerals at all the other churches. Karl sang in the choir; the director prized his clear, true tenor, and when he sang a solo tears welled up in many eyes. Choir practice, on Thursday evening for as long as anyone could remember, was changed to Tuesday evening because Thursday was press day, and work could not stop until the *News* was ready for mailing.

Sadie waded into the rickety old house. She puttied windows, scrubbed and sanded dirty woodwork, dug and scraped grease out of pantry corners. Her brothers helped: Roy patched the roof, and Tom and Paul cleaned the cellar. Everyone joined happily in burning the filthy old privy and building a new one. Mabel and Carolyn papered and painted, and the "little girls" ran errands and got in everybody's way. They made over some old curtains

Mamie wasn't using; Grandmother had some pots and pans she could spare and a worn Axminster rug for the living room. The house began to look good, and the yard was cleared of weeds.

The weather turned springlike early. Karl got a neighbor to plow and harrow most of the acreage; he planted a garden and set out little cherry and apple and peach trees, hardly more than switches.

When the weather was right Karl planted corn and alfalfa; by the time the alfalfa bloomed, he'd have two or three hives of bees. He exulted in the thought of the homegrown fruit there would be in a few years and the jars and pots of honey, enough to trade for credit at the grocery store. In time he'd build a little smokehouse to cure hams and sides of bacon with the corncobs. Everything would be used; there would be abundance.

"Why don't more people do this?" he asked Sadie. "Look at the money we'll save; think of the satisfaction of growing our own food. We're onto something here, honeybunch," he said. "A little garden patch and a chicken coop are all right for folks in town, but we're going to have a lot more than that."

The work on the land was backbreaking, and each task accomplished showed up something else that needed doing, but they were young, so young! and each new morning was full of hope and confidence.

Sadie began to get a few music lessons, and she went to Mamie's house to meet with her pupils at the old, square rosewood piano. She bought a secondhand sewing machine and yards and yards of lavender Indianhead cloth; she pedaled furiously making a pleated cover and cushions for an old daybed she'd found at a farm sale. This was for her sisters; the girls could come and stay overnight. Now that the house was in pretty good shape, staying home while Karl was at work made her restless and uneasy. There had always been so much to do at home and people tumbling over one another. It was too quiet.

"We missed Sadie at home," Uncle Tom told me. "She'd always been the hub of the house, with Mama ailing so much. There were still a lot of us—that was before Roy and Lula were married—but it didn't seem right without Sadie."

A special subscription price—a dollar a year—brought people in to sign up for the *Franklin County News;* if someone brought a broody hen to trade for a subscription, so much the better. Karl began to feel like a landed squire; he pictured his acres blooming and bearing plentifully for the family they'd have.

On press day, if he had time, Karl ducked around the corner for a sandwich and a cup of coffee at the cafe. Late in the day Sadie milked the cow, shut up the chickens, and brought supper out to the shop. Karl gulped down his food. Thursdays were always like that, Sadie thought resentfully—he'd work feverishly until the paper was printed and ready for mailing. He was happy, though, as the week's work reached a climax. He sang as he worked at the composing machine—"The Rose of Tralee" or "Kathleen Mavourneen." If he were at the press, he'd sing a popular song or a march, depending on whether the cranky old gas engine worked well or sputteringly. Even printing sale bills was fun for Karl.

For Sadie it was almost like being alone. There was little she could do until it was time to address and wrap the papers except to stay out of the way while Karl locked forms, inked the platen, and fed the press.

Sometimes as the evening wore on Sadie put her head down on the table and tried to sleep. She began to feel it was somehow unfair for her husband to be too busy to talk to her, too busy even to know she was alive.

There were other nights when job work had to be done. A lot of job work—things like advertisements, wedding announcements, a yearbook for a lodge—was beginning to come in. Karl prided himself on the quality of his work; getting things exactly right was essential for his business, he told Sadie.

"Ah," she said, "I don't know about that! Ninety-nine out of a hundred people don't even notice the difference."

"But *I* know," said Karl. It was the sort of thing Sadie said herself, but when it was thrown back at her she hated it.

She hated it when he'd do job work after supper. Thursday nights, when the paper went to press, were bad enough, but at least she had something to look forward to. On Fridays it was only the single-wraps—the papers that went out on the evening train—which needed to be taken to the post office. Then there was only the cleanup that remained to be done. After that they might have dinner at the cafe and visit with people and perhaps close up early, since there wasn't enough to keep them busy.

One evening as she lifted her head from the desk and started to rise, she felt dizzy; she slumped to the floor with a little whimper. Karl stopped feeding the press. He let the sheet of newsprint fall to the floor, leaped to her side, and put his arm under her head.

"Honeybunch, honeybunch! What's wrong, my darling?"

He left her only long enough to get water on a rather inky towel, and he patted her face with it, imploring her to be all right. Presently she was. Karl closed the shop, and they went home together.

"We've got to have a horse and something you can drive," he said next morning. "I can't have my girl walking home when she doesn't feel well."

Roy found a horse they could buy at a fair price; he helped Karl cobble up a decent little rig out of spare parts. Now Sadie could drive into town when Karl worked late and would be free to go home if she didn't feel well.

She did drive home a few times after that, but she didn't like it. She lay awake wondering when Karl would be home and why it was taking him so long to finish up a simple job. She wasn't afraid of staying alone; still, there were a lot of creaks and pops in the old house. She didn't like it at all. She thought she'd rather be at the shop waiting than at home alone waiting, but when she was at the shop, that too seemed unbearably tedious.

The next time she fainted, Karl grew anxious. "You'd better see Dr. Freese in the morning," he said. "I don't like this fainting, especially if my girl's pregnant."

"Pregnant!" Sadie said angrily. "I'm not in the family way, if that's what you mean!"

"That's what I mean, honeybunch," he said. "Would that be so bad?"

"I don't want to talk about it!" Sadie said.

The final faint occurred on a Thursday evening. When Sadie slumped, Karl finished his run before he went to her. He then took her by the ankles, dragged her into the back room, and carefully closed the door. He re-inked the platen, set up another run, and had it half-finished when Sadie came to, looking white and shaken.

"When are we going home?" she faltered.

"When the paper's ready to mail," Karl said.

Early in June a farmer from east of town brought Sadie two hives of bees and three geese and a gander, tied by their legs in the back of the wagon.

"But what . . . ?" said Sadie. "Why . . . ? I don't want any geese. I don't know what . . ."

"Didn't Karl tell you?" the farmer asked. "He made me a deal for these here geese and bees for a ten-year subscription. Didn't you know about it?" He laughed uproariously as he unloaded the hives and the geese. "Here's an old smoker you can use, and you better get yourself some long sleeves and mosquito netting. You got huskers' gloves, ain't you?" He laughed again as he said, "Giddap" to his horse. "Well, good luck!" And he drove away.

Sadie was aghast. She knew enough about geese to know the chicken pen would never hold them unless their wings were clipped. She knew Mrs. Wentworth picked down off the breasts of her struggling geese and made pillows; the thought of trying to do it herself made Sadie feel sick. She reached out to see if any wings were clipped and got a painful nip on her arm from the gander.

She was trying not to cry when Karl answered the phone.

"Oh honey, I'm sorry," he said. "I meant to tell you, and it just slipped my mind. Honeybunch, it'll be all right. I'll fix a pen when I get home tonight."

"Tonight!" Sadie wailed. "It's hot already, and it's not even eleven o'clock. They can't be tied down all day in this heat without water. Can't you come home right now?"

"Honeybunch, I can't, I just can't," Karl said. "This is Thursday, remember? Can you get Roy?"

"Roy's gone to Naponee! There isn't anybody home but Mama and the little girls!" Sadie cried.

At that moment Aunt Sarah turned in off the road. Sadie muttered something incoherent, hung up the phone, and ran to meet her.

"Well now, let's see," said Aunt Sarah. She put her hat and the large satchel—she called it her reticule—on a chair. She rolled up her sleeves as they walked to the shed.

"This'd never hold 'em, with no door and all those boards off," she said. "But look now, here's some woven wire. It ain't enough, but it'll have to do—if that corner's stout enough and we can find some more boards." She went outside and pushed on the corner.

"It'll hold," she announced. "Get the hammer, Sadie, and see if there's any staples."

There weren't, but there were enough boards with nails that could be pried out of them, straightened, and then clinched over the wire with a hammer. The big waterer from the chicken pen would do, and the chickens could get along with an old wash pan. Stakes pounded in with the flat of the axe would support some boards, and a couple of rocks would keep the geese from pushing them over.

"There," said Aunt Sarah, with satisfaction. "It's prob'ly not as much room as they'd like to have or oughter have, but it'll hold 'em till Karl fixes a better place."

She knew just where to grip the necks to keep the strong beaks from lashing out.

"Their wings are pretty well tied down with some old stockin's," she said. "Get your paring knife, Sadie, and cut the cord around their legs just as I push them into the pen. They'll settle down after a while when they get a drink and eat some oats, and if the stockin's work off then it won't hurt anything."

"Oh, Aunt Sarah!" Sadie said as they sat over fried eggs and canned peaches. "What am I going to do? Karl should have had a place ready for those nasty geese, and he didn't even tell me they were coming, nor the bees either. Sometimes I wonder if he even loves me at all." She was becoming teary.

"Well, he forgot," Aunt Sarah said calmly. "People forget things. He meant to tell you, I'm sure of that. He just forgot. O' course he loves you; he didn't give you or anybody else any rest till he got you. I wish I had a nickel for every time Gus forgot to tell me something he shoulda told me."

Uncle Gus, Aunt Sarah's husband, had died two years earlier. "But he loved me all right," she added stoutly. "Wasn't ever any doubt about that. You just put that out of your mind. Karl loves you too. He won't do it again. Maybe!" She looked up smiling, and Sadie smiled too. She didn't really think for a minute that Karl didn't love her. He was thoroughly penitent as he built a good pen for the geese and moved the hives to the alfalfa patch.

"I just had too much on my mind," he said. "The bids on the county printing and all that paper stock coming in. I shouldn't have forgotten; it won't happen again."

It did, of course, but Sadie had begun to see that it was a part of her life. It wasn't only his forgetfulness that troubled her; it was also Karl's willingness, eagerness even, to believe anything anybody told him. She had only a sketchy knowledge of sheep and their ways, but she seethed when Karl cheerfully told her that the two ewes he'd bought would be the foundation of a profitable flock.

"Those two?" She was incredulous. They were, to begin with, repulsive—vacant in expression, slobbering; the wool on their rear ends was matted with manure and weeds.

"They're old, both of them, old and dry; they're not going to lamb. Can't you see that?"

"The man told me—," said Karl, "he told me they'd been bred to a good young Corriedale ram just two weeks ago."

"Well, if they were," Sadie said, "all he got out of it was the exercise."

It was true. No pregnancy developed, no lamb was born, and a few weeks later one ewe lay down and died; the other, after walking around bleating a couple of days, followed her example.

"Old age," said Sadie. "Or pure cussedness. I'd say it was pure cussedness if they hadn't done us such a favor by dying."

The guinea fowl were not really a success either. Nobody had told Karl that guinea fowl make a hideous, persistent racket beginning at dawn; he had heard of them only as a delicacy and had pictured them, beautifully browned, on the table. Nobody told him that you couldn't catch them either; you had to shoot them, and you had to be a pretty good shot at that.

It was unfortunate that both the cow and the calf got into the alfalfa when it was exactly at the point where it causes bloat in cattle and that nobody knew of it until it was too late to save them. After that it seemed only a minor indignity that on the same day a queen had emerged from one of Dad's beehives and had led the whole swarm over the river into Kansas.

Even so the dream might have survived if it hadn't been for the flood. It came late in the year, when such a thing could not have been foreseen. It came in a flash and in unimaginable torrents. Both Sadie and Karl were in town; there was no possibility of getting home until the storm was over. When they did, in late afternoon under clearing skies, they found the house collapsed on the side nearest the creek and water standing in all the remaining rooms. The cellar was full, and eggs floated on the surface. The cave was gone entirely.

The sow hadn't made it out of her wallow at the creek's edge, and several of her piglets swirled about in the shallows where twigs and leaves had backed up. Only the horse, the geese, honking and hissing, and a few bedraggled guineas were on their feet.

By this time Sadie was pregnant. Mamie Humphreys said, "Well, you'll just come here to my house. Those upstairs rooms at the back will be fine for you, and you can pay rent if you like. By the time the baby comes, we'll have Mama's sewing room cleared out. She hasn't used it anyway, since her eyesight began to fail. It will be just right for a nursery."

CHAPTER FIVE

On a sunny day in November 1918 I was riding my tricycle up and down the sidewalk in front of our house, swerving back and forth just to touch the spears of the iris—we called them flags—which bordered the walk, when a great hullabaloo broke out. The town fire siren howled, people burst out of their houses, Mother ran past without noticing me, and far down the street I saw Dad running toward us from the shop. In a moment church bells began to ring, people ran around slapping one another on the back; they hugged, laughed, and cried. The war was over.

I couldn't remember when there hadn't been the war; it was the natural order of things. It was fun for me to go, dressed up in a Red Cross nurse's dress, cap, and apron, like Mother, to the Liberty Bond rallies in the park. Dad and Loris, dressed in khaki soldier uniforms, puttees, and campaign hats, went too. I liked seeing the bandstand draped in bunting and hearing the town band play "Over There," "Pack Up Your Troubles in Your Old Kit Bag," and, after the crowd was assembled, the "Star-Spangled Banner."

A minister from one of the churches gave the invocation, with fervent pleas for the safety of our boys, made in the absolute certainty of a just cause. There was always a speaker, a solid citizen from Holdrege or Red Cloud or Kearney; once a fireball from Omaha spoke. Everybody was a patriot; Liberty Bonds, lots of them, would be sold. There was, however, a final touch to heart and purse strings, and I liked that best of all.

A hush fell over the crowd as Dad lifted me up on a table at the foot of the bandstand. I loved that hush and standing there in Dad's arms while everyone looked at me.

Mother had coached me. I waited a moment after she struck the opening chord on the piano, then I began to sing. I sang "It's a Long Way to Tipperary," "Hello, Central, Get Me No Man's Land," and, finally, the one everybody waited for, "Just a Baby's Prayer at Twilight."

"Not a dry eye in the place, Karl," said Mr. Reed, our Congregational minister, as people began to line up to buy Liberty Bonds. "That little girl brings them to the mercy seat." Mr. Reed had a somewhat satirical attitude toward evangelical fervor, religious or patriotic.

"We'll exceed our goal," said Rashie Murray, the banker. He patted me on the head. "Little lady, you're one of our best weapons against the Hun."

The Hun. Huns were bad people, everyone knew that, and yet they were somehow connected with Germans. I couldn't figure it out. The Germans, I knew, were good. Frieda Eschenbrenner, our hired girl from time to time when Mother needed help, lived with her family on the Macon prairie, where a whole lot of Germans lived in neat farmhouses with big red barns. Frieda sometimes took me home with her for a day or two. I liked all the Eschenbrenners, especially Frieda's brother Herman. Herman was a stout, ruddy young man with huge red hands who sometimes let me ride in the wagon with him, behind the great rumps of the farm horses. All the Eschenbrenner children were grown or nearly grown, and all were still at home; the big oilcloth-covered table nearly filled the kitchen. I was seated like a queen on pillows between Mr. and Mrs. Eschenbrenner and fed with the best tidbits from the big steaming bowls the girls carried around the table. I liked the fried potatoes and side meat, and I liked being pampered and petted.

When I stayed overnight I slept between two of the girls on a bed puffy as a cloud, under smooth sheets and a quilt filled, they told me, with the *gansefeder* from their mama's geese. It seemed light as air, not like our own solid bedding, and I floated off to sleep to the sound of Bertha softly singing, "Schlaff, Mein Kleineschvester."

My best friend, Erma Fruhling, was German too, the youngest in her house full of brothers and sisters, where we were both *schvesterchen*. The Fruhlings said it a little differently; this, Erma told me proudly, was because they spoke High German, whereas the Eschenbrenners spoke only Low German. Erma's family was from Schleswig-Holstein, she said, *Fruhling* meant "spring", and she and all her family were full-blooded Germans. I loved staying with the Fruhlings too. German meant clean, quiet houses and grown-ups who indulged me.

I just didn't understand the other Germany I'd heard about—that of the Huns—until a few months after the armistice. Then my uncle Paul Doher returned from France, proud of having served in the Rainbow Division. When he showed us his war souvenirs, I understood better. He unpacked a German uniform coat, helmet, and scarf; the smell that rose from them was somehow bitter, unmistakably feral. This, then, was the Hun; this was the smell of evil. It had nothing to do with Germans as I knew them. To this day a whiff a scent similar to that in Uncle Paul's souvenirs brings me a sense of foreboding.

Erma was sure to be at Sunday school before I was; so was everybody else. The Spences always skidded into the church at the last possible moment before Mother was to begin playing the piano for opening exercises. Other families walked sedately toward the church, clean and clothed and in their right minds; I don't know how they did it. We were clean all right; there'd been the Saturday night bath, and in the morning Dad shook Loris and me down into the week's suit of clean underwear, shrunken by the wash. He cooked breakfast too, as he almost always did, but on Sunday it was a bigger and more leisurely meal—bacon and eggs and oven toast. In the spring and early summer we'd have little spears of creamed asparagus we'd cut only a few minutes before, not long after they started out of the earth, to eat over toast. Every morning there was the heavenly fragrance of the coffee Dad boiled in the pot, with an egg white mixed in to clarify it, and the bits of orange peel he'd dropped on the hot stove to scent the air. It was a lovely time until suddenly somebody noticed the clock; we had to scramble. Everybody's clothes had to be found, some had to have a lick and a promise with the iron, and I'd almost certainly get my ears burned with the curling iron.

"It wouldn't happen if you'd just stand still," Mother would say, putting the curling iron back in the chimney of the kerosene lamp she'd lit to heat it. If I'd stand still! How was I to stand still with Mother yanking my Dutch bob and brandishing the curling iron? My hair was frizzed only on Sundays. To this day the smell of scorched hair means Sunday school to me.

My pennies were tied up in a corner of my handkerchief, secured with a tiny safety pin under my sash. When I had a new dress Mother always said, "Now don't you switch!" I understood this admonition perfectly: I was not to sashay my behind around with pride for my fine raiment.

One Christmas Sunday I wore the new gloves Aunt Mabel had brought me from Lincoln, expensive kid gloves pushed and smoothed on just like ladies' gloves were. When Sunday school was over and we went upstairs to wait for church service, I was horrified to find that I'd chewed off three finger ends. I got spanked for that; fifty years later I found those tiny chewed gloves at the bottom of my mother's handkerchief box.

Sunday school was a decorous proceeding; with Mrs. Herman Platt in charge it couldn't be otherwise. She forbade the least hint of levity, even in the basement of God's house.

I don't know why the monthly church suppers, held in the same large basement room, were so different—Mrs. Platt was always there—but they were. The same kids who sat solemnly on the little red chairs on Sunday, and all the big kids as well, came to the church supper for fun—noisy, racing, hilarious fun. We ran up and down the stairs; once we even managed to get into the belfry and make a sort of ping on the bell. We played hide-and-seek, we tore in and out of the church's several doors and round the block—everywhere but the church sanctuary; nobody had to tell us that was out of bounds. On church supper evening nobody reproved us; we were all allowed to run wild until we were called in for supper.

While we shrieked and ran around, we didn't think of eating; when the summons came, we could think of nothing else. The smells were maddening: coffee—which none of us drank—meatloaf, chicken and noodles, hot bread, pickles, and baked beans. The grown-ups—they were always served first in those days—sat at white cloth–covered tables before well-filled plates, waiting for us to line up and bow our heads for the blessing.

The aproned ladies behind the long buffet table served us generously—too generously, I thought, if I got Mrs. Merrick's meatloaf, which was rock-solid and as pallid in flavor as it was in appearance. I hoped for my mother's meatloaf and to escape her baked beans, which were much admired. I'd seen them soaking and smelled the dry smell they gave off at first boiling and the spicy one they produced after hours in the oven. What I wanted was Mrs. Wentworth's beans. They were Van Camp's—right out of the can, Mother said scornfully—and I liked them best of all.

Mrs. Fruhling's chicken and noodles always went fast; you were lucky to get any of that. I liked Miss Emma Smith's salad—pineapple and grated carrot suspended in green Jell-O. As I carried my loaded plate to the table, I could hardly wait to attack it; not much later I was aghast at the amount of food I'd let the ladies pile on my plate, not that there was much I could have done to stop them; children were known to be always hungry. The prospect was awful when, suddenly, I was sated: little Armenians lurked in the background with hollow eyes and distended bellies. For some unknown reason we had to eat more than we wanted in order to help them.

Erma and I were five when we started first grade. Two or three nights a week we stayed overnight with each other, at her home or at mine. One of the best parts of going home with Erma was that we were almost always sent back downtown to Austin's store to buy food for supper. Better still, if either of Erma's brothers, Fred or Ehme, were home between shifts of their work for the railroad, they might give us a couple of pennies apiece or even a nickel for the two of us. This meant we'd have to hustle; the candy store was a block and a half farther down the street from Austin's, and deciding how to spend the windfall took time. While we pondered our options, Miss Geneva or Miss Mildred Hayes quietly waited behind the counter. I didn't like licorice, and Erma didn't like jawbreakers, because they took so long to eat. We could agree on jellybeans, gumdrops, or corn candy; for two cents you got a good scoopful in the bottom of the striped bag. The problem was how to spend the rest—banana-flavored hard marshmallows shaped like big peanuts, soft toasted coconut marshmallows, or bumpy sugar-coated peanuts, real peanuts. The tiny pink, white, or green hearts that said HOW ABOUT IT and OH YOU KID were tempting, but we didn't like their taste. We read as many of the mottoes as we could through the big glass jar, and, if we had a whole nickel, we'd buy a penny's worth. Miss Geneva, the plump sister and a soft touch, sometimes dropped a few in the bag anyway. We went out pushing and elbowing each other over which boy would like to make which smart remark to which girl.

At Austin's store we stopped the shoving and giggling. It wasn't that we were afraid of the Austins, but they were "nice" people, and their good opinion was something one valued without having to be told to do so. We thought Estel Austin, a tall boy who worked in his father's store, was as handsome as a movie star. We were sure he liked Eva Yatas; we wondered if they'd "go together" when they got older. Eva was the only one good enough for Estel; he couldn't possibly like anyone else. As he weighed and bagged five cents worth of sugar and ten cents worth of potatoes for the Fruhlings, his manner toward Erma and me was as grave and considerate as it might have been for Mrs. Campbell, the doctor's wife, who gave large dinner parties for out-of-town people.

My clothes were made over from suits and dresses sent home by Mother's young sisters, who worked in Lincoln and Omaha and bought pretty clothes. Mother didn't alter them; she loathed the sight of a needle. Mrs. Jensen sewed them, and the Jensen kids got piano lessons in return. I liked going home with them after school to be fitted; their mother could size up Aunt Esther's discarded dress, pin here, cut there, rip, and restitch, and before the week was out I'd have a dress to wear proudly.

I tried my best to keep those new dresses clean; I knew what happened to woolen dresses in our house. I tried sponging spots off, as I'd seen Mrs. Fruhling do with Erma's dresses, but, when the time came to take a stain out of a dress, no pleading of mine could avert its fate. Mother poured "high-test" gasoline in a dishpan in the back yard, put the dress in, and rubbed it vigorously. God knows why it didn't blow up. Then the dress was hung on the clothesline for a week, two weeks even, but no wind was ever enough to blow away the reek of gasoline. I smelled it most when I took my coat off in the hall at school; I was sure the other kids could smell it too. Running on the playground brought it out, and winter sunshine through the schoolroom window made it worse. I comforted myself by thinking of spring and starched cotton dresses.

The ugly black stockings everybody wore took on a greenish hue after the war, until the German dye industry recovered. The color wasn't as bad as the lumps and wrinkles. Everyone wore long underwear, and as the week wore on the legs of it became baggy from being pulled on over one's feet. Mother made a neat fold of the loose wrinkly knit and pulled the stockings up over it.

"There!" she'd say. "It'll never be noticed—from the back of a galloping horse!"

I knew this was supposed to be a joke, but, being the one with lumpy legs, I didn't find it funny. There was only one thing to do: step into the brushy little room formed by Sargent's immense lilac bushes, undo the supporters, roll up my underwear, and pull up my stockings. I knew I was lucky to have this refuge; Erma had to walk to school in plain view of the whole town and couldn't roll her underwear up out of sight until she got to the girls' toilet.

On a late May day when I was eight, I was sent to spend the day with Hay-Hay, a friend of my mother's. I knew what was up; I was about to get, I hoped, a baby sister.

I don't know how we got to calling her Hay-Hay; maybe some child couldn't say Mrs. Hevner. Anyway, to the Spence kids she was always Hay-Hay. She was a small, stocky, bustling woman who carried a basket over her arm, and she lived in the biggest house in town, with "Uncle" Clyde. Uncle Clyde made a lot of money manufacturing hog serum, and his plant east of town employed several men. I loved Hay-Hay's big, childless house. The kitchen, the dining room, the living room, all seemed immense, and there were porches on three sides, with smooth concrete floors you could roller-skate on. Best of all there was the den. I never saw anyone sit in the den—indeed, none of the chairs, handsomely upholstered in leather, invited sitting. But one feature drew me back again and again, even though I had to force myself to go clear inside the room to see it: a great bald eagle, mounted over the door in a pose and with a baleful glass glare that suggested imminent attack.

I was disappointed when Hay-Hay called me in from skating and told me I had a baby brother; I really had planned on a sister. What delighted and fascinated me were the honeybees that had moved into our house that same day. They were buzzing about furiously when I got home, falling all over one another in their eagerness to get in and out of some holes in the siding and make their housekeeping arrangements. They lived with us for years, building combs and gathering honey. From time to time Dad pulled off a few boards and collected a crock of it.

On the whole the bees were less of a bother than the baby. He bellowed and bawled night and day from the time he was born, with scarcely a pause for breath.

"He's hungry," said Dr. Feese. "Obviously, you can't nurse him, Sadie. It'll have to be cow's milk."

Cow's milk it was not. Mort threw it up within minutes of swallowing it. He had diarrhea too; I rinsed diapers out in the slopjar, and Dad started up the gasoline washer every evening when he got home.

Sometimes, when the baby was near exhaustion anyway, there was a little respite from the screaming if he was pushed around in the baby buggy. I pushed it around the neighborhood at a steady pace, skirting the big Conkling house because the old-maidish sisters had already asked somebody why Sadie Spence didn't feed the baby; they hadn't had a good night's sleep in weeks.

Dad finally called Uncle Tom Doher, now with a thriving medical practice in Wilsonville.

"What are we gonna do, Tom?" he asked. "Your baby okay? What are you feeding him?"

"He's okay," said Uncle Tom. "Fern's nursing him. But I haven't seen a baby yet that I couldn't modify cow's milk for. Let's see, this is Thursday," he went on in his slow, quiet way. "I'll talk to Fern. We'd better come up on the train tomorrow evening."

Aunt Fern was unbuttoning her blouse as she walked into the room where Mort, crying hoarsely, was turning his head from side to side on the pillow.

"The U.S. Cavalry has arrived," she announced. "Give me that baby," and, to me, "Get me a bath towel."

The towel was to catch the overflow. Milk ran from both breasts as the baby sucked and swallowed and nearly strangled in his eagerness for this bounty.

"Hungry little bugger, isn't he?" said Fern. "Go after it, kiddo, and maybe I won't have to pump them out."

Uncle Tom viewed the scene benignly, and so did the fat, placid baby he held on his arm.

"Fern," he said, "is a Holstein."

Fern was a very little Holstein, a tiny woman with enormous breasts. Wellington, five days older than Mort, had every reason to be placid; he'd never known want.

That night, his belly full for the first time in his life, Mort slept for ten hours. In the morning the babies, fed and bathed, were put toe to toe in the baby buggy for me to wheel out into the neighborhood.

"Well!" said Miss Fannie Conkling. "First time I've seen that child with his mouth shut and his eyes open. Blue-eyed like Karl, ain't he?"

I didn't like talking to Miss Fanny at the best of times. I muttered something and hurried on.

Uncle Tom, still sure he could make cow's milk work for the baby, tried everything he could think of. He boiled it; he added things. Mort threw it up and screamed until Fern fed him from her overflowing breasts.

"I've got to go back," he finally said. "Two confinements this week, and old Dr. Funston isn't well himself. You've got to find a goat. Fern can stay a few days and come home on the train, but you've got to get a goat. If that doesn't work, it'll have to be mare's milk. That's closest to human milk."

The word went out through country newspaper editors and all the churches. Our goat Nanny was brought all the way from a farm near Holdrege at a fearful price and was worth every dime of it. She gave her milk gladly, Mort drank it greedily, and quiet came to the neighborhood. I was grateful to Nanny for the quiet, for not having to push the baby buggy so much, and for not being a horse. I learned to squeeze a creamy stream into a saucepan while she looked back at me with gentle liquid eyes. I never could have done that with a mare.

Nanny lived with us a long time. The bees were left behind when Dad abruptly sold our house and bought a big, square, drafty one on the north edge of town, but Nanny went with us. She was introduced to the billy goat of a traveling photographer who stopped in town; the result was a tiny kid goat with melting brown eyes like his mother's.

When my brother Tommy was born, three years after Mort, he got Nanny's milk as a matter of course. That Christmas, for the Nativity scene, we tied a pillow on her back and tassels on her ears to play the camel. She behaved calmly and camelly, while Tommy, usually cherubic, squirmed and squawked instead of lying in the manger looking holy.

CHAPTER SIX

Aunt Sarah, for whom my mother was named, was born before the Civil War. She was the elder sister of Sadie's father, and she seemed ancient to me. She lived by herself on a tiny farm about two miles out in the country, and from time to time she would ride in with her neighbors, or perhaps walk in, for a couple of days' visit. I loved Aunt Sarah and was always glad to see her coming up the front walk, although I'd heard Mother remark that she had a gift for showing up at inopportune times.

Aunt Sarah was a strange figure who dressed in long skirts and high-laced shoes at a time when skirts were relatively short, shoes were low, and hair was bobbed. She had two hats, the felt one for winter and the straw one for summer, which were otherwise very much alike. I knew that in her reticule she carried her nightgown—outing flannel in winter, muslin in summer— and the few other things she needed for a visit of two or three days.

When Aunt Sarah came, it meant hot baking powder biscuits on the table three times a day. She was famous for her biscuits; no others were so light and tender, so crisp and freckled top and bottom. We ate them with butter, gravy, jam, or honey, we ate until we could eat no more, and still Aunt Sarah went round and round the table with the biscuit pan hot from the oven, urging us on.

Aunt Sarah never referred to her wonderful biscuits in the plural; they were always "the biscuit." "Have some more of the biscuit while they're hot," she'd say. "No more? You don't like the biscuit?"

After supper Aunt Sarah would say to me, "Let's wash 'em while they're hot."

Clearing the table and washing the supper dishes were my responsibilities, and usually I delayed the jobs, saying to Mother, "I'll do them, I'll do them. I know it's my job; as long as I do them, what do you care when it is?"

This was our nightly wrangle, yet when Aunt Sarah was there, I jumped up as soon as she started clearing the table. I had to hurry because I wanted to get to the dishpan first. Aunt Sarah figured the dishes were washed as soon as she got them wet, no scraping and little soap, and I couldn't stand that. I scraped furiously with a knife or the edge of an uneaten biscuit, I dipped hot water out of the reservoir of the wood stove, and I rolled the bar of soap around in my hands for a good lather, letting Aunt Sarah know that I wanted to wash rather than dry.

Aunt Sarah always slept with me, and to me her preparations for bed were one of the best parts of her visit. First she took off her skirt and shirtwaist and hung them over a chair, and then she took down her long gray hair and plaited it in two braids. Next the nightgown came out of the reticule to be put over her head; then she began actually undressing. From under the nightgown came first two or three underskirts. The outer one was always white gathered muslin, but in winter, depending on the weather, there would be at least one more of gray woolen knit, with bands of darker gray and red or blue and with black-machined scallops.

Then came the chemise, which she called her "shimmy," the corset cover, and the corset. This was a device made of heavy cotton drill, steel stays, and long white laces like shoestrings. Mother wore a corset, but it was not like Aunt Sarah's, wide at the top and bottom and narrow in the middle. When Aunt Sarah pushed the front parts together to release the steel clamps that held it together, she always gave a little sigh.

"Aunt Sarah," I'd say, "Why do you wear a corset? You're so little around, you don't need it."

Her reply was always the same: "I've worn a corset every day of my life since I was fourteen years old, and I'll wear a corset every day as long as I live."

The last garments to emerge from under the nightgown were the bloomers, black sateen or white muslin, depending on the season, and black cotton stockings. But I knew that Aunt Sarah wasn't nude underneath her nightgown. Except for her weekly bath, she never removed the union suit that was the foundation of all her clothing. In summer this was a short-sleeved, mid-calf, cotton knit garment that buttoned up the front and had an opening in the rear, where one side overlapped the other. In winter it was woolen, with long sleeves and legs. I knew this kind of union suit well; in winter I had to wear one too, and I hated it.

As she slipped her arms into her nightgown's long sleeves, Aunt Sarah would say, "Polly, where's the witch?" Or she might call it "the vessel" or even "the Wichita, Kansas," because that's where chamber pots were made. But to Aunt Sarah the term was crude, and when such things had to be mentioned at all they were always cloaked in language well removed from any reference to their actual function. This was not putting on airs; it was the reflection of a day when bodily functions were unmentionable. Body wastes were called number one and number two, and, if she had to speak of a bull, it was as "the animal." I understood this, and, while I was with her, I was careful to use terms she liked to use.

When the light was out and we were in bed, I'd hear Aunt Sarah take out her teeth and put them in the cup of water she'd brought up from the kitchen and put beside the bed. Then I'd say, "Tell me about a long time ago."

As she talked to me, the old woman became a young Irish girl who'd come west with her father, Mike Doherty; and her brother, Steve; my grandfather; and her sister, Bridget. She'd worked hard as a hired girl and thought a lot about clothes—how to change her old dress to make it look new or at least different, how to re-trim her hat with a bit of ribbon her "lady" had given her, and how to blacken her shoes with soot to hide the scuffs. She thought ill of women who "painted," but she and the other girls would pinch their cheeks to make them pink and would have a bit of cornstarch on a rag for secretly patting their shiny noses.

Above all, Aunt Sarah loved to dance. As we lay in the dark, I'd close my eyes and wait for the imaginary sound of the fiddle and the accordion to commence.

"Your Uncle Gus," Aunt Sarah would begin, speaking of her husband long gone, the great-uncle by marriage I'd never seen, "he played the fiddle for all the dances around here, and old Mr. Hoffman always brought his 'aycordeen' and played it till he got tired, and then Gus would pick it up and play it. He'd let Gee Eggert take the fiddle for a while. Gus could play anything—fiddle, squeeze box, organ, Jew's harp, banjo—he could play 'em all."

Aunt Sarah never said so, and I don't know how I knew it, but, when she said Mr. Hoffman got tired, she meant he got too drunk to play. Uncle Gus was a drinker too, I knew that, but, drunk or sober, he could play his fiddle or any other instrument he could lay his hands on, and Aunt Sarah never said that Gus got tired.

Now I was hearing the music, faint at first and then loud and clear. I saw a girl with brown hair and smooth skin and a tiny waist, a girl who never lacked partners, although Gus, who was courting her, stood up on a box and played the music they were dancing to. I pictured her being whirled until her skirts flew out, and my toes twitched under the covers.

Sometimes, when nobody was home, I'd crank the Victrola and play "Tales of the Vienna Woods" and whirl around the living room all by myself, seeing myself slim and pretty and wearing a long red velvet dress with a square neckline edged with filmy lace. Aunt Sarah had never had a velvet dress or danced to a Victrola, and I'd always had a Dutch bob and freckles, but as I danced round and round the room I couldn't tell where I left off and Aunt Sarah began. Or whether I—we—were dancing in a great hall with a long staircase among fashionably dressed people in a haze of perfume or in a one-room schoolhouse among hardworking farm people dressed in their best and smelling of sweat.

"Folks went visitin' a lot in those days," Aunt Sarah said. "After church we always went to somebody's place for dinner, or we had company for dinner. Papa'd say, 'Hurry, girls, get the house redded up before the company comes.'"

There were "literaries" and box socials and the Christmas program at the church. At the literaries there were debates on such topics as "Free Silver— Trade or Trap?" and even on the heretical theories of a man named Darwin. There were recitations and musical performances, and sometimes the ladies draped themselves in curtains and scarves and formed tableaux. And, if it occasionally turned out that some of the speakers only wanted to get up and spout off, on balance there was an air of earnest self-improvement and a good feeling that the tenor of prairie life was elevated by the literary. The evening ended with sandwiches and cakes that the ladies had brought and coffee boiled in a cloth in Mrs. Harris's preserving kettle.

The box social was a different matter. When the schoolhouse needed a new roof or times were good and agitation swelled for buying a reed organ, a box social was organized to raise money. Every maid and matron in the neighborhood prepared food for two, packed it in a box decorated, if possible, with colored paper, and brought it to the social shrouded in newspaper or flour sacking to conceal its appearance. After an evening of dancing, the boxes were to be auctioned off, and each high bidder, having paid the money, would find the hidden name and eat the food in the company of the lady who had prepared it.

The outer wrappings were removed behind a screen by the teacher, and the boxes were arranged on a long table for display and speculation. Mabel

Truesdale brought her potato salad and pickled beets and Augusta Marsden brought deviled eggs and angel food cake. The boxes these women prepared were sought for the quality of their contents, weighed against the personal idiosyncracies of the cooks. Mabel Truesdale was a widow on the prowl for a husband, and Augusta Marsden was sure to talk about her ailments while tears welled up in her eyes. It was a matter of deciding whether it was worth it or not to bid on a box.

"Oh hell, I don't mind ol' 'Gusta," Walter Miller said. "Her bladder's too close to her eyes, but she shore makes good angel food cake."

As the evening wore on, false rumors were spread, through waggishness or malice, and a luckless buyer, his mouth all set for Mrs. Sargent's fried chicken, might wind up eating supper with Edna Mayfield, whose bread was always stale—even when newly baked, some said—and whose beef was always greasy. Yet Edna was a jolly soul, and in any case there was nothing to do but to put a good face on it and remember that it was for a good cause—and one could always get even the next time.

The most fun came when a young man was known to be sweet on a certain girl or when they were "keeping company." The girl, if she liked the man, might let him know somehow which creation was hers, and he'd try to bid on other boxes just enough to avoid buying them and to put his fellows off the scent. Someone always seemed to get a good hunch, though, and then all the men united to make the swain pay through the nose.

If two young bucks were after the same girl, everyone could stand back and laugh and cheer while they fought it out. For the bachelors there was no risk of being left to pay too much money or incurring a wife's anger while he shared supper with a pretty girl.

"Tell me about Uncle Gus and Murray Winter, Aunt Sarah." I'd nudge her when she began to doze off.

"Well, it was when Gus first came to Franklin," Aunt Sarah said, meaning to the area. "I'd been out walking with Murray Winter about a year, and he was getting ready to pop the question, I knew that. I liked him too, and I might have said yes if it hadn't been for Gus. Gus took a shine to me right away. I was a fair-looking girl," she added shyly.

She didn't have to tell me that. Hadn't I seen her there behind my eyelids, looking wonderful as she danced, never missing a dance, not stopping until the music stopped?

"Times were hard that year," Aunt Sarah said. "But the schoolhouse roof had commenced to leak, and they'd patched it till it wouldn't hold a patch anymore."

I knew the story well. I knew that in those days everyone pitched in to do the work, but of course it took money to get the shingles and nails.

"Fanny Ostman told me there was a new feller working for Mr. Sargent, and she said he had a fiddle in his bedroll with him when he came to work," Aunt Sarah said. "All the girls were just waiting to get a look at him, and I was hoping he could play that fiddle and keep Mr. Hoffman going so we could dance."

"And could he play the fiddle?" I prompted.

"Could he play the fiddle!" Aunt Sarah said. "He stood up there, and he played that fiddle, and we danced and danced and danced, and nobody wanted him to stop. It was gettin' late—after 9:30, I know—when they let him stop. Some of the old folks wanted to get home, and the boxes still had to be auctioned off."

"Then what?" I said.

"Murray knew I'd brought the box with pink ribbons on it," she said. "It was all right for me to give him a hint, because we'd been keeping company, you see. But Gus had been watching me, I guess."

"You guess?" I asked.

"Oh well—yes, I knew he'd been watching me," Aunt Sarah admitted. "And somebody told him I was spoke for, I guess, or just as good as. And that got his dander up. When Murray started bidding on my box, Gus got right into it. The two of them went to bidding and the men whooped and hollered and egged 'em on. All us girls were standing at the back, and those girls giggled and carried on till I didn't know which way to look!"

There was certain complacency in her tone now, and I was no longer aware of the hissing sound she made when speaking without her teeth.

"Go on, go on," I said.

"Well, it ended up with Gus bidding more for that box than had ever been bid before," she said. "And he had to go to Mr. Sargent and ask for a month's pay in advance to pay for it. It set him back, but he always said it was worth it. And after that it was always Gus for me. I wouldn't walk out with Murray anymore, and he felt bad for a while, but he got over it and married Lucy Homrighausen in the spring. Gus and I didn't get married for a year."

"How much did he pay?" I asked, as if I didn't already know.

"Eight dollars and forty cents," Aunt Sarah said, with satisfaction. "It was over half of what they needed for the shingles and nails."

Before going to sleep, Aunt Sarah would say what she always said.

"Polly, don't you believe it when people say dancing's wrong. You can be just as much of a lady at a dance as you can in church. If people do bad things it's not because of the dancing; it's because they forget themselves."

I believed that, and I wanted to go to dances, but, by the time I became a girl, dances were no longer neighborhood, family affairs, and nice girls, my mother said, didn't go to public dances; it wasn't ladylike. It wasn't that Mother thought dancing was wrong; she and all her brothers and sisters loved to dance, and they'd taught me to dance almost as soon as I could walk. It was just that dances at Senter Park brought young fellows from Riverton and Bloomington and even Red Cloud, and girls wore dresses above their knees and showed their legs in silk stockings, and there was bootleg hooch being drunk out of fruit jars in the darkness outside.

I didn't know the word *fornication,* and I didn't know exactly what boys and girls did when they were in the back seat of a car outside the dance hall, but I knew it had something to do with the burning I often felt as I drifted off to sleep and that this was exactly what every mother of a daughter feared. Some mothers let their daughters go to dances, and some girls sneaked out and went to dances.

I always hoped to wake up in the morning in time to see Aunt Sarah putting on all those clothes that hung over the chair. Did she manage all those openings and laces and clamps under the nightgown, or, if I had been less of a sleepyhead, would I have seen her in only her union suit? It never happened; when Aunt Sarah woke me, she'd be in petticoats and corset cover, and she'd say, smiling, "Now let's see, what shall I wear today—my red dress or my blue dress or the dress I wore last night?" This was a joke among the girls and women of the early day; nobody had that many dresses to choose from.

Every spring, at the end of the cherry season, Aunt Sarah invited us all for Sunday dinner. She would have been busy canning and preserving the cherries and would have made the last of the fresh cherries into pies. There was always a hen or two that had chicks early, and by the time of our dinner the cockerels from these hens would be big enough to fry. Those Sunday mornings when we were coming to dinner Aunt Sarah must have been up early; she had no refrigeration except the cave, and so the chickens had to be killed and dressed that morning. She'd been to her garden and picked peas, and she searched out a few new potatoes hardly bigger than marbles to cream with them. There were mashed potatoes besides, and gravy made with milk in the fried chicken skillet. There was wilted lettuce with bits of bacon. There were baked beans, succotash made with dried corn and canned green beans, cole slaw with creamy dressing, tiny pickled beets, sweet cucumber pickles, bread-and-butter pickles with sliced onions, piccalilli, mustard pickles, little red radishes, green onions, tomato preserve and chokecherry jelly, wild plum jelly, and comb honey. Everything had grown near Aunt Sarah's dooryard except for the flour, salt, baking powder, and spices. Her chair sat empty, her plate untouched, as she carried food around and around the table, urging us to eat. Now and then somebody would say, "Why don't you sit down with us, Aunt Sarah? We've got everything we need." She always said she would, in a minute, but she never did until we'd had the last biscuit we could be persuaded to eat and the table had been partly cleared and the pie served.

By this time everyone was sluggish and glassy-eyed with overfeeding. Dad stretched out on the Brussels carpet in the parlor for a little nap, and Mother and I helped Aunt Sarah with the dishes. Aunt Sarah put the food away in the tin food safe with holes in it, for the supper we'd have before we went home.

Beyond Aunt Sarah's garden and tiny orchard of gnarled and unpruned trees was a creek. Here trees grew and lived and occasionally fell to lightning and wind. I thought Sherwood Forest must have been like this, and I crept through the grass and underbrush quietly, thinking of myself as Maid Marian and half-expecting the gallant Robin Hood or Friar Tuck or Little John to materialize. An abandoned house was in these woods. I thought of it as my secret place, where I would come to live if I ran away from home. The floors were rotten, and the windows were broken, but I could see myself living here in perfect comfort and never, never going back to live with my mother. By the time I'd played out my fantasy and wandered back, I could hear Mother playing the reed organ in the parlor. She had learned to play on this very organ. Uncle Gus had taught her to chord while he played his fiddle. She said he'd call out, "Sadie! Key of G!" and away they'd go, Mother pumping furiously to work the bellows, and Uncle Gus sawing away on his fiddle—a reel, a hymn, or a ballad.

A photo album with a painted rose on the padded velvet cover lay on the marble stand in Aunt Sarah's parlor, and while Mother played the organ I looked through the photographs mounted on the ivy-printed cardboard until I found Aunt Sarah and Uncle Gus, in a wedding pose no less stiff than the cardboard. Aunt Sarah was pretty, with curls escaping from her tightly combed and pinned hair. I couldn't imagine what she'd seen in this odd-looking fellow, neither young or old, standing expressionless before the camera with his hand on her shoulder. Not until I remembered the box social where he'd mortgaged a month's pay for the privilege of eating supper with a girl he'd never even met and Aunt Sarah's saying, "After that it was always Gus for me." She'd married him, and if he wasn't much of a farmer, and he wasn't, and if he drank too much, and he did, they managed, and I never heard Aunt Sarah complain of anything except her rheumatism.

Their son George was killed in the Spanish-American War, and their only daughter, Mary, who married Will Buster and always referred to herself as Mary Peak Buster, was not a favorite among her cousins. She was none too bright and was a big, bosomy woman not at all like her mother. She and Will had one son, Gordon, and Mary Peak Buster talked endlessly of him, ending every recital of his cuteness with "the little tyke." This resulted in his being nicknamed Tyke, an appellation he could never shake.

Mary Peak Buster kept her telephone party line tied up a good part of every day, talking of the little tyke and of her hens and her housekeeping. "I've washed the kitchen windows and mopped the floors and killed every fly in the house but one."

"Saving that one for seed," my mother remarked.

CHAPTER SEVEN

In 1924 the Ku Klux Klan came to Franklin in the person of LeRoy Simpson, a tall spindly man with a middle-aged potbelly and adolescent pimples. Simpson had been born in Macon, Georgia. He had scratched out a living on a hardscrabble farm until he began working as an organizer for the KKK. The Klan knew there were ten-dollar memberships to be gathered out there and that some people yearned for extralegal settlements of long-festering grudges. Simpson had come to town to organize the local Klan because of a postcard from Harry Grout in Franklin.

Harry Grout had written the postcard as soon as he'd heard the Klan was in business again, and Harry worked out the arrangements for LeRoy Simpson to come to Franklin. All his life Harry had heard about those nightriders who'd robed up and ridden out to punish wrongdoers and put the fear of God into "uppity niggers."

Most of Harry's information had come from Col. Ebert B. Ewing, who'd come to Franklin in the 1890s. As kids, Harry and Mel Spinney had sat for hours listening to old Colonel Ewing talk about the Civil War and the subsequent exploits of the mystic Knights of the Ku Klux Klan. They listened spellbound to Ewing's stories of battles and night forays by Gen. Nathan Bedford Forrest's men. They pictured Colonel Ewing, now an old man, as a dashing young fellow infiltrating the camps of enemy troops by night and leaving contemptuous notes where the Union soldiers would find them the next day, baffled and reluctantly impressed by the daring and skill of their night visitors. Colonel Ewing made the hardship and the comradeship and the dangers real and vivid to his listeners, and when he pictured the soldiers' homecoming and the horrors of Reconstruction, "with scallywags and niggers running the Guv'ment," they could see perfectly how the Klan movement had spread, as brave men found it necessary to take matters into their own hands. The colonel didn't brag; he simply told what had happened, and, when the boys whooped and hollered and wanted him to get more specific about his own acts of bravery, he just smiled and said, "Now, boys, that ain't the point—we was all in it together."

What "Colonel" Ewing didn't tell them—what he hadn't told anybody since he'd come to Franklin—was that he'd been born and raised on a hardscrabble farm, was only eleven when the war broke out, never left Hancock County, Tennessee, until he'd headed to Nebraska, and had never fired a shot at a living thing except squirrels and birds. As a kid, he'd heard about secession and the arguments for and against it, but the only part that really moved him was the talk about states' rights and sacred honor and what we'd show those boogers if they tried to push us around. He knew— he'd heard it often enough—that one Southerner could whip any fifteen of those "northern nigger lovers." He saw the men ride off to war, and he longed to go with them; he dreamed of them every night and day while they were gone and set the tone and flavor of the rest of his life upon those dreams. Gen. Nathan Bedford Forrest was his hero, and from the time he had whiskers he groomed them so that by age twenty, when he was getting married, he had a flowing mustache and beard just like the general's.

By that time all the soldiers were back who were coming back. They were more worn and bedraggled than dashing and romantic, but the ones Ewing admired most hadn't given up, not by a damn sight. They had some scores to settle, and they meant to settle them. Word came of "the mystic knights" who gathered and rode out under cover of darkness to take care of troublemakers, people who'd transgressed God's holy laws by treating blacks as if they were folks like anybody else. The Klan hated Catholics, immigrants, white men who were fornicators and wife beaters, and most of all, the blacks themselves.

Stories went around the countryside about these nighttime expeditions, and in the telling they grew and grew, and they filled the young boy Ebert Ewing's imagination with eagerness to be one of those strong men who went out and made things right for the God-fearing and right thinking. He determined to become just like them. He had a lot to learn, he knew that, and he set about it in earnest, hanging around the men as much as they'd let him and picking up ways of speaking that he hadn't learned from his own folks. If he had been too young to fight in the Civil War, he could at least help organize Klan "Klaverns" where they didn't exist.

By the time he came west, he and his wife, Mindy, had a brood of children, one born right after another. Mindy tried but seemed unable to keep up with the cooking and washing and cleaning it took for a family that big.

Memphis was a hub from which people of all kinds were heading west to begin their new lives, and it was there that Ebert Ewing's dreams crystallized, giving him his new persona. The high rollers who worked the riverboats and river towns brought the glamour Ewing imagined the antebellum South had all to life for him as the bedraggled men who had returned to Hancock County couldn't.

The man who epitomized all Ebert Ewing would like to have been was Fairburn Beauregard Fallbrook, who had been a real colonel in the Confederate army. Colonel Fallbrook was a tall, handsome man whose Panama suits were made in St. Louis and were said to cost two hundred dollars apiece. He wore a ruby the size of a pigeon's egg hanging from a heavy gold watch chain across his discreetly patterned waistcoat and another smaller one on his ring finger. His voice was soft, his manner courtly toward women, and courteous toward even the least prepossessing of the men who congregated around him in the saloon, hoping to hear him speak of his days with General Forrest at Chickamauga or Shiloh or of his experiences on the river since mustering out.

It was known that Colonel Fallbrook gambled for high stakes and did well at it, that women worshiped him, and that he was slow to anger but deadly when provoked, but he never spoke of these things. His way of speaking was self-deprecating and humorous; only an occasional word revealed the breadth of his experience in war, in love, and in defense of his honor. Others told these stories outside his hearing. When some listener, more pushy than the others, questioned him about details or urged him to enlarge upon his experiences, Colonel Fallbrook's eyes grew a little remote, and he replied mildly that he couldn't oblige. Others who'd seen and done more than he had would have to supply that sort of information.

It was in Memphis that Ebert Ewing bought his first Panama suit—not a tailor-made one like Colonel Fallbrook's but a fine-looking white suit and white shirts and a black string tie and a wide-brimmed white hat. It was in Memphis, too, that he added the *B.* to his name, and, though his wife hardly noticed it at first, she overheard him telling someone after they'd reached Nebraska that it stood for Beauregard.

In his own mind, now, Colonel Ewing had been a soldier in the great conflict, which he now thought of as the War Between the States, and, if some of his exploits seemed advanced for a boy, nobody questioned them. It was understood that the "colonel" title was honorary—he was too young to have really been one—but it didn't bother anybody; no animus existed anymore against the Confederacy. In time Mindy herself began to refer to her husband as the Colonel.

It was because of Colonel Ewing's stories of honor and the need to avenge injustices that Harry Grout had asked LeRoy Simpson, the KKK organizer, to come to Franklin. Simpson came on the train. He stayed at the little hotel near the tracks, where he held meetings in his room and distributed pamphlets. He was in Franklin only a few days, just long enough to collect ten dollars from each of the men Harry had been able to scrounge up and to give instructions for holding meetings and proceeding with the work of making America safe from the influence of blacks, Jews, foreigners, and Catholics. It was a feather in Harry's cap that he was able to get Horatio Murray, president and cashier of the Franklin State Bank, to join and to urge others to join. Rashie Murray, Horatio's son, also joined. Most of the men put a down payment on the costumes, which were to be shipped from Nashville, and all agreed to attend the first big public meeting.

There was a good crowd at the schoolhouse the Tuesday night of the meeting. Harry Grout, as chairman, began by recalling the glorious history of the original Ku Klux Klan, when brave men robed up in costumes, made of sheets by loyal wives and mothers, and rode out to scare the niggers and people known to be enemies of "real" Americans. Harry spoke at length of the fear and wonder and mystery the Klan aroused and of the power each Klansman felt upon silently greeting fellow members with the secret handgrip.

He read aloud from the printed material Leroy Simpson had left with him and then launched out on his own. "Old Harry's always been quite a talker," somebody whispered.

Harry made it plain that, unless suppressed by the God-fearing, right-thinking men of the country, "these elements" would bring America down.

"Some folks may think these people aren't dangerous," he said. "Some folks would like to hide their heads in the sand and refuse to face the facts. Some folks will say Harry Grout's stretching it," he went on. "But look here."

At this signal Mel Spinney passed packets of pamphlets to each row.

"There it is!" cried Harry. "In black-and-white. I guess when people see what's printed in black-and-white in this here literature they're going to start waking up and seeing what's been happening to America. And I say the whole thing's got to be stopped!"

The men were looking through the pamphlets; some pages had pictures.

"What are you gonna say when foreigners take over this town?" Harry demanded. "And when the Jew money interests foreclose on your business? How you gonna like it when a big buck nigger takes a shinin' to your daughters? And what are you gonna do when the pope tells you that you can't worship God unless you're Catholic?"

Catholic was the operative word here; there were no Jews or blacks in Franklin, and many of the men present were sons of immigrants. There was no Catholic Church either, but there was one in Campbell, a tiny French settlement eighteen miles northeast, and that, it seemed, was close enough.

Apprehension built. It was plain that the country was in danger and that these men must act to save it. There was no other choice.

"How many here are 100 percent Americans?" Harry cried. "Everybody stand up that's 100 percent Americans!"

All the men stood up except Dick Kretsinger, superintendent of the school; Art Campion, the plumber; and my dad.

"Anybody who don't believe in America for Americans can leave right now!" Harry thundered.

The three men got up and left the auditorium.

Dad was sweeping out the shop Friday when Harry Grout, Mel Spinney, and four or five other Klansmen came in the door.

"Well, Karl," Harry began. "You didn't have much about our meeting in the paper."

"I had everything about that meeting that was fit to print," Dad said. "I had the date and the time and the place and the number of people who attended."

"Now look ahere," Mel Spinney said, beginning to bluster, as he always did. "We want full coverage of our meetings, so's people will know what the Klan stands for."

"If you had any sense," said Dad, "you'd want to keep it quiet. I never heard so much nonsense in my life. You ought to be ashamed of yourselves."

Harry Grout attempted to take charge. He hadn't planned for Mel to speak at all; Mel and the others were just there to show Karl Spence that the Klan meant business.

"Karl," he said, "America needs the Klan."

"What in hell for?" Dad shot back.

"Why, to save it from the niggers and the Jew money interests and Rome!

It's time right-thinking Americans woke up and looked around at what's happening . . ."

"All I see's a bunch of half-baked boobs holdin' up my day's work," Dad said. "I clean the shop on Friday, and it looks like today it's gonna need a good one."

By this time his bright blue eyes were snapping, and he was holding his elbows out—like a gorilla, Mother said—as he always did when he was getting mad.

"Now Karl," Harry began in a conciliatory tone. "We need the cooperation of the press. We're going to help you, and we need you to help us. We have some press releases here we need you to run next week, and there's more coming from national headquarters all the time. They explain how the news should be handled, so's everybody can understand what we're up against."

"I know what I'm up against," said Dad. "I'm up against the sorriest bunch of no-goods in Franklin County. Goddamned Kluckers! And I can tell you pretty quick what you can do with your news releases. This is my newspaper, and, if you think I need help from a bunch of illiterate nincompoops who wouldn't know the Bill of Rights if it came up and bit them, you've got another think coming. And," here he reversed the broom and started toward them, "I've got enough crap to sweep out of this place today. You get your asses out of my shop, and you do it damned quick!"

The Klansmen were scattered out the door by this time, one of them hollering back, "I notice you didn't stand up with the 100 percent Americans the other night!"

"No," Dad shouted out the door after them. "I never stand up with horseshit!"

The meeting with the press hadn't gone at all as Klan organizer LeRoy Simpson had told his fledgling members it would. Simpson had led them to expect that all that was necessary was to explain that certain dangers loomed and certain actions must be taken. He'd said that the local newspaper would cooperate to muster an aroused citizenry and protect America. It had all been so plain, and yet here they were, their first meeting spoiled by the refusal of Karl Spence, Art Campion, and Dick Kretsinger to stand up for America; a barely minimal account of the meeting in the newspaper; and a point-blank refusal by its editor to print what the Klan was about. Worse, the editor had all but threatened them with violence. And the new Klan members didn't even have their robes yet.

They fell to bickering after they were well away from the shop and the other businesses. Dad heard fragments of what the men had said and filled in the rest. "Why didn't you keep out of it, Mel?" said Harry. "Everybody knows Karl Spence is a hothead, and everybody knows he don't like you, anyway."

Mel was in no mood to take the blame. They all felt sore and shaky, remembering what Karl had called them and remembering too that they'd turned and run from a little paunchy guy waving a broom at them. The Knights of the Ku Klux Klan hadn't come off well, and, with Karl shouting dirty words at them right out where everybody could hear and could see them scuttling, the whole town would know of it before dinnertime.

Mel said, "Let's go up to the Odd Fellows Hall."

Mel was a member of the Odd Fellows, and he got a little something, duly noted in the treasurer's report, for folding the chairs and sweeping up after meetings. They all trooped up the outside stairs to the meeting room over Sam Chittick's store. It wasn't a formal meeting; Harry almost wished it were because he could use the practice. It was just crabbing and complaining, and the others seemed to blame him for not handling things better.

"You know Karl'll write some of them mean editorials of his, and folks are liable to get the wrong idea about the Klan," said Osie Medlow.

Finally, Harry said, "Listen, everybody. This isn't getting us anywhere. There's got to be some way to get things going. We've got to find some way to make Spence back down because we need newspaper support."

Direct, head-on action wasn't going to work, obviously, but everybody had a weak spot if only you could find it.

"How about him being pro-German?" Osie asked.

Osie was referring to a story in the Bloomington paper in 1917 that Karl L. Spence was probably pro-German because he spelled his first name with a K.

"Nah," said Harry. "That sort of stuff was silly at the time, and that's years ago. Nobody'd go for that anymore."

At this Elmer Wyatt spoke up. "I think Karl's got a weak spot all right." They all looked at him.

"I think he's got a weak spot for Mary Eads," Elmer said. "She's kinda cute, you know."

It caught on at once.

"Yeah," Mel said. "She's pretty, and she works late with him sometimes on Wednesday nights when he's tryin' to get the paper out."

"Or when he's got some extra job work," Elmer said. "I'm down that way sometimes in the evening."

They all knew he was; his wife was an invalid, and he sometimes went to visit Ona Magee, a cretinous offshoot of the Bargerson family who lived in a run-down house near the railroad tracks.

It was Mel who had the idea of writing the letter and Mel who volunteered to carry it out. He knew it was true Karl didn't like him, and he knew Sadie was contemptuous of his wife, Ella. Maybe Ella was kind of a silly woman, but the Dohers and the Ewings had been neighbors out in the country, and Sadie and Ella had grown up together. Ella had never been invited to become a PEO, and she felt it wouldn't have hurt Sadie to do that much for her.

"Sadie Spence has always held her head pretty high," he said. "Maybe she needs to know what's goin' on when Karl works late at the shop."

Somebody had a pencil and an old envelope. Mel would have liked to put in specific dates and times, but Elmer wasn't willing to say just when he'd gone past the shop in the evening.

"Anyway, Mel," said Harry. "The main thing is just to give her something to think about. Don't mention Mary Eads by name. Just ask Sadie how she likes her husband spendin' time at night with a young, good-looking girl."

Edgar Bowman, usually silent, spoke up. "But, Mel, when she gets this letter she might tell Karl you wrote her, and it'll make him mad as hell."

"I wrote her?" Mel demanded. "How's she gonna know I wrote to her? Good Lord, Edgar, you must think I'm as crazy as you are. I ain't gonna sign my name to it."

Everybody else had understood this from the first; it was only poor old Edgar who hadn't got it, and of course everybody knew he wasn't especially bright.

Mel tore off the back of the envelope and printed a few words on the scrap of paper. Not too much, they all agreed, but plenty to put a bee in Sadie's bonnet and, if they knew women—here some snickers—to put a burr under Karl's blanket. Just could be the Klan would get the kind of publicity it needed, after all.

That noon the discussion at our house, as at probably every house in town, was of the Klan's visit to Dad's shop. I could hardly contain my pride. We'd heard earlier about the meeting he'd walked out of, and I already knew how Dad felt about the newspaper: news was news and got printed no matter whose toes got stepped on; policy was his alone as editor; the proper function of a newspaper was to stand up for decency and good government; and Benjamin Franklin and William Allen White were at the top of a newspaperman's pantheon—I'd learned these things from the time I could understand the talk at our table.

I'd seen him mad; I could almost see him now, elbows out, blue eyes blazing, as he ran those Kluckers off. I was glad the whole street had seen them scuttling; it was what you could expect of people who snuck around in bed sheets and tried to scare people. I thought to myself, "I guess they found out a few things that day!"

Mother wasn't so confident. She felt sure the Bill of Rights was a good thing, and she meant to find out more about it at some point, but she had also known Dad to bristle up and go off half-cocked before.

Mother was contemptuous of the Spinneys, always had been. She and Ella Spinney had gone to country school and then to Franklin Academy together. Ella had been a giggly, flighty girl, always trying to get in with the Sadie Doher–Ruby White–Christy Dill group, the girls who did everything, had the most fun and the most beaux, and unofficially set the social tone of the academy. Ella couldn't get in that group. When she married Mel Spinney she started producing babies one right after another. She said, giggling, "I guess we've got the baby bug!" and Mother's distaste was complete.

The Grouts, too, although members of our church and respectable people, were as far distant from my parents' circle as it's possible to be in a town of twelve hundred people. Blanche Grout was a fanatical housekeeper. Her shelves bristled with Brillo, Brasso, Dippo, Dutch Cleanser, Bon Ami, and steel wool. Crocheted antimacassars were on all her chair backs and arms; doilies and scarves and French knots and tatted edging adorned every dresser and tabletop. Her china was swaddled in flannel, and her silver plate was in tarnish-proof chests, but she polished it anyway. She waxed the gray-painted floors of her front and back porches and grew zinnias in stiff rows in the beds around their edges. Her family would as soon have dumped a dead rat in the parlor as to touch one of the cutwork guest towels in the bathroom, and no guest was known to have ever done so. Mother considered Mrs. Grout a Dumb Dora, and she did a wicked takeoff of her bringing her recipe, "Blanche Grout's Queen of Lemon Pies," to the committee that was getting up the Woman's Club Community cookbook. I could fairly see Mrs. Grout's angular frame and her pursed lips, the starched print dress, and the varnished straw hat with the viscera-colored grapes.

Still Mother thought Dad might have been too vehement in his denunciation and treatment of the delegation that had come to the shop. Unlike me, she felt a little embarrassed that he'd shouted and chased them into the street. The Grouts and Spinneys weren't much, of course, but Horatio Murray was cashier of the bank, and there was no use antagonizing him. Rashie Murray, Horatio's son, had a good job at the bank. Couldn't Dad see his way clear to getting along with these men and just handle their announcements as he did the ones that thePEO and the Woman's Club sent in about their meetings?

"Good God!" Dad shouted. "This is nothing like the PEO or the Woman's Club! They want me to use my paper to lump people together by religion and race and set folks against one another. Next thing you know they'll be beating up on people, never mind due process or courts of law. And, on top of that, having the gall to think they can tell me what I should put in the paper, my own paper! Bunch of goddamned Kluckers!"

Mother raised her hand. "Please! The children!" Just then Mort dumped his plate of food off his high-chair tray, so that ended that.

It wasn't long afterward that I began to realize something was terribly wrong at home. Mother was silent and withdrawn, and sometimes in the morning her eyelids were red and puffy. It crossed my mind that maybe she was pregnant, but she hadn't acted this way before Mort was born. Then she'd been the glowing Madonna, conscious of the elevated state of motherhood, Dear Little Baby under her heart and all that. Now sometimes I woke up and heard my parents talking, and there was weeping in Mother's voice. Loris felt the tension too; I knew he did, but I couldn't ask him about it. Anyway, I felt sure he was as much in the dark as I was.

One Sunday evening we went to church, and all through the first hymn I kept wondering what was keeping Uncle George and Aunt Belle Austin, who usually sat next to Dad and me while Mother played the piano for the service. The Austins weren't really my aunt and uncle, but I called them that, as I did all my parents' friends.

The Austins were something solid in my life. They lived up the street in a house that seemed opulently furnished to me. There were fine carpets in the living room and the library, and the chairs were upholstered in blue velvet. Steel engravings, framed in pale gold, hung on the walls—the Acropolis, the Cathedral of Rheims.

Sometimes Aunt Belle called to me as I was passing her house and invited me to sit in the exquisite parlor. She'd give me a cookie and ask me about my schoolwork.

Austin's Store—groceries, dry goods, and general merchandise—was the main one in Franklin County, and each morning precisely at 7:30 Uncle George left for the store, dressed in a suit with a vest. He always wore a white shirt and a necktie. I sometimes saw him unpacking cartons with his suit coat off and sleeve garters holding his cuffs up out of the way, but when he waited on customers he always put his coat back on. As a first- and second-grader, I'd worn shoes called Roman sandals, with six buttoned straps from the instep to above the ankle. When a button came off, Mother always said, "Stop in the store and ask Uncle George please to put another button on."

I liked an excuse to stop in the store. I liked the smells that floated across from the grocery side—coffee, vinegar, bacon, apples, oranges—to the dry goods side, where the shoe button machine was. I liked helping Uncle George search through the drawers of buttons to find the right one. And, if he weren't busy, he'd let me drift behind the counter and finger the bolts of fabrics with the lovely names—challis, chambray, madras, domestic (how right it looked for its name!), muslin, lawn (stretches of green grass and ladies in long dresses with parasols), drill (soldiers marching in close order), drab, duck, nainsook, batiste, and dotted Swiss. Uncle George seemed to like my wanting to know what they were called. And when a customer came in and he told me, "Better run along home now; your mother will be wondering where you are," I didn't mind. I always went out through the grocery side, where Estel, the tall, handsome Austin son, worked. I hoped he'd notice me; if he did, he'd smile and give me a gumdrop or a Fig Newton from one of the boxes with glass fronts.

Aunt Belle and Uncle George hadn't appeared at church as Mother struck the final chord of the first hymn, and, in the hush before she began playing the next one, there was a stir at the back of the church. Everyone looked around as a procession of hooded, white-clad figures walked slowly down the aisle. I knew instantly this was the Ku Klux Klan. Some kids at school had been talking about the Klan, and I'd jeered and called them Kluckers, just as Dad did.

Lucille Spinney had said lots of people had plenty to learn. Her grandpa, she said, helped start the Klan in Tennessee, and her grandpa knew all about what had happened there when blacks, Jews, and other foreigners got too smart. Things were going to start happening here in Nebraska, too, she said.

This, the eerie appearance of a troop of masked men dressed in sheets, was apparently one of the things she'd been talking about. The hair on the back of my neck bristled, and, as the silent procession walked down the aisle, I glimpsed a figure I thought I knew. With the sickening drop of something heavy into my belly, I became sure that this masked, sheeted figure was Uncle George Austin. I wanted to shriek "No! No!" but I couldn't make my dry mouth form even a whisper to ask Dad if he'd seen Uncle George. I sat dumbly while Mother began the introduction to the hymn. Wild dismay choked me when Dad's clear tenor soared out in the words of the old song. It was Mother's job to play for church, and she would do her duty if the roof fell in, but how could Dad sing? Why didn't somebody, the preacher or Herman Platt, the deacon, order these dirty sneaks out of God's house? And when the offertory began and one of the Klansmen advanced to the altar and put a naked green bill on the table before it, why didn't someone tell the Kluckers that the Congregational Church didn't need the money of people who had to hide their faces to go to church? In all my life I'd never seen my parents lie or sneak or slink; how could they bear it? Wasn't anybody going to do something?

I sat through the rest of the service in a stupor of shame and bitterness. Immediately after the announcements the Klansmen rose as one and silently left the church before the sermon began. The sermon was brief and made no mention of the visitation. As always, the benediction was welcome, more after that service than any other I could remember, and for once Mother didn't take long in gathering up her music and getting ready for the short walk home.

The dam broke as we reached the front door. The sobs were dry and tore my throat; I gagged and choked. Dad took me on his lap in the Morris chair and said, "It's all right, baby; it'll pass, they can't last long."

"But Uncle George!" I cried. "Uncle George was there!"

"No, no," Mother said. "The Austins went to Hildreth today. They weren't there."

It took a while to make my parents understand that I was sure I'd seen Uncle George, seen his shoes peeking out from under the white robe.

"No," Mother said. "The Austins went to Hildreth today to see Belle's niece. They wouldn't have gotten home in time for church."

"Look, baby," Dad said. "George Austin wouldn't touch the Klan with a ten-foot pole. He'd never be a Klucker."

"He's not that kind of man," Mother said. "And lots of people have shoes like that."

She went to the kitchen to make cocoa, and Dad held me tight until the sobbing and shuddering stopped. I drank the cocoa, and Mother played the piano while Dad sang "Listen to the Mockingbird," my favorite, whistling in all the right places. Loris came in from wherever he'd been, and we all went to bed at last. I slept at once and deeply, until the dreams came and woke me up, and then I couldn't sleep.

In the morning I went to school tired, and I looked with loathing on Lucille Spinney's smug face.

It was an endless day before I could plod home and fall on my bed.

When I woke I smelled ham frying for supper and heard Dad whistling in the kitchen, as somebody finished a music lesson with Mother in the living room.

I went downstairs, and Dad said, "Mr. and Mrs. Austin would like you to run over for a minute. They want to see you."

This was formal; it didn't seem ominous, but I knew it was important. I washed my face and combed my hair and changed my rumpled dress. I went to the Austins' house and rang the bell. Aunt Belle smiled when she opened the door, and, when she indicated I should sit on the high-backed chair I'd always admired, I knew it was no cookie-and-conversation visit. She went to bring Uncle George, who was settling his coat on his shoulders as he came to the parlor and sat down.

"Polly, your father told me about the men who dressed up and came to church last evening," Uncle George said. "He said it was very upsetting to the whole congregation."

"Yes," I whispered.

"We want you to know, Aunt Belle and I, that we were not in the church yesterday. We went to Hildreth for the day and were too late to go to church when we got home."

Aunt Belle added, "Your Uncle George would not be a part of anything like that in any case."

My Uncle George! They knew, then, how I felt about them, that they were something solid, something right, for me.

"No," Uncle George said slowly. "I would have no truck with any such group. I have too much respect for my church and myself. Those men had good reason to hide their faces; they're a disgrace in the house of God."

I sighed deeply. Uncle George and Aunt Belle had respect for my Dad, even though he did shout and threaten people right out on Main Street. And they had respect for me as a person, even though my feet didn't quite touch the floor when I sat in the high-backed chair.

Uncle George came to me and took my hand and shook it as he would a grown-up's. The meeting was over, and Aunt Belle saw me to the door. Aunt Belle wasn't much for hugging, but there on the porch I got a hug, the first, and perhaps the only one ever, from her.

I walked home slowly, thinking about it, feeling good about it, and when I opened my own door and smelled supper on the table, I rushed into the kitchen and hugged my dad around his big, comfortable middle. At supper I ate two pieces of ham, mounds of mashed potatoes, a helping of peas, and a big dish of applesauce.

We all went to the piano, where Mother played and I sang "Loch Lomond" and "The Rose of Tralee" with Dad, and Loris played "Traumerei" on his fiddle. I fell asleep over the arm of the sofa and was led off to bed.

Nobody questioned me about the visit to the Austins, and nobody ever mentioned that I didn't wash the supper dishes that night.

In the morning I went to school calm and joyous. Nothing Hazel Grout or Lucille Spinney said or thought could touch me now. I didn't care that the two of them whispered a lot at afternoon recess, looking at me. When I got tired of it, I stared at them until they turned and went back into the schoolhouse, still whispering.

I heard Dad in the kitchen when he came home.

"Oh Karl!" Mother cried. "Did you have to do that? Wasn't it enough when you chased them out of the shop and cussed them out in front of everybody? Did you have to dirty your hands brawling in the street with Harry Grout?"

"It wasn't much of a brawl," Dad said, and I could hear the grin in his voice. "He was down with a bloody nose before he knew what hit him, and, when I yanked him up and punched him again, he took off like a scalded rat. Must have headed for Swede Jensen's office just as soon as he washed his bloody nose."

"Clyde Jensen?" Mother faltered. "He's going to get Clyde to sue you?"

"Nah," Dad said, and the grin bubbled up in his voice. "Clyde Jensen in his judge's job, not Clyde as a lawyer. Swore out a warrant for my arrest, had me hauled in to Judge Clyde Jensen's court."

"Arrested?" Mother was almost crying now. "What did Clyde do?"

"Fined me," Dad said. "Five dollars and costs. Smallest fine he could assess on a guilty plea."

I heard the noises of weeping and murmuring my mother made and then Dad's guffaw.

"Harry scuttled out of there almost as fast as he scuttled before," Dad said. "And Swede told me he'd like to have given me an award. But he said if I headlined the story 'FIVE DOLLARS AND WORTH THE MONEY,' he'd have me up for contempt of court."

"Headline!" Mother shrieked. "Surely you're not going to put it in the paper!"

"Of course I am," Dad said. "Court procedures are on the public record. I always print court proceedings, you know that."

Mother was weeping again. "Everyone will know you were arrested," she cried. "What about the children? What will people think?"

"Think?" Dad demanded. "Do you think there's a soul in this town who doesn't already know what's been going on? Anybody with any sense'll know I love my girl too much to let those SOB's make her unhappy!"

For gosh sake, I thought, why is Dad acting so silly! His girl! I snuck up the stairs. Parents could be embarrassing; I was glad nobody would know about this.

On Thursday the front page of the *Franklin County News* carried a box headed, "KARL L. SPENCE PLEADS GUILTY TO ASSAULT AND BATTERY." The story read: "In Franklin Municipal Court Tuesday Karl L. Spence entered a plea of guilty to a charge of assault and battery, brought by Harry Grout. The battery took place earlier the same day on the sidewalk in front of the Franklin State Bank, and resulted in numerous bruises and contusions to the plaintiff. Judge Clyde A. Jensen imposed a fine of $5 and court costs on the defendant."

On Friday afternoon Mel Spinney, spotting Karl Spence heading for him, ran up the outside stairs of Sam Chittick's store and into the Odd Fellows' meeting room, where he barricaded the door with furniture and stayed until nightfall.

The Klan had not had a very good week in Franklin, and it eventually died out but not for many years. Whether it was the stupidity of its "philosophy" or the general ineptness of its members that caused its demise, I don't know. I wish I could say that prejudice died out in small-town Nebraska with the withering of the Klan, but that's not true.

CHAPTER EIGHT

I remember little about the house I was born in except that the outside was covered with brown-stained shingles, and the inside was highly varnished: floors, woodwork, and furniture. When they refurbished it, it must have been my parents' dream house. Maybe Mother knew, before it happened, that Dad might sell it. Maybe he had a good reason, I don't know. At any rate we moved rather suddenly to an old house that Dad had bought "for a song," as he put it. Later, a time or two, Dad simply made the announcement that we were moving, and away we went. When he jumped, he was always optimistic; if his optimism flagged later, we never knew it.

Mother's must have flagged when she got inside Dad's old bargain house and saw the falling plaster and the warped floors. The ceilings were high, the kitchen cupboards tall and unhandy. There was no bathroom. She put on her painting and cleaning hat and waded in.

That hat! She'd loved it the moment she and Dad had spotted it years before in a Holdrege store window. It was a cloche of "dusty rose" satin, stitched all over with swirls of gold cord.

"It's too expensive," said Mother.

"Nonsense," said Dad, "nothing's too good for my honeybunch."

He walked in and bought it. We children were dazzled by its beauty, and we felt everybody in church must share our admiration when Mother sat up front playing the piano in that splendid hat and the new dress she'd bought to go with it. But that had been years ago. Now it was a source of shame and embarrassment to Loris and me—spotted with calcimine and stained with God knows what all. We pleaded with Mother not to wear it. Why wear the nasty thing at all? "It covers my hair," said Mother matter-of-factly. That hat was as embarrassing as the hoarse, penetrating "Hoo-hoo!" with which she summoned us.

The abrupt moves we made from time to time were always Dad's idea. I don't know how Mother felt about it. If she protested or raged or cried— she must have—we children didn't hear it. Maybe she learned not to; by the time Dad announced a move, I'm sure the deed was done: the house we were in would already have been sold, papers would have been signed, money accepted, bridges burned.

It must have been about money. We were always short of it. When financial trouble was bearing down, selling our house may have averted disaster. Dad was always optimistic, even ebullient, about the move; when a new idea hit him, caution never held him back. Of course we can do it; jump in now and figure it out later, seemed to be his motto.

I didn't hear Mother say anything about money either except when I wanted some wildly impractical thing. Then she'd say, "No, we can't afford it." I know her attitude toward debt was a lot different from Dad's.

Maybe it was her feeling of relief which kept her quiet. When Dad got a good price for the house we'd been living in and bought another one for a low price, it meant there would be money to apply toward paying off debts. It was Mother who said no, Mother who managed to run the household with so little cash, and Mother who waded into all those dilapidated, dirty houses we moved into and made them clean.

The things that had to be done to those houses! First of all, and always, we needed a bathroom. In the time and place when those houses were built, bathrooms weren't considered essential. One woman said, "A toilet right in the house—ugh, that's dirty! I'd rather go out back."

Some houses had a big closet or storeroom that could be fitted up for a bathroom, but sometimes structural changes had to be made. Dad did what he could, of course, but he was inept at anything mechanical except making printing machinery run. There were carpenters and handymen around, and he made deals for their work in exchange for ads or extended subscriptions or something of the sort. But lumber and plumbing fixtures cost money, and Mother must have sweated getting the cash applied to the renovations before it slipped away from Dad.

Roofs had to be mended; outsides had to be painted. Loris and I scraped and sanded and re-puttied the window sashes. Mother painted walls with a wide brush. All of us painted woodwork and stair steps. And every time, when it was finished, or as near finished as it ever got, it looked right. The old familiar hit-or-miss rag rugs, glass-front bookcases, and mission oak library table were in place. And always there was the piano, with Ludwig von Beethoven glowering over everything in the room.

It was the piano, of course, which made everything so right. Certainly our furniture was ordinary and shabby compared to what many people had. Some families had pianos, but none rang and reverberated through the life of the house as ours did—practice for church music, soloists and groups throughout the week, and kids for lessons as soon as school was out. Every evening we all trooped to the piano after supper, leaving the dishes on the table.

We sang in parts, we sang solo, and Loris played his violin. The goose flesh popped out on my arms when Dad sang alone. It was the tender beauty of the words in the songs he sang—"Kathleen Mavourneen," "Loch Lomond," "Last Night the Nightingale Woke Me," and, most of all, "Drink to Me Only with Thine Eyes"—and the melting sound of his soaring tenor voice. We felt warm and secure at home with the piano.

Mother's first piano was a graduation present from her parents. After that first move back to town, it went with her as she and Dad moved here and there in Franklin. It was a tall, dark upright. The wide bench was full of exercise books and sheet music.

The baby grand was a bombshell in our lives; that was the way Dad planned it. It was delivered while Mother was in Holdrege at a long-planned music teachers' conference. When I got home, my mother's sister, Aunt Carolyn, was almost gibbering with excitement as she met me.

"If you come in," she babbled, "you have to stay in. Karl says it's a surprise. Sadie can't get wind of it." I had no idea what she was talking about.

The piano was beautiful, all curving mahogany and dazzling ivory keys. "Mother'll die," I said when I saw it. "She'll just die."

"Yes," said Aunt Carolyn. "Isn't it wonderful?"

Mother wouldn't be home until late. We ate our supper in gulps and watched Mr. Perlow, the piano tuner, work on the piano. He tapped his tuning fork, tightening first one pin then another. Dad was nervous as a cat.

Finally, there was the flourish of arpeggios which signaled that Mr. Perlow was satisfied with his work, and at almost the same moment a car stopped outside. We grinned at one another, we fidgeted, we stood in a row where we could see Mother's expression as she saw the piano. Her reaction was as good as we had hoped it would be. She screamed and cried and ran to it.

The upright was a good piano, but the baby grand was classy. The academy had a concert grand, of course, and other upright pianos—I think our old one wound up there—but nobody else in town had a grand except the old Conkling sisters, and its keyboard and pins hadn't been touched in years; nobody ever saw it or played it.

Dad's surprise for Mother was all he'd hoped for. If paying for it was a problem, we children didn't know that. Mother was proud and happy. We all were.

Mother never apologized for our furniture or her makeshifts. It wasn't that she didn't care about nice furniture and nice houses. She admired fine things as much as anybody; the way she felt about herself, however, didn't depend upon her having them. Digging mouse turds out of cupboard corners or plugging up the holes in the old houses we moved into didn't diminish her. That it might seem degrading to some people probably never crossed her mind. The packets of cottage cheese she made and traded for credit at Austin's store had no connection, either, with the engraved cards— MRS. KARL LORIS SPENCE—she left for ladies who had just moved to Franklin. She knew who she was; she thought it only right that they should know too.

The piano was another matter. There had always been a piano; there always would be a piano. The baby grand was simply the ultimate tangible expression of Dad's love for Mother and of the importance both of them attached to music in our lives. When John McCormack or the Minneapolis Symphony or John Philip Sousa made concert tours in the hinterlands, we always went to Holdrege to hear them. The tickets might have been comps—country newspapers got complimentary tickets for many things— or, then again, they might not have been. Still, whatever they cost, we had them.

If we didn't have a car when musicians came to Holdrege, Dad got Will Humphreys to drive us. If the concert were scheduled for a Thursday, the paper came out on Wednesday, with Thursday's date. If the weather were freezing or the roads muddy, Dad put on the side curtains. Mother heated soapstones and warmed blankets, and we started early. In the concert hall, after riding sixty miles in a Model T, our hands and feet tingled as feeling came back to them. But, when ten violinists in white tie and tails lifted ten bows as one, nothing else mattered. Sound surged through us and carried us up and up and up. When it was over I stumbled out into the cold after Loris and our parents, fairly dazed with beauty. I thought of the plain young woman who sat in her evening dress plucking gorgeous tones from a great harp, and she was touched with glory too. I saw myself sitting in her place, drawing that lovely sound out of the vibrating strings.

There was money for books and money for stacks of music. Magazines—the *Atlantic,* the *Literary Digest, Collier's, Liberty,* the *Ladies' Home Journal, Delineator,* the *American, Youth's Companion*—came to us through an advertising arrangement with a jobber in Omaha.

We got goods and services from almost every merchant in our town in exchange for advertising or subscriptions, some as gifts to good customers. Mr. Eghoff, the cobbler, had a permanent "card," a small advertisement, in the paper in exchange for fixing our shoes. His card said, "GOOD WORK, REASONABLE RATES," and it was truth in advertising on both counts. No price was put on the work he did for us, and no books were kept on either side. I heard him tell other customers, "That'll be eighteen cents. Twenty's too much, and fifteen ain't enough." He lived near us, and if it was close to noon he'd say, "Wait a minute, I'll walk along with you. Time to see if the hens laid a egg or the neighbors fetched in something." He didn't lock up when he went home for dinner, just hung the card on the doorknob that said, "BACK SOON." Mr. Eghoff explained, "Somebody might want to leave their shoes, and, if their work's ready, they'll see it on the back table and help theirselves."

Many of Dad's ideas were exasperating. There were the raspberries, six crates of them, which he'd bought off a passing truck. They were dead ripe and had to be made into jam at once. Mother had all the curtains down for washing because she was having PEO the next day. She made the jam and ironed the curtains after choir practice that evening—she ironed until midnight and got them hung up at 1:30 A.M.

I suppose the bargain for roasting ears, fifty dozen of them, sticks in my mind because Loris and I sat on the cellar door all one afternoon husking and silking them. In the 1920s sweet corn wasn't like the strains that agricultural colleges developed later on. In those days corn had silk over and between the kernels thick as the hair on a dog's back, tenacious silk that had to be pulled off first in wads, then in strands, and at last thread by thread. That was a long night too. Every ear had to be put in boiling water, cooled in tap water, and shorn of kernels with a knife.

There weren't enough jars to can it all; it had to be dried. I was sent to Austin's store for twenty yards of mosquito netting at five cents a yard to put the corn on. Every window screen in the house came down and had corn spread on it. By morning the kitchen floor was covered with drying corn. It had to be watched and turned for days, and it came out dark and hard as a bullet. "Ugh," I thought, "all that work for nothing." But in the winter, after a soak in hot water and a long simmer, it was delicious. I forgave Dad—of course, I'd long since done that—and Mother did too. Still, she must have wanted to whack him at the time.

Mother canned some hens one fall day, and it gave my brother Mort, our visiting cousin Wellington, and a couple of neighborhood urchins an idea. It had been a long time since I'd played with my doll, Betsy Anne, but even so I wept when I saw her dismembered limbs swimming in fruit jars full of water. The only thing that saved her lovely head was its being china, too large to slip unbroken into a fruit jar, and some failure of nerve on the part of the wretched brats who'd murdered her.

CHAPTER NINE

Dad was nine when his parents brought him to Nebraska. He was born in Williamson County, Illinois—it was called bloody Williamson in the 1870s because of backwoods feuds and in the 1920s because of labor violence in the coalmines. It seemed to me that Jenny McBride and Charley Spence, each from a family of ten children who'd grown up as neighbors, married for the express purpose of becoming my grandparents, and the bonus was that I got two great-uncles I wouldn't have missed for the world.

On my mother's side, Uncle Jim McBride was a big, heavy man whose blue eyes and black hair seemed to be the model for Dad's. He wore pin-stripe suits and shirts with starched collars and cuffs, and each May he bought a new straw "katy"—a straw hat—with a striped grosgrain ribbon around the crown. He smelled of cigars and bourbon, and he loved me in the same open, expansive way he loved his own daughters. His big, round voice rolled through any house he was in, and my mother's prim notions of what was suitable for children's ears affected him not at all. Uncle Jim said and did whatever he liked; so did Aunt Lottie and all the McBride kids. There were six of them, and they lived in Cowles, not too far for visits. I had a crush on every one of the four boys, and so did every other girl who met them; they cut a wide swath. I loved it when they caught me up and hugged me half to death and when they teased me at the long dinner table, abundantly piled with food.

My uncle on Dad's side, Ernest Spence, was a tiny grasshopper of a man, thin to the point of emaciation. His suits were conservative; his speech was soft and dignified. As a matter of strong personal conviction, he didn't smoke or drink, and he wouldn't accept advertising for tobacco or liquor in his newspapers. Those substances, he said, defiled the temple of the body, and he would not be a party to their promotion. He was a pillar of the Bladen Methodist Church, and he never used profanity. "It wasn't always that way," said Aunt Lottie. "Belle and Mag could give you an earful about Jim and Ernest when they were kids together back in Illinois. Ernest was as much of a scamp as Jim was, fooling around with the girls just the same way."

I never knew Aunt Belle, Aunt Mag, or any of the other McBride sisters and brothers except for Uncle Jim and my grandmother.

"They were a wild bunch," said Aunt Lottie. "Always up to something, girls and all. Still are, for that matter." She smiled. "When we went back there to see them, and they all got to talking . . . well, you can imagine."

I could imagine that part, the talking, and I wished I'd been there to hear it. It was easy enough to see Uncle Jim as a boy, easy enough to see him doing almost any crazy thing. But Uncle Ernest—we called him "Unk"—only occasionally could I catch a glimpse in my mind of a skinny little boy. Even then I couldn't imagine an ornery skinny little boy. I knew he couldn't have worn conservative suits and starched collars then—they were all barefoot, out-at-the-elbows kids back there in Illinois—but the picture of him as a boy eluded me. This slight, dignified man with steel-rim glasses—he'd chased girls? And caught them?

I saw him twinkle now and then, though, when Uncle Jim and Grandmother got to talking about life in those days—how poor they were, how much fun they'd had. He never denied anything; could it all have been true?

"We had a team of mules," Grandmother said. "That was about all we had, old Mack and Molly. You couldn't farm without mules or horses. Pa sent Jim and Ernest to get some seed corn. They were supposed to lock the wheel going down the hills to slow the wagon down. Instead, they whipped the mules to keep the wagon from running into them and got them into a lather by the time they got home. They told Pa the mules bolted at a jackrabbit and they only saved the corn and the wagon by good driving." She laughed. "I don't know if Pa believed them or not; I didn't. I felt sorry for the mules."

"Sorry for a mule?" Uncle Jim demanded. "Jenny, you know better than that. Before the week was up old Mack caught me bent over a manger and like to bit my butt off. I never turned my back on him after that."

"What we did to those mules wasn't as bad," said Uncle Ernest, "as what Jim did to another mule your Pa had. That mule had a miserable disposition, and Jim hated him."

"You didn't like him much yourself," said Uncle Jim.

"No, I didn't," Unk admitted. "But I'm not the one who shot him."

"Shot him!" I said.

"Yes, shot him," said Unk. "That was an aggravating mule, and Jim just lost his patience. Fortunately," he added, "Jim never was much of a shot. He just grazed the mule, but his intentions were purely murder."

Both of those boys from the backwoods of Illinois came to Nebraska determined to get ahead. Ernest was full of ideas; he had been from the time he was a kid. There were only three business buildings in Bladen when he got there, but from the first he saw the place as the hub of an agricultural empire. Somehow along the way he'd picked up barbering, printing, watch repairing, and optometry. He was nineteen when he set up a barbershop in Bladen, the newspaper the *Bladen Enterprise* in the back room of the barbershop, and in a year or two a watch repair and optometrist's bench.

Ernest urged his brothers-in-law—Charley, Frank, and Amzi—and Jim McBride to come west. There were fortunes to be made, he declared; a man would have to be a fool not to get in on it.

There were opportunities, to be sure. Homesteaders had flooded in, busted up the sod, and raised crops. Towns sprang up and fought over the location of county seats. Nebraska was dotted with little towns, and almost every one of them had a newspaper, a contentious, scrambling newspaper. In Nebraska a town of fifteen hundred was a big town; it still is in western Nebraska. In those days a town over two thousand might have had two newspapers.

Settlers, whether in town or in the country, were litigious, and the county printing—legal notices, delinquent tax lists, and the like—was the backbone of the newspaper business. The county printing, if you could get it—and only one newspaper per county could—was the principal and indeed the only sure support of a country newspaper. Advertising you had to get out and hustle for. Job work such as sale bills, advertising flyers, and wedding invitations helped, but the county printing was what kept most country newspapers afloat.

By the time Jim McBride arrived, Ernest Spence was running himself ragged. He hurried from one job to another: fitting a pair of eyeglasses, selling ads, scribbling notes for news items, while lather dried on a customer's face. On Saturday evening farmers in work clothes sprawled on benches in the back, waiting their turns to be trimmed and shaved. And all around, in every direction, were opportunities just waiting to be seized!

Jim came in on the train on a Friday evening. Ernest showed him around town and expounded on the possibilities.

"This country's a gold mine, Jim," he said. "People are coming in and building. Bladen can be the queen city of southern Nebraska."

Jim wanted to know more. He liked the countryside, what he'd seen of it, and he wanted to see more. He suggested getting a rig from the livery stable and going for a drive in the morning.

"Let's do it Sunday," said Ernest. "We'll go to church, and you can meet some people, and then we'll drive all over. Tomorrow I've got to get out two orders of job printing. Printers come in and work a week or two and then take off. We need somebody steady."

Steady was exactly what most itinerant printers were not. They called themselves journeymen, and some of them were topnotch at their trade; the common denominator was itchy feet and a great thirst. "Tramp" printers, if sober, would do a good day's work; if broke and sober, a good week's work. Payday meant a damned good drunk; freight trains rattling through town might be the signal to leave. One wanderer dressed like a fashion plate, complete with Malacca walking stick. He quoted Scripture like an archbishop, Shakespeare like Edwin Booth. Ernest had high hopes for him until the morning after payday, when he was found dead drunk in a ditch east of town.

He had high hopes for Jim McBride, too.

"The *Enterprise* is the key to the whole thing, Jim," he said. "The key to bringing people in, the key to keeping them here, the key to building a community. It'll make money, but, more than that, it'll set the tone for this part of the state. Here, let me show you how to set type."

Jim looked startled.

"Not that you'll be doing much typesetting," Ernest added hastily. "We'll get somebody steady; this is just so you'll know how to do it in a pinch."

Jim's main interest was in the land. It was being transferred right and left, to new people and between settled owners. He began to know people and to learn about options. Young as he was, Jim McBride exuded an air of confidence which reassured people; he moved surely into real estate transactions, and he helped Ernest set up a display case for his brand new stock of jewelry.

It was about that time that Charley and Jenny Spence moved their family to Bladen. Charley began at once to manage a lumberyard Ernest had an interest in. Their son Fred, age eleven, helped with the jewelry and watch repair business; his nine-year-old younger brother Karl, my dad, began to learn the printer's trade.

In no time Karl had learned to set type and to "throw it in"—sort it back into the compartments of the case—with astonishing speed. He liked to set type, and he liked to read, so he propped a book up beside his copy and read it while he set type perched on a high stool in front of the case.

"This boy's a natural," Uncle Ernest said, and he put him on an upturned goods box before the composing stone to learn the compositor's craft.

By the time he was twelve, Karl Spence was a full-fledged printer. Now tall enough to pump the foot pedal while he fed sheets into the press, he could, and sometimes did, all the work of getting out the *Enterprise*. It was then that he began the habits that were to be with him his whole life; the week, every week, culminated on Thursday, the day the paper came out. The paper had to come out on Thursday no matter how he or anyone else felt and no matter what was happening at home or in the world outside. Karl took pride in his responsibility. In addition, meeting the Thursday deadline was the only way he could keep the county printing contract.

Bladen is in Webster County. It was Uncle Ernest's thirst for Franklin County's printing that made Karl Spence, at fourteen, a country newspaper publisher. Supplying Karl with hardly more than a wheelbarrow load of type and tools, Ernest set the boy up in business to publish the *Upland Eagle* in Franklin, the county seat.

"You can do it, Karl," he'd said. And indeed the boy never doubted that he could. At fourteen, bursting with energy and high spirits, he went to Upland, got acquainted with the storekeeper, the preacher, the banker, and everybody else in town, gathered news items and set them into type straight out of his head or his notes, solicited advertising, editorialized, made up his displays, set it all up, composed it all on the stone, locked it into the forms, and printed the *Upland Eagle*, pumping the foot pedal as he fed the sheets into the press.

On Friday he finished the mailing, swept up the shop, and took the train home to Bladen. He liked being an independent businessman in front of his family and friends, but at the same time he was a fourteen-year-old kid who wanted to put his arms around his mother and his feet under her table. Home was a bigger house now, and there were two little brothers to tease and show off for.

Nothing was like it had been in Illinois. Charley Spence had caught fire from his young brother's way of looking at things and was handling sales of land from Manitoba, Canada, to Tampico, Mexico. His wife Jenny dressed stylishly and went with her husband to see the land in Mexico. There were limitless projects and prospects.

Ernest Spence had married Nell Bennett and settled in a house next door to his brother and across the alley from Nell's brother, Dr. Will Bennett. Nell, a tiny woman, gave birth to her first two boys and a girl with surprising ease and speed; the next accouchement caught everyone off guard.

"The first we knew of it," Grandmother said, "was Ernest pounding on our door at two in the morning. 'Jenny, Jenny, come quick!' he was hollering, 'there's babies all over the place!'"

There were only two. By the time Dr. Bennett got there, his sister's twin boys were wrapped in a shawl, and Ernest's teeth were still chattering.

"You wouldn't have known him," Grandmother said. "He's usually so sure of himself. Did me good to see him stand there babbling, just like anybody else."

Jim McBride was married too, to Lottie Doyle, and they had three little boys. From being a clerk in banks here and there around the county, Jim had become a banker, owning a good part of the Cowles bank, and dealing in farmland and grain. Frank and Amzi Spence had come to Webster County, too, and settled on farms. Family visiting was easy, even with a change of trains at Blue Hill, and Ernest was thinking of buying an automobile. It was the coming thing, he said.

He built a business block for the *Enterprise*, with a barbershop and post office on the first floor as well as offices upstairs for a doctor, a dentist, and the telephone company. He built living quarters for the telephone operator next to her office. Ernest and Charley were working on their dream of making Bladen an important city, and they boosted its advantages far and wide in those pre–chamber of commerce days. As the town's leading citizens, they ran it pretty much to suit themselves, as they did the Methodist Church.

In 1908 they built a general merchandise store and stocked it with groceries, dry goods, millinery, patent remedies, hardware, and sundries. Among the stock that came in on the train was a case filled with cigars, pipes, and a variety of smoking and chewing tobacco. Of course, as deacons in the church, they could not sell the filthy weed and profit from corruption. Returning it for credit would be, in their minds, countenancing corruption, too. There was only one thing to do: pitch it into the furnace.

"Into the furnace," said Aunt Lottie. "My brother Miner clerked for them, and he had to help. It was a long time before he could talk about it without choking up. Miner," she added, "I don't remember ever seeing him without a chaw in his cheek. He was eighteen when I was born, and he was chewing then."

Aunt Lottie was a heavy woman. She served three enormous meals each day, collected recipes, and often said, "You know what's good?" then answered her own question.

"I was a fat girl when I married Jim," she said. "All the Doyles were fat but Miner, and in those days, if you were fat, you were fat. We didn't think anything about it. All the girls, fat or thin, wore corsets."

Aunt Lottie wore a corset with stays and laces and print housedresses starched and ironed to a gloss. She kept her house shining clean; she sewed, baked, churned, canned, and preserved and never had a hired girl except when her babies were born. She took no guff from her husband or anybody else. Her boys teased and cajoled her but never put anything over on her.

"I was always proud of my butter," Aunt Lottie said. "I always liked to turn it out into that big blue crock and put my mark on it with the paddle. I don't know what possessed those boys to do what they did."

She went into the pantry and brought out the angel food cake pans, two of them.

"They were about nine and ten, I guess," she said. "Don and Shep. It was their job to milk the cow and turn the separator. They never complained— wouldn't have done them any good if they had, and they knew it."

She began separating egg whites into the blue crock.

"Cowles used to have a baseball team," she said. "Red Cloud, Guide Rock, Blue Hill, Bladen—all the towns around here had teams, and they had ball games over there in the fairgrounds. The bleachers were put up that spring. They're kind of rickety now, but they were new that spring."

She began to beat the egg whites with a wire whisk.

"I'd just churned," she said. "I'd had those two stomping the dasher. I didn't have a Dazey churn with a crank then; it was an old-fashioned kind with a wood dasher you pulled up and down by hand. But I always had my cream the right temperature—I didn't have a thermometer then, but I could tell—and, if the temperature's right, it doesn't take long to come to butter. I don't know what got into them."

"What did they do?" I asked. But Aunt Lottie wasn't to be hurried in telling her story.

"I washed the butter," she said. "Salted it, just a little, you know; you can spoil the flavor with too much salt, and working it too much makes it greasy. It looked so nice sitting there on the table. I was always proud of my butter. But I left the room a minute, went to the backhouse, I guess. When I came back the butter was gone."

"Nobody was around," she said. "There was nobody in the house that I knew of, and I hadn't seen anybody come in. I started looking, and Jim came home for dinner, and we both looked for those boys. They didn't come home till suppertime, and they didn't say a word when I was telling about the butter disappearing. But the next morning," she said, folding sugar into the egg whites, "I found the crock under the porch, and Jim called and said somebody'd been in the bank and said there was butter or something all over the bleachers at the ballpark. Somebody'd sat in it when the team was practicing the night before. I went out and found those two," she said, sifting cake flour into the batter, "and first I whaled 'em. Then I started heating water and melting lye soap into it. They carried buckets of water and worked with scrub brushes till their dad came home at noon. He didn't let them quit till he was satisfied those bleachers were as clean as hot water and soap and elbow grease could make them. Musta been two o'clock when he let them stop scrubbing and come home for some dinner. They were pretty tired and subdued."

She slipped a spatula into the batter, poured it into pans, and smiled with satisfaction as she slipped the pans into the oven.

"You never know what kids'll do," she said.

Don and Shep were grown young men now. They'd worked and earned money from the time they could deliver handbills or clean the back room of the drugstore. All the McBrides worked, even their brother Buns, but Buns figured there were other ways to make a buck.

"He's a snake oil artist," I heard someone say. "Buns could sell the Brooklyn Bridge to J. P. Morgan." I could believe it; nobody could say no to Buns.

From my first remembrance of visits to Uncle Ernest's family in Bladen, it was a motherless home. Aunt Nell had died in 1919, and I had no real memory of her. I do remember hearing Mother say that she and Dad had decided to ask Uncle Ernest to let his daughter Marjorie come live with us. Uncle Ernest needed help, Mother said. I'd have the sister I'd always wanted.

Unk's answer was a firm no. He appreciated the thought, but he reassured all the well-meaning people who wanted to help that he and the children could manage nicely. The church ladies who clucked over him, wondering what possessed a man with six motherless children to think they could manage by themselves, must have been astonished at the strength of this small, quiet man. When I was old enough to realize what it had meant, I was astonished, too.

In the early years of his marriage Unk had built a substantial home for the family he meant to have and did have. Whatever his pain, this home, this family, would endure. There was never any possibility that he'd let his children be split up or any possibility that they couldn't manage by themselves.

They did, too. Each one had work to do; each one did what he or she was expected to do and did it quietly. No arguing, no fighting—I marveled at it. The house was orderly, the kitchen was clean, and the meals were ready on time. Rolland, Harold, and the twins worked at the *Enterprise;* they did their chores at home, too. The oldest daughter, Vera, sat at one end of the long dining room table and Unk at the other, smiling at the talk and the laughter.

I hardly remembered Rolland, either. He was the eldest but died when he was twenty-two, a couple of years after his mother's death. I was a grown woman, with children of my own, when I learned that Uncle Ernest had had a wife before Aunt Nell and that she and their two little girls all died within a year or so of one another.

"Ernest's had a lot of sorrow," Aunt Lottie said. "His first wife was a nice woman, and Nell was a nice woman. Folks thought sure he'd fall apart when he lost Nell."

My Uncle Jim McBride told me, "Mina Riggins thought sure I'd broke down when Nell died. At the funeral, damn, was it cold, and Polly, how old were you then? Let's see, five or six, I guess. The preacher got started on one of those long-winded prayers the Methodists go for," he said. "Cold enough to freeze the balls off a brass monkey, and he just kept going."

He smiled at me.

"There you were, standing right in front of me," he said, "shivering in your little coat and hood, and you let out a teeny little fart, just about this long." He held two fingers about an inch apart. "I had my head bowed, of course, wishing to Christ the preacher'd quit, and I had my handkerchief in my hand. I was laughing so hard I put it over my face, but I knew I was shaking; I barely made it through. Mina told Lottie later she never dreamed I'd take Nell's death so hard."

By the time I knew him, Uncle Ernest didn't do much physical work; indeed, his health wasn't up to it. In spite of all the work he did, he'd been "poorly" all his life, claiming gastric disorders of several sorts. A lifelong insomniac, he sometimes declared that he hadn't slept a wink for more than seventy-two hours, and, when I took my children to see him in 1944, he told me he hadn't had a well day in his life.

In 1907 an item in the *Bladen Enterprise* announced that Ernest Spence, former editor of the paper, had been forced by poor health to retire but would fit a few eyeglasses as strength permitted. That was about the time he and my grandfather Charley opened their big general merchandise store and not long before Ernest, with various partners, built two residential developments and several business buildings in Bladen. During World War I he would often set off with a load of prospects in his Overland 90 automobile, to show citrus land in Texas, timberland in Arkansas, or wheat land in Kansas or eastern Colorado, while Rolland and Harold got the paper out. He bought a sawmill in Arkansas, opened a mill in Bladen to make Little Red Hen chicken feed, and dispatched salesmen far and wide to promote both the chicken feed and Glassweave, a building fabric he'd developed. In 1925 he found white clay in a bog on Uncle Amzi's Wyoming farm, had it analyzed, and learned that it was identical in composition to the beauty clay women used. If cleaned of a little grit and a few bones, the stuff could be packaged and marketed and would make a man a fortune. This plan never reached fruition, however. There were midnight calls about leasing the Texas citrus land for test wells; this plan also came to nothing. But a coal deal with Charlie Bryan, a former governor of Nebraska, worked out well; Unk traveled all over the state, selling rail carloads of coal to schools, factories, and power plants.

As Unk aged, his hearing failed, until eventually he became deaf; his mind remained alert, however, and his eyesight keen. He died in 1963 at the age of ninety-one, having just completed a holiday trip by train to California with his two daughters and forty-six years after poor health had forced him to retire.

CHAPTER TEN

I adored my brother Loris. There were just the two of us for the long time before the little boys were born. For Loris's first four years there hadn't even been me, so at first he must have had that only-child feeling that's different, I understand, from any other.

My brother was my main source of learning until I went to school, both because I believed everything he told me and because he taught me to read so early in life that I can't remember not reading.

That must have given Mother satisfaction because, while she read little herself, she knew "literature" was important. She may have learned that at the academy, or she may have learned it from the pages of the *Ladies'*

Home Journal or other uplifting women's magazines of the day. She earnestly wanted us to have the best, and we did, insofar as she and Dad were able to give it to us.

I started school when I was five, and suddenly everything was different. I didn't like the change. My brother had his own friends—Owen Cross, Charles Bloedorn, and others—and he didn't want me following him around. I had Erma, of course, and Benita Harrington and the younger Cross boys, but I wanted it all. I sensed his distaste for me, but I kept trying for a long time to hang around him.

What rankled me most was the clubhouse. It began as a pit the big boys dug in Bloedorn's yard, cattycorner from ours. They worked like dogs all one Saturday and drove the younger kids off when we tried to find out what they were up to. We saw an old tin heater come out of our shed and go down into the pit; we saw scrap boards and bricks carried from Bloedorn's lumberyard. We pleaded and promised not to touch anything and to keep our mouths shut if only they'd let us in, but it was no go. Finally, when we saw a length of stovepipe stuck up through the mounded earth and smelled the smoke rising in the chilly dusk, we pounded with sticks and bats until Mr. Bloedorn stepped out on his porch and suggested we run on home to supper. That clubhouse survived for years. We saw potatoes and salt being carried in and were sure we could smell the potatoes roasting, but we never were admitted, even for a peek.

I thought my brother was ten feet tall, but he wasn't; he was small for his age. He was handsome too: he had rosy cheeks, and old ladies spoke of him as that "pretty Spence boy." There was nothing he could do but pretend he hadn't heard, while he flushed beet red. He hated it in the same way I hated hearing myself described, by the same well-meaning old ladies, as "wholesome."

Besides that he was a "good" boy. He worked hard at the shop and learned the printer's trade. By the time he was ten or twelve he was writing and setting up news stories and ad copy without making a fuss about it. He didn't want to be a bother to anybody. When he fell out of a tree in our yard, he picked himself up, walked into our house white as a sheet, and said, "I think I've broken my arm." The jagged bone was sticking out through the skin on his arm.

Loris's teachers didn't send notes home from school; mine did. There were parent-teacher conferences about my "attitude," none about Loris's. He didn't mouth off in class; I did. He didn't punch other kids; I did.

I was an embarrassment to my brother, and he avoided me as much as he could. We argued and fought at home, but elsewhere Loris was quiet and mannerly. Other things bothered him too. It wasn't just the ridiculous old hat Mother wore for cleaning and painting or her raucous "Hoo-hoo" when she wanted us home. The Friday evening family excursions to the movies were agony to Loris.

The only reason he went with us at all was because of the ticket arrangement Dad had with Fred Hutchins, who owned the theater, the furniture store, and the funeral parlor. As soon as we got inside, Loris moved away from us to sit with his friends or by himself.

We went early so as not to miss "the comedy," but he knew what would happen when it got under way. In a theater that small there really was no place to hide.

The comedy was a short subject before the feature. Dad and I thought it the best part of the whole show. It might be Harold Lloyd or Charlie Chaplin or somebody you'd never seen before and wouldn't see again. It invariably had a chase, on foot, on horseback, by train, or by motorcar. There were shrieking close calls as locomotives bore down; there were pratfalls and trapdoors. There were buckets of water dumped on fat ladies in evening gowns, banana peels lying in wait for clerical gentlemen. The feature, even one with Fred Thompson and his white horse, couldn't compare.

And Dad laughed. It began with a gurgle and went on to high-pitched whoops. He gasped; he choked; he got his breath and began again. Everybody got caught up in it; many stopped looking at the screen to crane their necks and smile at us. Loris ducked his head, and, when the movie was over, he got out as quickly as he could. He ducked his head again if, a day or two later, he overheard a remark somebody was sure to make: "Had a good time at the show the other evenin', didn't you, Karl? I heard you all right! Bet they heard you in Riverton! Bloomington, anyway!"

A test devised in 1904 by a psychologist at the Sorbonne in Paris complicated things for people all over America in the 1920s; certainly it made things worse for Loris. It was the Stanford-Binet IQ test, and it became all the rage. Newspapers and magazines, scientists and politicians, educators and physicians, all proclaimed this test the indispensable, foolproof way to peg everybody into his proper slot: in the army, the trades and professions, and at Ellis Island, where arriving immigrants could be quickly sorted out as desirable or undesirable. Almost nobody pointed out that the test was simplistic, that it was heavily weighted against certain segments of any population, and that it failed to take into account dozens of factors that might reasonably be supposed to affect the results. That its originator never advised or envisioned the kinds of uses it was put to in America never crossed anybody's mind. As pop science, it was a huge success, and almost nobody questioned it.

Certainly nobody in Franklin, Nebraska, questioned it. The whole school was tested. Those who tested high were promptly reassigned from their grades into higher ones, where they felt lost and awkward among children who were older, more experienced, and more knowledgeable, it seemed, in the things that really mattered.

It happened twice to Loris and me, but it was worse for him. I was big for my age, not small like him. Best of all, Erma and I were shifted together both times, along with our classmates Jimmy Burton and Ralph Staten. Like Loris, Jimmy was small for his age. Whether it bothered him as much as Loris I don't know. At home I saw Loris tie weights on his feet and hang by his arms from a bar in the doorway, trying to stretch himself.

Loris was fifteen when he got out of high school. He was the valedictorian and the smallest boy in the class. He wanted with all his heart to be tall, to be grown-up; he wanted to do everything.

In the fall he went to Lincoln, to enter the University of Nebraska. He got a job as a reporter on the *Nebraska State Journal* and another as a printer on the *Lincoln Star*. He joined a fraternity and went to parties and football games. He studied hard and got good grades, just as he'd done in high school.

Until he was gone, I had no idea that I'd miss him, but I did, every day, like a tender tooth you can't help biting down on. I couldn't remember why I'd been so mean, why I'd never let him alone, why we'd argued and fought. I saw him only once that whole year, briefly, on a school trip to Lincoln. There was no time to say anything, and if there had been, I thought disgustedly on the way out of the city, I would have stood there like a clod, mute and dry mouthed. I hardly heard what the other girls were saying.

"He's so collegiate, so smooth," said Pauline Jensen. "When will he be home? I wish I wasn't so tall."

I knew she was thinking about the dances at Senter Park. Her mother let her go to them, if her sisters went along.

"June," I said indifferently. "That's when the term's over." I didn't say what I felt—that the three months in between looked like forever.

He didn't come home in June. He didn't come home at all that summer. I couldn't believe it.

"It's his job," Dad said. "They want him full-time at the *Journal*. Youngest full-time reporter in the state of Nebraska," he added proudly. "Probably in the country."

The idea came to me while I was sitting in church, not listening to the sermon—I almost never did—not thinking, but watching the motes in the purple sunlight streaming onto Mr. Eberhardt's bald head. I'd put it right in God's lap. Hadn't I heard all my life, "Ask and ye shall receive?" So, I'd ask. As soon as I could get home by myself, I would. I couldn't ask right there, with Mr. Eberhardt's bald head getting in the way.

I made the proposition straight out. "God, I promise if you'll let Loris come home, just long enough for me to get things straightened out, I promise I'll be a different person. There'll be no more arguing, no more fighting. I promise everything will be different. God," I said to myself, "I won't do it anymore. I promise, God. You'll see."

In September Mr. Newell, who'd been our pastor in Franklin but had moved to Lincoln, wrote to my parents. "Loris was at our house awhile Sunday evening," he wrote. "Wife and I both think he seems somewhat tired and drawn."

Mother knew immediately he'd overdone it and damaged his heart.

"You know he's never been strong," she cried. "All that studying, two jobs, parties, those fraternity boys. They've encouraged him to do everything the stronger ones can do. He's delicate!"

"He's small," said Dad, "and wiry. He's not weak. You don't know yet. A year at home, and he'll be fine. You'll see."

My relief that Loris was coming home was so great I hardly listened to Mother. It was irrelevant, anyway; she couldn't know that I'd made a deal with God. Let her think what she pleased.

Mother was given to these alarms about her children; we were used to it. There was, for example, her unflagging insistence that Mort had been a "blue baby." Uncle Tom tried to reason with her. "Sadie, that's a congenital heart defect," he'd say, and give the technical term for the condition. "No 'blue baby' has ever survived infancy; Mort wouldn't be out there racing around with Wellington if he'd been a blue baby."

He didn't make even a dent in her certainty. This was something Mother knew, and she bristled at the presumption that medical doctors knew more than a mother.

It was true that Mort often screamed and held his breath until he turned blue in the face. He'd done it from the beginning, when ordinary baby formula hadn't agreed with him and he was half-starved. He was a perfectly healthy kid once he got milk he could digest, but he hung onto the habit of holding his breath when he got hurt or wanted attention. He liked the hullabaloo. His color became normal when he ran out of breath and had caused enough excitement. Then he started to breathe again.

I was trembling with eagerness when the car carrying Loris stopped in front of the house. I didn't want to act like a little puppy dog, wagging my tail, whimpering with delight, but I had to make Loris understand that I was a new person.

He kissed Mother, and then he hugged me, hard.

"What are you up to, sport?" he said, and grinned.

It was absurdly easy. I was bursting with happiness, and I hadn't cried or anything. What's more, he understood without my telling him that I'd changed.

As for him, he just wanted to be left alone. He didn't want every mouthful of food and drink supervised, he didn't want to account for every minute of his time, and he didn't want to be reminded that it was time to rest.

"I'll rest when I'm tired, Mother!" he snapped once, in a tone we'd never heard from him before.

The year in Lincoln had changed him. It wasn't only his snarling at Mother. There was more to it than that. We all felt the change.

Mother was appalled by Loris's appearance, which I thought was dazzlingly modish. She objected to his smoothing his hair down with brilliantine; I thought it made him look romantic, like Rudolph Valentino. He wore a plaid pullover and trousers with cuffs so wide they almost hid his shoes. Nothing like it had been seen in Franklin.

"Don't worry about it," Dad said to Mother. "Remember how upset you were about those narrow pants legs Tom and Paul wore when they came home from France? They couldn't take them off or put them on with their shoes on, remember? And they don't wear those tight pants anymore."

"It's just a phase," said Hay-Hay. "A little extreme, but all things pass."

Loris smoked too, openly and casually. I was thunderstruck. I knew he and the other boys had smoked in Bloedorn's backyard for years, but to smoke in front of Mother, in front of anyone, to be unmoved by Mother's tears and lamentations—I could hardly believe it.

"He was too young to go away from home," Mother cried. My boy's changed! I should have kept him with me! Dr. Feese says too much strain on a young heart—"

"You can't keep him with you forever," Dad said. "He's a man. You can't stop a boy from becoming a man."

"A man!" Mother said. "Is that what it takes to be a man—to smoke and ruin his health and wear outlandish clothes? If that's being a man, I'm not sure I want him to be a man!"

"You can't stop it," Dad said gently. "You can't keep apples green. He's all right." Dad didn't tell Mother he sometimes took a cigarette with Loris at the shop.

There was a nickname now too: Rosy. Loris liked it, and I thought I'd get used to it. "The guys at the frat house hung it on me," he said, smiling. "I never liked *Loris*. That's a monkey."

I decided he was taller than before. We measured everybody on the dining room door frame, where all the marks and dates were kept. I was an inch and a half taller; Loris was a quarter of an inch taller, and he smiled about it.

"You're not going to outgrow me, are you?" he demanded. "You do, and I'll knock your block off and bring you down to size!"

He slept until ten or eleven and went to the shop when he felt like it. Now and then he took me with him to a farm where the owner let him ride a horse.

"It's too bad he doesn't have a mount for you," he said.

"Oh, that's okay," I said quickly. "I like to watch you, and I don't mind waiting." I didn't much like horses in the first place. The thought of getting on one terrified me.

Mother was dead set against the horseback riding, but it didn't make any difference. There was a row when he went to a dance at Senter Park with a bunch of boys, and that didn't make any difference either.

For me the greatest, most wonderful change was that my brother talked to me.

He told me about a philosophy teacher who'd brought up ideas so new, so dazzling, to a bunch of Nebraska kids that his whole class was in ferment. He told me about covering news stories—celebrities even—for the *State Journal* and about working half the night as compositor at the *Star*, two blocks away. He told me about the drinking and dancing and partying at the fraternity. He told me he'd met the love of his life.

"She thinks I'm too serious," he said. "She thinks we're too young to be thinking of marriage, but I know I'll never love anyone else."

I was awestruck. My brother in love! And thinking of being married. I could hardly believe it, and I swore a great oath that nobody would hear of it from me. I could imagine only too well how Mother would hit the ceiling. I'd already heard enough scornful remarks about puppy love, intended, I was sure, to put a damper on my frequent crushes. I even suspected, and felt a little disloyal in doing so, that seventeen was a bit young to be thinking seriously about marriage.

"Do you think that sometime . . . ?" I faltered.

"Oh yes," said Loris, "Someday. Dorothy likes me; she told me she likes me. I realize we're a little young now, but later . . . She's promised to write to me."

She did, now and then, not as often as Loris wrote to her, but sometimes there was a cream-colored square envelope in the mail, addressed in an impossibly elegant backhand. I had to bite my tongue not to ask questions.

We all went to the October church supper. When the tables were cleared and Mr. Platt had made the month's announcements, he paused and said, "We have with us this evening one of our own, back from a year in our great state university. Loris Doher Spence, will you kindly stand and tell us what you mean to do with your life?"

I almost gasped. I'd seen Mr. Platt do it before; he was fond of requiring young people to give definite statements about their beliefs and life plans in public.

Loris hardly hesitated. He stood, nodded to Mr. Platt, looked out over the people craning to see him from the tables, and said easily, "It's a little early to say, Mr. Platt. I'm working with my dad in the shop at present, and I haven't made any long-term plans. I'm glad to be home." He smiled and sat down.

It wasn't what anybody expected. It was seemly for a youth, upon being questioned by Mr. Platt, to falter a bit, to reply humbly and even with some frustration. To be downright cool, to give a sort of nonanswer, caused a rustle in the room. Mr. Platt collected himself.

"We are told," he said portentously, "that the Russian Bolsheviks are moving to take over America's institutions of higher learning. What can you tell us about that, young man?"

"Nothing," said Loris. "I don't know anything about it."

Mr. Platt went on. "I'm sure you are aware, young Loris," he said, "that our churches are working to stop the desecration of the Sabbath in our capital city. Please tell us what you are doing to help in that work."

"Nothing," said Loris. "Most of the students think, and I do too, that it would be better to have movies shown on Sunday than for the kids to be wandering around with nothing to do."

The churches Mr. Platt spoke of—Protestant denominations all across the state—believed Lincoln theater owners were trying to make money by corrupting Nebraska youth with showing Sunday movies. They'd circulated petitions—Mother had signed readily, Dad hadn't—imploring the Lincoln city council to deny permission to show movies on Sunday. That there might be a contrary opinion among right-thinking people, that students might have an opinion at all, had, I suppose, hardly occurred to these good people.

"I wrote an article for the *Daily Cornhusker*," Loris added, "supporting Sunday movies in Lincoln. For keeping the Sabbath, movies are better than beer parties."

It was strange and wonderful. My brother really was ten feet tall, and I was the one who'd known it all along.

The last letter from Dorothy came a few days before Christmas. I'd never read any of her letters. I hadn't expected to read this one, but I did, the day after Christmas, when Loris and I were burning gift wrappings in the barrel behind the house.

"Here," he said abruptly, handing it to me. "Go ahead, read it."

I looked at him and saw that he meant it. I lifted the creamy flap, with its DMH pressed into red sealing wax.

"Dear Loris," it said. "I know you realize how fond I am of you. We've been such good friends this past year, that's why I want you to be first to know, after Mummy and Daddy, that Walt and I are going to be married in June. He's giving me his pin for Christmas, and there'll be a big announcement party New Year's Eve. He goes to Washington January 5—a wonderful job with AP! I want you to be happy for us, Loris. After all, you and Walt have been best friends too. With every good wish for Christmas and the New Year, Aff'ly, Dorothy."

Loris took a packet of the envelopes out of his jacket pocket.

"See," he said. "Not tied with pink ribbon or anything, just a rubber band." He laughed a little. "Walt is a good guy," he said. "He helped me get started at the *Journal*. I owe him a lot."

He tore the notepaper and envelopes into strips and fed them into the blaze. The blobs of sealing wax melted.

"I introduced him to Dorothy," he added. "I didn't know . . . she'd have had a long wait for me, especially—" His voice trailed off, and then he stirred the burning paper with a stick. "Put the lid on," he said. "Let's go out to the farm. I'm glad Christmas is over."

CHAPTER ELEVEN

In 1929, when I was fifteen, Dad sold the little weekly newspaper and moved us to Crawford, a town about two hundred miles northwest of Franklin, near the Wyoming and South Dakota borders. I was ready to fall in love, and I did several times during those first years in Northwest Nebraska. I was full of romantic notions, dazzled by the beauty and strangeness of this new place, and thrilled to be the new girl in town, to be asked for dates by boys I'd just met, and, wonder of wonders, to be allowed to go out with them.

Everything was different. Crawford was hardly larger than Franklin, but two miles from town there was Fort Robinson, an army cavalry remount station. At the fort a lively social life had begun as soon as the commissioned officers first brought their ladies to the post in the 1880s. There were teas, luncheons, dinners, receptions, polo matches, horse shows, dances, and cocktail parties, and everyone played bridge passionately.

Dad was exuberant; he almost never regretted his impulsive actions. He was delighted with the cowboys and Indians, delighted with the vast expanse of plains and buttes and pine-clad hills, delighted with the violent and bawdy history of the area. He loved driving out to Toadstool Park and looking for fossils in the badlands. He loved stopping in at isolated ranches and talking to the people, who welcomed him warmly, as ranch people do. He wanted to get acquainted, and he wanted to show what a really good newspaper, which he renamed the *Northwest Nebraska News,* could do for the area and the people.

Loris loved it too. This was his cup of tea—all the space, herds of horses at the fort and on the ranches, horsy men to talk to. He absorbed all the new and wonderful things about Northwest Nebraska. He bought a filly he named Lina and began to work with her twice a day, as the men of the United States Equestrian team did. He took her over the jumps at the fort and began to talk about polo equipment. He bought smart riding clothes and an English saddle and, for the parties, a tuxedo, which he instructed me to call a dinner jacket. He loved the partying, the drinking, and the girls so much I began to think he might get over the girl he'd loved in Lincoln. There was absolutely nothing he could not do here. He'd be strong and well, and, who knew, he might grow a couple of inches. He was only nineteen. We all loved our new life so much, anything was possible.

All of us but Mother. Life was great for Dad, Loris, and me. Yet now and then I caught a glimpse of something I'd never seen in my mother before, but I was having too much fun to think about it. It was years before I realized that the very changes that were so exciting and stimulating for the rest of us had skewed and rocked the foundation of Mother's life.

Mother was born in Franklin, and she'd lived all her life there until we moved to Crawford. All her life she'd been at the top of the pecking order: the eldest daughter and strongest sibling in a large, well-regarded family; a moving spirit in a group of girls who took the lead in everything in Franklin Academy; the mainstay of her church and all its activities; an instigator of good works; and a leader and worker in every worthy project in our little town. She played the piano for every possible occasion, took charge, and did everything that needed to be done and did it willingly. She had an overpowering sense of duty, of moral superiority, and of *noblesse oblige*. She was, in fact, a *grande dame*, but she'd have been astonished and probably outraged if anybody had suggested such a thing. She really had no idea of it; it was just the way things were. If anybody had remarked upon it, she'd have said there was no such thing as an aristocracy in Franklin, and she believed that. She was truly unaware of it because she was part of it—right up at the top—and always had been.

In Crawford worth was calibrated by a different standard. There were the families who had arrived early. They had settled in the 1880s and 1890s, lived through the hard times and the Indian scares, stood fast through many changes, and put down family roots early on. And these were the valued things. By comparison everything else hardly mattered. There might be skeletons and shady dealings in a family's past, questionable conduct or antecedents, deficiencies of all sorts, but the cachet of having arrived early and settled early could never be tarnished. To have arrived in 1884, the year of the big die-up, when thousands of head of livestock had perished in a blizzard, and to have stuck it out—that's what counted, and nothing else quite filled the bill.

In Crawford we were rank newcomers, made even more suspect by Dad's having bought the *Crawford Courier*, a ragged little newspaper that had limped along in competition with the *Crawford Tribune*. The *Tribune* was published by Millie and Emma Lindeman, two middle-aged maiden ladies, and their ancient father. The Lindemans had come to Crawford in the early day.

It was probably being Congregationalists that opened doors for the Spences. Some of the earliest settlers were Congregationalists, and, as soon as people found out that Mother was a willing and accomplished pianist and a piano teacher, there were invitations from townspeople and from the officers' families at Fort Robinson.

Mother had never been a questioner; what she knew was what she knew. Yet here the best people were casual, indifferent really, in their attitudes and in beliefs that for Mother were immutable. There'd been no open social drinking in Franklin. Mother had never had a drink in her life and probably had never been offered one. Only a few young women had ever been seen puffing a cigarette, and they were of a group known to be "fast," whom my mother and her friends frowned upon. My mother knew that, back in Franklin, Mim Fruhling and some of his cronies played cards in the old section house down by the tracks and children played Old Maid; however, ladies didn't play cards. In Crawford there were huge bridge luncheons for women and bridge dinners for couples. Sherry was served at the ladies' luncheons, cocktails at the evening parties. Most of the men and many of the women smoked. It was a different world.

Whatever Mother may have felt inside, she didn't let it show. She bought a book, and she and Dad set about learning to play auction bridge. He liked it so much that day after day, when I got home from school at noon, he had a bridge hand dealt out on the table, and we played furiously until I simply had to leave for school again and he had to go to the shop.

I'd never thought much about Mother's clothes or her looks. I knew she had an imposing bearing, and, obviously, Dad thought her beautiful. She'd grayed so early that I'd never seen her with the dark hair of her graduation and wedding pictures. She was heavier than she'd been in those pictures and now wore the short skirts of the 1920s rather than the tucked, high-necked shirtwaists and long skirts of 1908. In Crawford I saw outfits I'd never seen before. Mother's clothes weren't really dowdy, but they weren't quite right.

One look at Mrs. Ellsworth was enough to show me that. She was unimaginably thin, impossibly chic, and completely casual about it. The other army wives were stylish too, in their dress and manner. They'd been everywhere with their husbands; they knew how things were done. their air of ease about the world filled me with longing. Why was I so awkward? Could I ever learn to fit in? How did one become so smooth—that was the word in 1929—so cool and cosmopolitan?

Mother and I didn't talk about it; I knew I couldn't ask her. But she bought a *Harper's Bazaar* at Beans & Lindeman's drugstore, and she bought new clothes; there wasn't much money, but the things she got were right. She got evening dresses for both of us, and Dad got a tuxedo. I saw something I'd never seen before: my parents dancing—Dad not very well, Mother well enough to make his efforts look good.

My evening dress was scarlet chiffon, with pointed petals dipping well below my knees. Wearing it, dancing in it, I felt smart and sophisticated. Standing in a group of girls, all of us with dance programs, while the boys and young officers clustered around and jockeyed for position, made me feel, for the moment at least, as popular and desirable as I'd always dreamed of being.

That scarlet chiffon was one of Mother's triumphs; I could find no fault with it nor with the drop-waisted blue-on-white dress that had a pleated skirt only nine or ten inches long. It was above my knees when I was standing; of course, when I sat down, it was well above them. I was conscious of all the boys in school but most conscious of Levi Richardson, the first boy I'd dated when we got to town. When I wore that skirt, it hiked up. Levi half-turned in his seat in study hall and looked at me steadily with a smile that was not quite a leer, while I primmed my knees together and felt a little flustered. I had good legs and I knew it, and it was delicious having Levi notice them. I felt pretty and charming; I felt like a woman. And I liked the feeling and sense of power that went with it.

Not all mother's buys were so successful. There was the black wool coat with a fur collar she bought at a clearance sale in November. It was a pretty coat and a great bargain. I liked the luxurious feel of the fur as I pushed it up to my face the way Mrs. Ellsworth did; I only wished I had a beau to send me fresh violets to pin on the coat like she did. But in January *Harper's Bazaar* reported that hemlines had taken a dive. I hardly knew, and didn't care, that the stock market had crashed in October; I was devastated, as I'd been more than once before by one of mother's bargains. There was simply no way to fix it. Even Mrs. Jensen in Franklin couldn't have lengthened that coat into something you could fool yourself into thinking would get by.

The market crash hadn't yet sent its ripples as far as Northwest Nebraska. Hoover was president, and Dad, a Teddy Roosevelt Bull Mooser but still a Republican, believed it when Hoover said prosperity was just around the corner. Of course Dad always felt that way, even in our hardest times; he always wanted to believe it. Yet he was having a hard time convincing Crawford businessmen that advertising in the *Northwest Nebraska News* would be better than advertising in the *Crawford Tribune*. Advertising was advertising, wasn't it? The Lindeman girls had been born and raised in Crawford; their father had come to Dawes County in the early day; it was only right to give them the advertising. As for persuading them about the value of an advertising program, to get the most business out of their advertising dollar, that idea made no headway at all. Dad felt the pinch, and I was stuck with that wretched coat. I grew to loathe it.

Summer clothes were better. Robert Henry had come to the area only a few years earlier than we did, and he stocked his Golden Rule Store with fresh new fashions. Being a newcomer didn't hurt his business; the officers' wives and well-to-do ranchers had money to spend for clothes. Mr. Henry had a representative from the Ed V. Price Tailoring Company of Philadelphia come out twice a year to measure suits for those who wanted them and could afford them. I had heard that Levi Richardson got all his suits tailor-made; he loved good clothes, and his parents could afford them.

Unlike other Crawford businessmen, Mr. Henry saw advertising as a way to sell more merchandise. Dad and Loris proposed an advertising program with special features every week; they offered to take payment in trade.

Barter had been a way of life for us as long as I could remember, and Bob Henry, short of cash like everyone else, liked the idea. I got another evening dress of white tulle caught up with appliquéd taffeta roses, for graduation a blue moiré silk with pleated ruche around neck and hemline, and for summer a white shantung with a shawl collar. I got a brassiere, my first, a garter belt, and a box—three pairs—of rayon hose that I pulled on carefully, wearing old gloves so as not to snag them. I got a white Panama hat and white gloves and a straw basket purse. Everyone was wearing white Panama hats for the polo matches and the horse shows and the cocktail parties at the Officers Club.

Fran Lawson's father was commanding officer at the post, and, as her friends, a lot of us got invited to parties at the Officers Club. Of course, the barman at the club served us only soft drinks, but we knew the boys had bootleg hooch in flasks. They went outside from time to time, and when they came back we could smell the raw whiskey as we danced with them. I tried to find out more about it from Levi.

"Sure," he said, smiling. "It's not hard to find. Check these guys' front teeth; we've all got at least one nick in a front tooth from drinking out of a fruit jar, tearing down Smiley Canyon in Buzz Confer's Model T."

The bachelor officers weren't much older, but they were different somehow. It wasn't just the West Point education; they weren't all West Pointers. It wasn't just being from the East; some of them weren't. And it wasn't that they'd been so many places besides Nebraska that they'd become so sophisticated. It had to be the tantalizingly worldly atmosphere the army carried with it, even to a frontier post at the edge of Wyoming and South Dakota. I was fascinated and frightened being around these men. They had an air of being in a world I'd hardly known enough about to dream of. Thank God I could dance. I could follow anyone on the dance floor. I wondered where a date with an officer might lead me.

My ideas about what I'd do after graduation were as vague as all my other notions. My parents were determined that I should go to college. How the money was to be managed wasn't clear and didn't bother me in any case because I wasn't sure I wanted to go and had no idea what I'd study if I did go. Mother was as sure as I was uncertain; of course, I'd go to college, she said. But she was equally vague about what I might study.

"Just take a regular course," she said. "You can decide on a career later. Maybe you'll go into nursing, like my sisters."

"Like hell," I thought. I'd heard enough from my aunts about bedpans and vomit and dirty old men to shudder at the very idea. They were good nurses, all of them, but only Carolyn really liked caring for the sick. The others, I figured, had taken up nursing only because it was the standard thing for girls to do or because their older brother was a doctor. Not me!

And a career—I wasn't sure I wanted one of those either. When I thought about it at all, I saw myself in some office or other, being efficient; I was good at both typing and shorthand. My persistent, favorite fantasy was being divinely happy as a wife. There was a shadowy man, always changing, in this picture; the only clear part was that I was the most wonderful wife ever known and that my husband considered himself the luckiest man in the world. We were a marvel to all who knew us. The work in the office was to be only before marriage; afterward, I'd be devoting myself only to my husband and children.

CHAPTER TWELVE

It's hard to say where the Middle West ends and the West begins. Geographically, ecologically, botanically, and politically, the Midwest stretches across the middle of America for some twelve hundred miles. In Nebraska the cow country West begins at about the 100th Meridian. East of this line is the farming area of Nebraska, where corn and dairy cattle are raised in this relatively wet part of the state. The Pine Ridge of Northwest Nebraska is more like Wyoming and Montana than like Omaha and the farm areas nearer the Missouri River.

It isn't only that the ranchers wear high-heeled boots and tight Levis and battered Stetsons. The real differences are cultural; the tempo and texture of life are different. The speech of the cow country Westerner is different in its flavor and color and violence. Political attitudes are conservative; personal attitudes are loose and relaxed. Gossip abounds, but the prevailing stance is live and let live. Everyone knows about "irregular" sexual liaisons that have gone on for years, long before today's live-in arrangements became accepted and usual, but the talk about them is bawdy and jocular, rather than indignant and self-righteous.

I was fifteen and a senior in high school in 1929, when we moved to Northwest Nebraska, and suddenly my whole world was different. We'd lived all our lives in a tiny town where the only male teachers were the superintendent and principal of the school and where female teachers were forbidden to marry or smoke or dance or play cards and were required, as a condition of their contract, to teach a Sunday school class.

Now we lived in a town that had been known all over the West for its gambling and sporting houses. Crawford was only three miles from the frontier army post Fort Robinson, where Crazy Horse had been murdered in 1877 and where the black Tenth Cavalry, a tough outfit, was stationed during the early years of the century. The black soldiers were gone, the ruts of the Sidney-Deadwood trail were grass grown, the seven or eight open bordellos were down to two or three rather subdued establishments, and high-stakes poker games were infrequent. But the Fourth Field Artillery, the Seventy-sixth Field Artillery, and the Remount Depot were at Fort Robinson. In 1929 the United States Equestrian Team was there to train for the 1932 Berlin Olympic Games. There were teas, cocktail and bridge parties, dances and polo matches, and, before I knew it, my mother had an evening dress, and my dad had a dinner jacket. The young army officers dated the local girls, and it was understood that nice girls didn't go with enlisted men.

In several long-standing liaisons the couple was treated much as they would have been if they'd been married, and, if it was known that Mrs. Lenhardt met the town's young banker for a dalliance somewhere up near White River, nobody "cut" her, and the good ladies of the PEO never took it up as a matter for their concern.

I was deliciously shocked and titillated by the Fort Robinson gossip. Was it possible that the beautiful Mrs. King, gracious and lovely when "pouring" at a tea in the Officers Club, was really having an affair with her husband's aide-de-camp? Didn't Captain King know about it? Everyone else seemed to. I noticed Mrs. King danced a lot with Lieutenant Rogers, perhaps more than with the other junior officers. I'd seen the two of them taking their horses over the jumps at the exercise ring, but I was sure there was more to it than that, and I was wildly curious. It all reminded me of Kipling's *Tales from the Hills*, but these, too, were maddeningly unspecific. I wondered if my mother knew what was really going on, but she wouldn't have told me if she had known, and there'd be that haughty, lofty tone I hated.

I knew how I felt, at the dances and the parties. Suddenly I was being allowed to go out with boys—men, really—when only a few months before, in Franklin, there'd been an awful flap in my family because Skeeter Ready had asked me to go to a party with him. Now I was being rushed by boys at school and by young army officers and local guys and was allowed to go out with them. I was in a whirl of excitement and uncertainty and feelings that until now I had only fantasized about.

I was dazzled by the perquisites accruing to Frances Lawson. Sometimes, dressed in formal riding habit or a more casual all-white costume, she rode to school horseback, followed at a respectful distance by an enlisted man detailed to escort her. When she dismounted in front of the school, he departed, leading her horse. At four o'clock a chauffeur-driven car came for her.

Fran could have a party anytime she liked. Her father and other officers could hire a man out of the ranks to act as a personal servant: Colonel Lawson could supply as many men as his daughters needed, to cook and wait at table for a dinner party at home or to serve at the Officers Club for a larger party. Fran could even have a combo from the Fourth Field Artillery Band to play for dancing.

Fran's mother was a semi-invalid, and from time to time Fran and her sister acted as their father's hostesses. I suppose these circumstances developed in Fran a superior social presence; at any rate she had one. She was completely at ease with anyone, chatting inconsequentially, making little jokes at her own expense, apparently untouched by the awkwardness and self-consciousness that beset me and almost all of the other girls I knew. She didn't question anything, as I was continually doing; she wasn't angry about anything, as I was half the time; and, indeed, it seemed to me that she had nothing to be angry about. Her father was a large, dignified man who spoke kindly to us when we were introduced to him and whenever he noticed us. He was responsible, by his position, for this wonderful life Fran had, and, if her mother seldom appeared and then seemed vague and grandmotherly in a sort of decayed, Southern belle way, and if her older sister was given to startling behavior now and then, it didn't seem to touch Fran.

Irene was another matter. She was the illegitimate but acknowledged daughter of a well-to-do rancher who had died a couple of years before we moved to Crawford. Irene's mother, Mrs. Davidson, had come to Mr. Jones's ranch with her husband when he was hired to work in the hayfield, and she took over the kitchen and the cooking for the hired hands and the neighborhood crews. After a time Mr. Davidson went away, and Mrs. Davidson stayed on with her daughter, Opal. Presently Billy was born, then Irene.

I'd learned all this about Irene's history from the kids at school. It explained why she had beautiful clothes and a car of her own. She had money, with complete freedom to spend it any way she liked. In some ways, though, it seemed to me Irene's upbringing had been much like my own. She said once, "I wasn't allowed to go to dances till I was sixteen. Billy went, of course—he had his own car when he was just fourteen—but Mr. Jones always said, 'No, Irene. No dances yet for our little Irene.'"

This was the way she spoke of her father: "Mr. Jones." I wondered what she called him at home. It was to me bizarre, romantic even, to have a father you knew and everybody else knew was your father and yet to refer to him as Mr. Jones. And it was somehow comforting to know that he wouldn't let her go to dances until she was sixteen, just as my dad wouldn't let me go to dances when we lived in Franklin. Certainly, there was nothing new about an older brother being allowed to do things a girl was denied; that's just the way it was.

By the time we moved to Crawford, Billy Jones was a grown-up man, and Irene was in high school. She and her mother had moved to town, into the McKelvey house. Paul McKelvey was Irene's boyfriend. He was one of "our football boys." There were a lot of them, not boys really but full-grown men, nineteen- or twenty-year-olds, who'd been kept on in high school because they were good for the football team. With no eight-semester rule to hamper them, everyone—superintendent, principal, teachers, parents, and businessmen—colluded to stretch out our boys' years in high school. They were state champions who played and beat teams from towns ten times the size of Crawford. They traveled as far as Sheridan in north-central Wyoming to play, first-class all the way. Nothing was too good for our boys.

Paul McKelvey's mother had moved to Lincoln, so Mrs. Davidson kept house and cooked and washed and ironed for Irene and Paul. This seemed like a good arrangement to me. When I went home with Irene, I thought of Erma's home in Franklin—everything clean and orderly, good cooking smells coming from the kitchen, and my friend's mother placid and ready to serve her children and their friends.

I liked Irene; I'd liked her from the first. She was a small, lively girl with a button nose, bursting with laughter and energy. I liked Paul McKelvey too. He was handsome and intelligent and a good dancer. I thought him a good boyfriend for Irene. I might have envied her except that I was having such a whirl myself.

Irene went home with me now and then. Mother wasn't cordial to her, but she wasn't rude. I was sure she'd heard Irene's history from somebody, and I knew what the Franklin attitude would have been. But here we were in new territory, where everything was different. Mother herself was becoming different. And, besides, she wouldn't have met Irene's mother, who went only to the Lutheran Church and the Lutheran Ladies Aid.

But the day she found out I'd been stopping in at Irene's house after school, she told me, tight-lipped, that I was never to do that again.

"But why?" I screeched. "Why?"

"We won't discuss it," said Mother. "It's just not a suitable home for you to visit."

"If you mean Mrs. Davidson," I said, "she's just . . . she's just like Erma's mother. She's not good-looking or anything."

I was trying to convey to my mother that Mrs. Davidson was anything but a fast woman, a *femme fatale*. She was fat and combed her hair back into a tight knot and wore cotton print housedresses and aprons and no makeup. She wasn't a "bad woman." I knew what bad women were like; they were like Cecile Henning in Franklin, who wore lots of makeup and dyed her hair and looked fast. It was Mother herself who had told me that Cecile Henning and Jess Hawkins, the father of a kid in my class, had been caught together in "compromising circumstances." She'd stopped right there, of course. She never went on with the interesting parts or gave the least clue about what compromising circumstances were, or what the two were doing when they were caught in them.

This was different, though, and I tried to explain that to my mother. Mrs. Davidson and Mr. Jones hadn't done anything sneaky; they'd just lived together when Mrs. Davidson's husband had gone away. They went to church, and Mrs. Davidson kept house for Mr. Jones. Even if there'd been no divorce and remarriage, it was all aboveboard. And Irene had had nothing to do with it. Irene wasn't a bad girl; she was funny and generous.

Here my mother interrupted. "Yes," she said. "I hear she's very generous."

This set me back on my heels for a moment, but only a moment. I demanded to know what she meant. Was there something wrong with being generous?

"There can be," said Mother. "Now we won't discuss it anymore."

This was my mother's invariable response when I asked questions she didn't want to answer. I stormed, and I raged, but it was no use. Finally, she gave the *coup de grâce*, the remark that always sent me choking and gasping to my room: "Let's talk about something else. Let's talk," she said brightly, "about something good to eat."

Things were different for Irene's brother, Billy. Billy dated Mary Jo Shepherd, daughter of the local banker, or any other girl he wanted to. Angrily, I tried to find out from my mother why the Shepherds, who were at the top of the heap socially and financially, made Billy welcome while innumerable slights were heaped on Irene. Her answer was another of the stock replies that enraged me: "You'll understand all these things when you're older. Now we won't talk about it anymore."

I knew what it was, of course; it was the old double standard, coupled with the fact that Billy had inherited a large, well-stocked ranch and most of the rest of Mr. Jones's property.

I seethed and burned and did all I could to show Irene that we were friends. I continued to take her home with me, daring my mother, with glares, to do anything about it. I didn't know whether Irene knew that she was the subject of a quarrel between my mother and me. Irene was as friendly as a puppy, and I thought, wistfully, that she took it for granted that people liked her and wanted her around. Fifty years passed before I learned that she'd known what they were thinking all along.

CHAPTER THIRTEEN

A job fell into my lap before graduation. Mr. Porter, an elderly man of senatorial mien, spoke to my father about having me work in his law office. Dad and Mother were intensely pleased. The Porters were "best people." To begin work in the office of a gentleman like J. E. Porter would give the nebulous career they envisioned for me an imprimatur nothing else could. And the thought of having my own money was a heady one. Occasionally, I might even stay downtown for lunch at Schwartz's Café with the other girls who worked in stores and offices.

Mr. Porter was going to be away the first month. I thought I just might start reading law, as Grandmother wanted me to do. I saw myself as a serious law student, cramming learning into my head, preparing for the bar examination, finally practicing law with my Uncle Paul in Franklin: SPENCE & SPENCE, ATTORNEYS AT LAW. I'd never crammed, of course; I never had to. And did I really want to go back to Franklin, dear as it was or as it had been? Well, I didn't have to decide right away.

When Mr. Porter had gone, I began to look through the hundreds of books on the shelves all around the room and found I could make almost nothing out of what I read. I'd been reading before I started school; I knew most of the words I saw before me, yet I couldn't make sense out of them. How on earth did people read law? There must be a trick to it, and I didn't know the trick. I'd look through the files.

In the files I saw some names I knew or had read in the paper, and I leafed through the pages in a desultory way. Mortgages, boundary disputes, nothing interesting until I came to a divorce action headed *Ames v. Ames*. In the back of my mind was a teasing notion that I'd heard the name. Where? How? Mrs. Ames? Sioux County? Deadman Creek? What?

It all fell into place when I saw the name Ben Caldwell. This was Betsy's dad, a good-looking, charming man I'd met at her mother's house one day. Betsy's mother was an attractive, charming woman; no wonder Betsy was so good-looking and so much fun. Her mother's more than two hundred pounds didn't keep her from doing the hula when she felt like it, and sometimes, while she sang, she played popular songs like "Springtime in the Rockies" on their rickety, out-of-tune piano. When talking to her, you forgot she was your friend's mother or anybody's mother. She received her ex-husband's visits casually; they sometimes played pinochle with Winston, her present husband. This was a revelation to me. It was bad enough to be divorced, but, if you were, you were supposed to be spiteful and vindictive toward your ex-spouse. Of course, I hoped Mother wouldn't find out that Betsy's divorced parents were on casual live-and-let-live terms, or that house might be off-limits to me too.

This—the Ames affair—must be what Betsy had meant when she shook her head and said, "Oh, that dad of mine!" There, typed on the legal-size onionskin carbon copies of a court document, was the allegation that Mr. Ames had found his wife and Ben Caldwell in bed at their home. I read on eagerly, but the dry legal phrases didn't flesh out the scandal; it took my inflamed, stumbling imagination to do that. I could see how any woman might find this man's attention exciting; to do what Mrs. Ames had done, or what her husband alleged she had done, was stunning to me. So, this was what people did; this was what an affair was. The things I'd suspected really did happen, and they happened to, or were done by, people I knew—not just movie stars or faceless names in the newspaper but a friend's dad. It opened up possibilities of conduct by real people in a way that made my head swim.

On Mr. Porter's return to the office, I had my first chance at taking dictation—real letters, real legal documents—in shorthand. This, I decided, was for me. To take notes, even at the glacial pace of Mr. Porter's dictation; to sit, alert and businesslike, before my typewriter, transforming them quickly into neat, smart-looking copy just as trim as the examples we'd had in our textbook—it was fun, and I was good at it. I didn't even mind Mr. Porter telling me, every time I began my work, to remember that the shiny side of the carbon paper should face me as I sat rolling it into the machine. I simply said, "Yes, Mr. Porter," as any professional secretary—what a fine, ringing sound the words had!—would do. I was caught up in the job, and I wanted to talk shop when I had lunch with the other girls.

The others weren't all that interested in shoptalk, and the excitement soon wore off for me too. I couldn't keep up indefinitely my smartly efficient pose in an office where not a dozen people a week climbed the stairs to come in, an office where there wasn't enough work to keep even half a secretary busy. None of the people who visited Mr. Porter's office cared how brisk and businesslike I was. My mother's determination that I should go to college began to appeal to me.

What really absorbed all the girls I knew was the idea of getting married. Jessamine was in the midst of wedding plans. She was going to live in Aruba, an island near Venezuela, where her fiancé had a job with an oil company. We talked endlessly about what her new life would be like, but the only thing we were most curious about we didn't mention at all. Except Betsy.

"Amy Randall's done it," she told me, "and she says there's nothing to it."

I thought about Owen Wister's *The Virginian* and the tent he prepared for his first night with his bride when they rode off into the inexpressibly beautiful, remote Wyoming wilderness. I thought about the principal we'd had at Franklin, a lean young man of ugliness so elemental in its maleness you could only shiver with delight at the black hairs on his long, spatulate-fingered hands. Every girl in school had a crush on him. He wasn't the first crush in my life by a long shot, but the others had been just girl-boy stuff, not this consuming, driving eagerness to know what love could be like with a man.

Clara Bow was the "It Girl" in those days, when we were still in Franklin. We saw her on the screen and on the posters in front of the movie, we read about her in the *Silver Screen* and *Photoplay* magazines that Maddy Ehlers had at the beauty shop. She was cute, and she had personality, but there was more to it than that. None of the articles in Maddy's magazines really explained what "it" was. I got Maddy to paint a cupid's bow on my mouth and to make spit curls, with an infusion she made by pouring boiling water over flaxseed, in stiff circles that dried on my cheeks. I had to rub the lipstick off and brush the tight rings back into my hair before I went home, but they didn't make a real difference anyway. "It" was, I began to sense, something you felt about yourself inside, something so strong and real that other people would feel it too—especially men.

But here, a few years later, talking with grown-up girls about marriage, planning a shower for a girl who was actually going to get married, I was just as ignorant as that twelve-year-old had been. I hadn't learned a thing.

Every now and then, however, I felt a stirring. It had happened when Levi Richardson caught my eye across the study hall and made a detour to drop a note on my desk. It had happened when Dick Roberts kissed me behind the scenes at the senior play. It happened when I walked down the street and saw a knot of fellows watching as I walked by. "Get an eyeful," I thought, as I glanced at them, and I swung my hips. "Get an eyeful, you guys."

I went out with boys not much older than I was, and after Christmas I went out with Tony Parks, an officer stationed at the post. He was neither the Virginian nor Principal Van Dyke. At twenty-nine he was too old, Mother said at first, for me to go out with at all. Loris liked Tony, and I tried to match his easy disregard of Mother's pronouncements, but it was Mrs. Porter's open approval of Lieutenant Parks which made the difference to her. A West Pointer, an older man—what more could a mother want?

It was strange. The certainties Mother had lived and ruled by in Franklin, even the basic certainty that she knew precisely what people should think and how they should behave, all quietly, imperceptibly crumbled—vanished really—before Mrs. Porter's assuredness. Her world was wider than the one we'd left. That it was the real world, the right world, couldn't be doubted. Mrs. Porter's quiet confidence was total. It didn't occur to Mother, or to anybody else, to question it.

I liked going to the post with Loris when he went to exercise Lina, his mare. Lina was one of the breaks—the most precious one—which had come to Loris because of the officers and men of the units stationed at Fort Robinson and the members of the United States Olympic Equestrian Team. These people liked Loris. Partly it was because of the coverage he gave their activities in our paper and other area newspapers and the feature stories that went out on the AP wire. But mostly it was because of him. They liked his eagerness to learn all he could about horses and horsemanship. They liked his intelligence, and they liked him for being tough and tenacious. Whatever he was proving as a small man, he was doing so without bluster or pretense. They gave him breaks he didn't ask for, including the chance to buy his lovely little mare before she went up for auction. Loris named her Lina for some obscure Italian singer whose contours he admired.

Loris's satisfaction was complete when Lina was bred to the Fort's best stud, Mark Master, courtesy of a friend in Remount. He explained the procedure and the precautions matter-of-factly. "She's nervous about the whole thing, you see. Excited but nervous. The egg's in place, and biology tells her she wants a baby, but when that big horse comes at her . . ."

"Yes," I breathed.

"There's a lot of kicking and whistling and neighing, but at the right time Mark mounts her and plants the seed."

"Gosh," I said. "It's not so simple, is it . . . that book Mother gave me . . . ?"

"Oh, that one!" Loris laughed. "The birds and the bees, for God's sake. Written by a bunch of maiden ladies of both genders. What do they know about sex?"

It seemed all right: being interested about sex in horses and in people. For babies to be born there had to be sex, I knew that much. I was excited along with being interested. I'd have to think about how much of the excitement was love.

"Come on," said Loris. "Let's drive up Smiley Canyon. Race you to the car!"

The Smiley Canyon road went from the plains and escarpments to the high tablelands of Sioux County and on into Wyoming. It was easy to drive up that road, but driving a truck down was sometimes impossible. Trucks got to going too fast, or the driver took it too close to the edge of a hairpin curve. When word went out: "Nash-Finch truck jackknifed!" people headed out with sacks and baskets. Who couldn't use a peck of oranges or a few dented cans of vegetables or salmon or, if the labels had come off, who knew what? Times were hard; two old women went out with a coffee can of cracked corn when a chicken truck tipped over and broke some crates. They caught eight or ten of the fryers, too, and popped them into a gunnysack.

The drive down always took my breath away, not its danger but its magnificence. Loris stopped at a place where we could see for sixty miles.

"There can't be anything better in the world," he said. "For me anyway. I hope I can stay right here my whole life. You may like some other place better. Anyway, for a woman—who you marry makes a difference." He thought a while. "It's not right that it should, but that's the way it is. Biology, I guess. Women have babies, and babies have to be taken care of. It's kind of a gyp. You'll have a lot of chances, and I hope you won't be in a hurry to decide."

He got out of the car, and I did too. The wind swept down the canyon as if it were a funnel. We leaned into the side of the car.

"Now, Tony," he said, "he's a nice guy, really a nice guy. I don't want to ask you how you feel about him—" he paused for a long time. "But maybe you'd better ask yourself. He's so much in earnest."

Earnest. Yes, that was the word for Tony. What was my brother getting at? It didn't seem like a lecture, yet.

"You're, let's see, not quite seventeen," he said. "You're just coming to the woman part. And you're curious. About everything." Whatever he wanted to say seemed to be bothering him. He took a deep breath. "You know what *C.T.* means?" he asked. "Have you heard that expression?"

I shook my head no.

"Well," Loris said, "it's not the kind of term I'd normally use around my kid sister, but it means 'cock teaser.' It means a girl who leads a guy on and then backs off when he wants to go all the way." Loris went on, "Men have a higher sex drive than most women, nice girls anyway. Flirting, that's not what I'm talking about. And I'm not suggesting that you'd do that—cock teasing."

He was not being smooth about this. In fact, he was floundering. I wanted to find out what was bothering him. I began to feel uneasy myself.

"It's just that Tony is . . . well, of course he's a good deal older than you. But he's so . . . vulnerable. Yes. That's it. He's vulnerable. He could get hurt."

I hardly knew what to say. It wasn't really advice or a lecture. Loris and I had talked about a lot of things; I wanted to talk about everything, but I just didn't know what to say. We both looked out toward the sweep of sky and earth. I saw the thunderheads behind the far buttes, the ones this side of Dead Horse. They rolled up puffy, glistening white. A few stabs of far-off lightning played behind them.

"Dorothy . . . ," I said. "Was Dorothy a C.T.?"

"No," Loris said carefully. "No, she wasn't that kind. She was more mature, I guess. Just a few months older than me, but I was such a cub! Damn it, such a cub!"

He turned away and searched the ground until he found a smooth, gray stone. We watched it sail over the crowns of the pine trees in the canyon. An eagle rose from a shelf of butte rock almost beneath us, and we felt a few drops of rain.

"Let's go!" Loris said. "There isn't enough gravel on this road anymore to fill a wheelbarrow. I don't want to drive down Smiley Canyon in a rainstorm."

CHAPTER FOURTEEN

That whole summer felt fuzzy. Nothing had sharp edges. Everything was blurry. "This fall," Loris said, "You're going to Lincoln. We'll manage it one way or another. Can't let you stay ignorant all your life." He paused. "Try to get Bousma for philosophy. I hope he's still there. He uses the Socratic method in class. You know, one leading question after another, to get you to think about things. Wouldn't hurt you to do a little thinking."

He was kidding. I hadn't told him, but he knew, that mostly I felt things, tumbled up against woolly half-formed notions, rolled back and stumbled off in some other direction. I always wondered what I was getting into, but I didn't really know what I wanted to get into.

The thing I knew I didn't want to get into was marrying Tony. I really didn't, but I was tempted to say yes when he asked me. I liked him and his gentle decency, but I wasn't in love with him, and everybody knows you ought to be in love with a man to marry him. All the books, all the stories, said so. And I just wasn't. I felt relief when I learned that his unit, the Fourth Field Artillery, was moving to Fort Bragg in the fall.

Fort Bragg, North Carolina—a big post. It was a world in itself, people who'd lived there said, not at all like Fort Robinson, a small outpost in the middle of nowhere. I'd never been East—never been anywhere really. Omaha, Lincoln, Grand Island, and North Platte. Those places weren't "East." East was Washington, DC. It was New York and Boston, the Carolina Banks and the Everglades.

If I married Tony, I'd have the army life I thought of as glamorous. I'd have the travel, the socializing with sophisticated, worldly people who'd been around and who were at ease in any situation. It might mean I'd learn that kind of ease. But I didn't want it. I loved the idea of it, but I didn't want to marry Tony.

In August Mother got a seamstress in to get my clothes ready for college. There wasn't money enough to buy many new clothes.

In Lincoln, at my first sorority rush party, I found that nobody, but nobody, would dream of wearing summer clothes that sweltering September. That first party, looking around the room, I knew that most of what I'd brought was all wrong. This was the University of Nebraska. It wasn't a little cow town or a frontier army post. It was simply up to me to change what I had enough to get by on, to write to Loris to see if he could get me a little cash to fill in with, and in the meantime to keep myself from looking downright dowdy in a world where everybody knew the rules but me. All I had that was really right was the box of hats and gloves. Hats and gloves were, I learned, de rigueur for parties and classes.

The rush parties were fun as soon as I got the clothes part right. I liked meeting people, and I was good at the small talk that kept things going. I'd learned that at the Fort Robinson parties. All of us, the rushees, walked from one sorority house to another, from luncheons to teas to dinners and evening parties, walking in little gaggles, seeing someone we'd met at another party, comparing notes on where we'd been and where we were going.

The faces were different, but the routine was much the same everywhere we went: a warm greeting at the door, introductions, a swift and efficient escorted passage through the room, and a sense of being appraised. I thought of the cattle the ranchers paraded around the ring at the sale barn, the

narrowed eyes that viewed them, and the smiles that went around the
bleachers when a critter let out a plop onto the straw of the runway. One
or two "actives" in each house were in charge, yet even they deferred to the
smartly dressed older women called "alums." Alums had been—oh, years
and years before—green rushees like us. They'd learned the rules and lived
by them. They'd married well and had children; they'd made lives as young
matrons with husbands who'd belonged to the right fraternities. And, in
the Nebraska towns of Grand Island and Lincoln and Omaha and Weeping
Water, they'd never forgotten that they were Pi Phis, Kappas, or Alpha Phis.

At the Alpha Phi house I met a girl I didn't have to make small talk with.
She was Margaret Sawyer, a junior from Broken Bow and a philosophy
major.

"Oh, Crawford," she said. "Near Chadron, right? I was beginning to
wonder if we were rushing any westerners this year. Most of the girls think
it's quaint to live where people make a living punching cows."

"I've noticed," I said. "You're the first person who knows where I live.
Do you know a teacher named Bousma?"

"Bousma! Yes!" she said. "I had a class under him last year. How do you
know about him?"

"My brother had a class under him when he was here, oh, four or five
years ago," I said. "He thinks Bousma's about the best teacher in the world."

"He is, he is," Margaret said. "It's great that you know of him. But if
you're thinking of getting into a class of his . . . it ain't easy," she said. "A lot
of people want to get into Bousma's classes. And for a freshman—I don't
know. But, look, a friend of mine—you won't meet her here because she's
a 'barb'—works for him part-time. Maybe she could pull some strings."

"Margaret, please," said a tall, thin girl who'd been making her way across
the room to us. "You've got to circulate. You're on the committee. There
are twenty-eight new girls here. Circulate."

"Oh God," said Margaret. "Duty calls. Listen: Before you register I want
to see what I can do. I mean what Lou can do. Your last name is Spence,
isn't it? I won't forget. I'll be in touch with you before Monday."

She started to leave, but I had to ask a question.

"What's a barb?" I asked.

"Oh," Margaret laughed. "*Barb's* short for *barbarian*. All this," she
waved her hand, "this is Greek. Sororities, fraternities, all Greek. The ones
who aren't in fraternities or sororities, they're considered barbarians." She
laughed again. "But sometimes you wonder. Lou—that's my friend—any
sorority would be lucky to get her, and yet she didn't get even one bid. She

couldn't have lived in the house anyway; she's too short of money. Still, it makes you wonder."

"Margaret," a warning voice said. "Twenty-eight. Circulate."

"Bye," said Margaret. "I'll be in touch."

I got a bid to Alpha Phi, and I moved into the house. It was what Loris wanted for me. I was welcomed by an active named Jo.

"Polly!" she gushed. "We've been watching for you. Margaret Sawyer made it clear we had to get you. 'Get her.' That's what she said, right in committee meeting. 'Be sure you get Polly.'"

I was flattered, particularly since it was the only bid I'd had.

"Is Margaret here?" I asked.

"No," Jo said, with a little frown. "She doesn't live here at the house. She lives in a kind of flat in a run-down old house, with a barb, of all people. Let's see, your roommates are Alice Brown and Janet Vlcek. You'll like them; they're lovely girls. The three of you get the biggest bedroom in the house. Of course," she giggled, "it's the only three-girl room in the house. You'll like them; you'll really like them."

I did like them. Alice was a tall, almost raw-boned girl from Omaha, Janet a statuesque brunette from Wahoo. They claimed never to have heard of Nebraska's Pine Ridge and derided the notion that there was anything worthwhile west of Grand Island. I was dubbed "The Girl of the Golden West," aka Annie Oakley.

As I stood in line waiting to register for classes, I looked around. There were people walking around, looking for something, then going where somebody told them to go. Nobody except the women at the registration desks seemed to know what was going on.

How did I get here, I wondered? My family had told me this was the next step, and I took it. But the next step to what? I hadn't minded the job in Mr. Porter's office, but I'd been glad enough to leave it. I didn't want to marry Tony, and his outfit's transfer to Fort Bragg had taken him away. I wasn't homesick, as some of the pledges had been; one had cried so much the housemother had called her parents, and they'd come and taken her home. But I was doing something I didn't particularly want to do, for no reason that I knew of or cared about.

I'm a damned minnow, I thought, a stupid minnow in a stream. Minnows dart here and there, or they lie motionless in the shade for a moment, or the current catches them and they get swept downstream.

CHAPTER FIFTEEN

All that fall I'd had signals that times were hard in Northwest Nebraska. Mother wrote every week and never failed to caution me about keeping expenses down. Loris wrote often too; his references to money and advertising revenues were guarded. Dad's letters were infrequent but optimistic; I had a nagging sense that they'd have been more frequent if there'd been more to be optimistic about.

It didn't hit me how hard times were until one day early in December. The first jolt came that morning. Marjorie Voorheis, our sorority chapter treasurer stopped me at breakfast and said, "This is the third. We haven't received the check from your family yet for your board and room." The second jolt was Margaret Sawyer's casual remark that Lou would be going home with her for Christmas.

"We've got a ride with a friend of my brother's," she said. "We'll chip in a couple of bucks apiece for gas. Lou'd spend more than that for food if she stayed by herself over Christmas vacation."

Stay by herself over Christmas vacation! That really hit me.

"Her family's in McCook, aren't they?" I asked.

"Yes, but getting there would cost more than she's got," Margaret said. "It's hard enough for her family to make it in the best of times. She has to stick with it to get her degree. We always have a houseful anyway, and Mom'll manage a present for her. It could be worse."

It could, of course. She could be stuck in Lincoln by herself. But not to get home for Christmas! I'd had all those hints about hard times at home. I faced almost five hundred miles of sitting up all night in a railway coach to get home, and I didn't even know how much the ticket cost.

The check for my room and board, twenty dollars, came that same day. It was the letter with it which gave me the third jolt. Loris wrote, "Get a round-trip ticket. We can turn it in for a refund if you don't go back."

"*If* I don't go back!" I almost screamed aloud, "What the hell are you talking about? Whose idea was this anyway? Did I beg to go to college? I don't even know what I'm here for, and now that I'm having a good time, making good—well, adequate—grades, you're talking about maybe I won't come back and finish the semester. I won't see Benners, my boyfriend from Omaha, again."

I was angry the rest of the day. It was so unfair. I was still angry when I went to bed, but a couple of hours later, waking up suddenly after that first deep sleep, my rage seemed to have evaporated. I tried to whip it up, but I couldn't. I thought about a lot of things, and I just couldn't get angry.

I thought about the buck or two that was usually in Loris's letters; there'd been nothing in this one. I thought about the check to Alpha Phi for my room and board; this was the first time it had been late. I thought about the check that always came with it, made out to me, for books and clothes and spending money, usually ten dollars, once twelve dollars. I always cashed it at once and put some of it in the drawer under my blouses. And what did I do with the rest? Sometimes I bought food at the cafeteria instead of going back to the house for lunch. Several times, on Tuesday or Thursday, when I had no classes in the afternoon, I'd ridden the streetcar downtown to Miller & Paine's department store, bought something I'd had my eye on, and treated myself to the special in the department store's tearoom. It was always a lovely lunch, but I wished I had those quarters back. I really didn't know what I had done with the money.

I was on the edge of dropping back into sleep when my heart gave a lurch: twenty dollars this month; it had never been that much before. I had to buy my ticket out of it. I didn't know how much it would cost, and I had no presents for anybody.

I woke up three or four more times before morning. Each time my mind scurried around, totting up figures, making wild guesses about the price of the ticket, trying to remember if there was a dollar bill left under the blouses. Each time I told myself it was useless to worry about it until I knew how much the ticket cost, and each time I started onto the squirrel cage again.

I could forget the book I was supposed to buy for English literature. It would be at least forty cents secondhand, but, if I weren't coming back, I wouldn't need it. Alice, Jan, and I had decided not to exchange gifts. We were all supposed to chip in fifty cents for a gift for the housemother. I wouldn't go to see my Uncle Charley and Aunt Ellen, Dad's brother and sister-in-law, without something for their kids, and I wanted a present for my little cousin Mary Margaret, Aunt Marg's daughter. The most expensive, though, were the gifts I'd picked out for my family; why hadn't I bought them before last month's money got away from me? The book on the Plains Indians for Dad was $1.25. The paisley ascot for Loris was $1.50; it was from Miller & Paine. The china lemon squeezer for mother, shaped and painted like a lemon with three green leaves, was ninety cents, and the little rubber trucks, with wheels that turned, one for each of the little boys, were sixty cents each—it all came to almost five dollars. I knew if I didn't bring home any gifts Mother would say, when I got there, "We'll just put your name along with mine on the presents I got," but it wasn't the same.

I was easing the blouse drawer open when the alarm went off—nothing there. I dug into my pocketbook: fifty-seven cents. I called the Burlington: seventeen dollars round-trip Lincoln-Crawford. That would leave me three dollars.

I was stunned. I thought of telling Benners I'd decided not to go with him to Omaha that weekend, but I wanted to see my aunts, and most of all I wanted to see my cousin Mary Margaret. Besides, not going wouldn't save any money; my aunts Esther and Marg never let me pay for anything anyway.

"Oh hi, Baby," Zoe said, when I went into the apartment Esther shared with Zoe and another woman. "I'm glad you're here. I'm just leaving. Esther's out on a date with her new guy. Make yourself at home. You know where everything is. You're bunking with Esther in the double so Enid and I won't wake you up when we come in. Esther won't be late. Bye!"

I was drowsy when Esther came in and sat down by the bed.

"Hey, you're an early bird to bed, kiddo!" she said, stroking my arm as she always did. "I thought you'd be up playing my new record. Why, honey! You've been crying! What's the matter, sweetie? Tell Aunt Et what's the matter."

I spilled it all while she stroked my arm. I'd planned to make a joke of it, how dumb I'd been, letting Christmas sneak up on me, not putting a few dollars back for Christmas presents. I'd planned to be matter-of-fact about asking for a loan. Five dollars now, because it's now that I need it, and even if I don't come back to college, I'll send you the money, at least a dollar every month, maybe more. I'll get a job. I was babbling.

"Loan, my foot," said Aunt Esther. "I know just how you feel, baby, that's just the kind of thing I've done a lot of times, and it makes you feel shitty, doesn't it? Nobody knows it better than me. I was going to take you down to Brandeis's tomorrow and help you pick out a new dress for a Christmas present. But money's more important right now, isn't it, kiddo?" She dug into her pocketbook and folded a five and a one into my fist.

"You've got your presents all picked out; fine, buy them in Lincoln. Or, if you see something downtown tomorrow you like better, get it here. It's for you to do whatever you want to do with it. Remember, it's not a loan. It's Merry Christmas, kiddo!"

I wept while she brushed her teeth and creamed her face and told me about the fellow she'd been out with. I wept while she hung up her clothes and put trees in her shoes and washed out her pants and stockings. I wept while she put on her nightgown and hairnet, and I wept when she put her arms around me in bed and told me there was nothing to cry about.

The next thing I saw was light at the edges of the blinds, and Esther was sitting on the bed again.

"Time to get up, lazybones," she said. "Get your bath and get dressed while I make up the bed, and then we'll go. You can grab a piece of toast on the way out. Zoe and Enid are still asleep; they were out till all hours."

I felt rich. I spent almost a dollar on a brown teddy bear for Mary Marg, and put it in her arms as soon as I saw her. She looked like a lady in her new coat and hat, Esther told her.

When we got to Northrup-Jones for lunch, little Mary Marg wouldn't allow the tray of the highchair to be swung over in front of her. "No," she said firmly. "I'm the mother."

CHAPTER SIXTEEN

I didn't go back after Christmas. It just wasn't possible; even I could see that. To finish the semester would have meant another round-trip ticket to Lincoln, a month and a half of room and board at the house, and miscellaneous expenses, all totaling around eighty or ninety dollars. It just wasn't there.

It was hard for Dad to talk about it.

"We didn't want to disappoint you, honey," he said. "We want you to do all the things other girls do. Mama wants it, Loris wants it, and I want it. But cash money. . . ." His voice trailed off.

"Dad!" I cried, and I hugged him. We weren't a hugging family, but I hugged him. "Don't feel bad. I don't. I wanted to come home. I was homesick; I was even lonesome for the brats. I wanted to come home."

It wasn't true, of course. But I couldn't tell anybody what I wanted when I didn't really know myself.

I walked downtown with Loris and saw the vacant buildings in the three business blocks: a hardware store gone, a gift shop gone, one of the lumberyards going.

"The Elite shows a movie Friday and Saturday night, and that's all," Loris said. "Mrs. Strohmeyer thinks they may have to quit even that. People just don't have the money to go to the show, even with free dishes."

The two drugstores were still open, and so was the Golden Rule, but the clothes racks that remained had been moved forward to make their scantiness less obvious.

"I guess you see some changes, Polly," Mr. Henry said. "Crawford merchants are scratching to keep alive. The only one doing any good is Chewie." He laughed.

I was glad to hear it. I liked Chewie.

"Chew-Tobacco" Childers was the junk and secondhand man. He had his nickname from his most noticeable personal habit: he almost always had a chew of tobacco in his mouth.

"He don't so much chaw his tobacca," Ray Hamaker remarked, "as he just wallers it around in his mouth."

The creases at either edge of Chewie's mouth were stained a deep brown and were more or less permanent; Chewie wasn't much given to washing. His shaving, too, was infrequent and sketchy, with the patches he'd missed, maybe more than once, showing the erratic course of his razor.

It wasn't Chewie's personal hygiene that bothered people; it was his habit of discharging great gobbets of brown fluid in almost any direction, without any warning. Folks were uneasy around him.

I myself had seen what could happen. I was standing in front of the shop, waiting for Dad, when Chewie drove his old pickup into the filling station next door. He told the new kid to fill it up and called out to a couple of the old men who hung around the station to come and see what he had in the back end of his pickup.

The kid pumped the gas, checked the oil, washed the windshield, and started on the side windows. Finally, Chewie paid for the gas, got back in his pickup, and started grinding on the starter. I happened to be looking directly at him. Just before it happened I had an instant of premonitory horror. Then Chewie spit.

The window was closed; I'd seen the kid washing and polishing it. The brown blob hit the glass. It spattered all over Chewie and the inside of the pickup. It took him a moment to realize what had happened and to get the window rolled down.

"Well, Jumpin' H. Jesus Christ!" he bawled. And, to the kid, who rushed over to apologize and rewash the window, "Get lost, ya punk!" He was fairly trembling. "God-damned knot-headed kid, ain't got the sense enough to pound sand in a rat hole! Man can't turn his back." The rest was lost in the roar of the engine.

Mrs. Childers kept the shop when Chewie was out buying junk and old furniture. If her husband stopped in one of the bars and failed to show up when she expected him, it made her mad, and she belabored him, sometimes physically, when he returned. One Saturday afternoon when half the farm and ranch families of Dawes and Sioux Counties were in town, Chewie had to retreat from her wrath. He'd made it through the door, but she caught him front of the shop, knocked him to the sidewalk, and sat on him. She held him by both his ears and began pounding his head on the concrete. Mrs. Childers was a tall, strong woman, but Chewie was game.

"Ah, you wanna fight, do ya!" he cried, to the unsmotherable delight of the onlookers. "You wanna fight, I'll fight ya!"

Stocks were meager in all the stores that were still open. Shorty Craig had closed his bakeshop, but he still got up at 1:30 A.M. and poked his yeast sponge down. By 8:30 he was on his way, ringing his bell, a little man with a heavy cart full of fresh loaves, five cents each. He pushed hard uphill and clung to the handlebar all the way down, tacking back and forth. He stopped at every back door in town, and, if he was lucky, he sold most of his stock. There were always a few loaves left, though; he had planned it that way. They were for the Indians who camped between the railroad tracks and White River.

At home we ate as well as ever. The Star Grocery's weekly special and a few other purchases pretty well covered our needs. It was just that everything was cut nearer the bone.

The army people still got their pay. The Frittses probably didn't feel the pinch; Mr. Fritts was manager of Nash-Finch Wholesale Grocery Company and was said to make five thousand dollars a year. People with that kind of money didn't have to worry.

Cash money. Everybody talked about it, but nobody had any. County legal notices brought in what little cash Dad and Loris saw at the shop, and the talk was that the county might go to warrants, in place of cash, which would have to be discounted, if you could find anyone to take them. Foreclosures were up. Handbills were printed for farm sales, the listing of feed and livestock, plows and harrows, curtains and dishes, fruit jars and tools. This meant another family had decided to load up and head someplace else. There had to be work somewhere. Everybody knew that in America you could get a job if you were willing to work. Certainly *I* knew it. I wasn't surprised to get a job as a part-time clerk-secretary. The office was in a corner of a warehouse full of alfalfa seed, right beside the Northwestern tracks. I went to work at eight, typed whatever there was to type, answered the phone, and tried to fill up the time until four o'clock.

I saw the open boxcars with feet and legs hanging down in the doorway. Little feet, some of them; bare legs, some of them, with cracked and broken shoes. The boxcars were occupied by slack-faced women with babies on their laps and dusty men who needed a haircut.

Sometimes people got off the boxcars and came to the door of the office to ask if I would look at something they wanted to sell. Once I bought a square cotton lace tablecloth from an old man and a young woman with thick northern England accents. And once I gave an old man a quarter for three two-cent stamps he'd had in his wallet a long time. It was all he had to sell and all I had to give.

CHAPTER SEVENTEEN

That was the summer I found out what I wanted. It was the first Levi Richardson summer. It was the beginning of love, real honest-to-God love. It began with a casual date on the third of July. On the Fourth of July, as we watched the fireworks, Levi said, "If we still feel this way next year, will you marry me?"

Of course I would. Yes, yes, yes. There was nothing else, and never had been anything else that I wanted. I'd never known, until then, what wanting was.

Levi had always been there on the edge of my life ever since we'd moved to Crawford. He was the first boy I went out with. At parties and dances he always led me onto the floor, two or three times. He was a smooth dancer, easy to follow. I liked being in the circle of his arms. I liked the smell of his skin and the little kiss he gave me at the end of each dance. I'd liked him from the start; suddenly I loved him. I wanted him with all my heart, and I'd never wanted anybody else. We told each other we'd never want anybody else.

Talk about hearts on sleeves! Anyone could see to look at us that we were in love. Every morning my eyes opened to sweet, shattering eagerness for love, for all of life. Twenty times a day I nearly burst with it.

I suppose times were as hard, after the Fourth, as they'd been before, but we didn't notice; we didn't care. I'll live anywhere, I declared grandly. Every abandoned shack we passed on the road had possibilities.

When we told my folks, Mother cried. When Levi had gone, she cried out to Dad and me, "But we don't know his people!"

Dad said gently, "They don't know Polly's people, either."

Sometimes that summer I went to Fort Robinson and watched Loris take Lina around the circle and over the jumps. The foal he'd named Mark's April capered after, at times stopping short, planting her feet for a moment, only to buck and kick just for the joy of bucking and kicking. Her legs were so long, she seemed to be on stilts; her eyes were scraps of brown velvet bordered with curling fringe.

"She's got the best of both of 'em," said Sergeant Rowbright. "Fine-boned like her dam, strong and classy like her sire. You've got a filly you can be proud of."

Loris was proud of the colt. He was uneasy about me getting married.

"You're so young," he said. "I like Levi, like him a lot. But you're so young."

"Young" I cried. "And how did you get so old so quick? I'm older than you were when you were in love with Dorothy. And you wanted to get married. I thought you'd understand how it is."

"I do understand," he said. "I do. But a few years, maybe another year, in Lincoln before you get tied down."

"I want to be tied down," I cried. "To Levi. It's what we both want! Don't you remember what it's like?"

"Yes, I remember," he said, softly. "Boy, do I remember! It's just that I want you not to be in a hurry. The waiting won't change anything. It hasn't changed me. It's been over three years since I saw Dorothy; she's got a husband and probably a baby by now, and I still feel the same. She didn't want to marry me, but I haven't changed. Love doesn't change. Just give yourself some time."

"Everybody's against us!" I wanted to shout, but I knew it wasn't true. My mother and dad, Loris, nobody had said we couldn't get married. They just wanted us to wait.

Wait. All my life the hardest thing I ever had to do was wait. And marrying Levi was so right that the waiting would be nothing but torture.

"Go to Lincoln one more year," Loris said. "Pick up those classes you had to drop. You don't want to leave it unfinished."

Yes I did. I wanted to leave it just where it was.

"A year will go so fast, you won't believe it," said Loris. "We'll get you back for Christmas, and before you know it the year will be over." He put his arm around me. "Maybe Levi and I can drive down and see you some weekend."

I was edgy the Sunday afternoon Levi took me to meet his folks.

"I've told them about us," he said, and laughed. "Mom's just as nervous as you are."

I'd driven on most of the canyon roads in Dawes and Sioux Counties with Dad or Loris or Levi. I was sure I'd seen the Richardson place, but I couldn't sort it out of all the scattered houses and farm buildings I'd passed.

But I knew it when we came to it though. I'd noticed the wide red barn and the neat white clapboard house.

"My grandfather built the house," Levi told me, "sometime in the 1890s. You can't tell to look at it, but it's built of logs set up stockade fashion. Dad and Uncle Will put the siding on later. It was tough enough for my granddad to get the studding and boards for the floors and roof. Times were hard then, too. He probably traded something to my other granddad and Uncle John Britton for the sawed lumber." He went on, "That's my mother's father and brother. They had a sawmill. Uncle John still lives up the canyon a ways."

Levi's mother was standing at the open front door when we drove up, but Levi took me around to the back.

"Well, Levi!" she scolded. "I thought this first time you might bring Polly in through the front room! Welcome," she said, putting her arm around me.

We went through the screened back porch, the kitchen, and into the front room. It was a huge dining room, with flowered paper on the walls, a big round oak table and buffet at the kitchen end, a black leather lounge against one wall, and two or three rocking chairs.

Levi's dad and Uncle Will rose as we came in. Both men shook my hand.

Uncle Will wore blue-and-white hickory-stripe overalls. His hand was large and horny. Charley wore suit pants and a white shirt, and I felt no calluses on his hand.

"I tried to get these men into coats and ties," Levi's mother went on, "but they balked. Said if you were going to be in the family you'd just as well get used to them as they are."

"Oh yes," I said in relief, now that the reason for our visit was out in the open. "It's much too hot for coats and ties. I wouldn't want you to—"

"No," Levi's mother went on, "You must take us as we are," although I had the feeling that the printed linoleum floor had been mopped no more than an hour before. It was a pleasant room, light and high ceilinged. There were ecru lace panels at the windows and a corner china closet with a curved glass door and insets.

I admired the banjo clock on the wall.

"Yes," said Levi's mother, pleased. "That's the very first thing I got for my house just for the fun of it. That clock was in the Sears Roebuck catalogs, year after year, and I'd had my eye on it a long time." She was remembering. "I saved pennies and nickels when I could, but it seemed like something always came up and the money had to go for something else.

Helen was about nine the year we made our first good crop. We needed a lot of things—it had been slim pickings for so long—but Charley thought it was about time I got my clock." She and Charley smiled at each other. "When it came, Charley hung it up, right there where it is now. I'll tell you, I thought I had the world on a string with a downhill pull. Keeps good time, too," she added.

The nervousness was gone. It felt good to be here with Levi's family, right and comfortable.

"You've lived here a long time, haven't you?" I asked them all.

"Since 1884," said Levi's dad. "Richardsons and Brittons—that's Jenny's family. Will and I were kids when the folks started talking about coming out here. That was back in Blair, at the eastern end of the state, on the Missouri River. The word was that if you could get out here and prove up on a homestead, you could run sheep and cattle and raise most anything."

"That's what folks were saying back where we lived too," said Levi's mother. "My pa and brother John ran a ferryboat across the Missouri River, and, when the Blair bridge was built, they decided it was time to move on. Pa and John began to feel crowded. I was just four or five, and Brother John was a grown man then. I was excited to hear him talk about how things would be out in the West."

"Uncle John's a talker," Levi said, and they all laughed.

"Will and I were just kids, but we were rarin' to go," said Charley. "Ma and Pa and the rest of us went by train to Valentine in the Sandhills—that was as far as the railroad went then—and Will walked the rest of the way."

"Walked?" I asked incredulously.

"Yes," said Uncle Will. "Fella we knew name of Connell had a big band of sheep he wanted to move out here. Get started making his fortune, I guess," he said, and laughed. "So, Fred and me and a couple of other fellows, we loaded those sheep on the railroad and went to Valentine, as far as track had been laid up to then. There were five hundred head of those sheep when we started out from Valentine in Cherry Country on April 23. We didn't get here till late August. You can push 'em only so fast."

"You walked?" I asked, still not believing. "From Cherry County? Why, that must be 250 miles!"

"Nearer 300," said Uncle Will, smiling. "Not counting the backtracking, chasing them out of the brush, trying to hold them together. Yeah, we walked and ran, fell down and got up, and cussed them. But we finally got 'em here, most of 'em."

"Walked!" I repeated. "Halfway across the state!"

I began to understand the pride old-timers felt (I never heard any of them speak of themselves as pioneers), the pride of having come early, of having stuck it out. I understood it better when Levi's dad told me the rest of the story of those sheep.

"They were all dead by spring," he said. "It was a terrible winter. I never saw a worse one. That's why they call 1884–85 the year of the big die-up. A lot of people lost all they had and couldn't do anything but go back where they came from.

"A bad winter," Uncle Will said mildly. "Blizzards one right after another. High winds piling up the snow till you couldn't find the stock, couldn't even get through the canyons sometimes to look for 'em. There were five hundred head when we started out and not one head of 'em alive by spring." He ruminated a moment. "Fred was real disappointed," he said.

Disappointed.

"Did he stay?" I asked.

"Oh yes," said Uncle Will. "He got a job freighting stuff from Valentine. I did too. He proved up on a claim, got a little stake together, and did real well. Still livin' in Crawford. Has a room at the Gate City Hotel."

"Pa brought us out on the train to Valentine," Jenny said. "Emigrant trains, they called them then. Folks had their livestock, a plow, stove, bedding, grain for seed and to eat—all on the train. And, of course, Pa and Brother John had the sawmill. Me, I was the baby of the family, and I stuck pretty close to Ma. The older kids liked to talk about the Indians, watching out the windows, hoping they'd see some wild Indians. When we finally did see some, it was sure a disappointment. No feathers, no war paint, no nothing."

"We saw a burial bundle in a tree on White River," Charley said. "That's all the Indian we saw the first year or two. And we didn't bother the bundle; we were kind of superstitious, didn't want to get a curse or something." He chuckled.

"Pa had this place picked out, and he and Charley had already filed their claims when Fred and I got here with the sheep," Uncle Will said. "Charley was a big, rangy kid—passed for a full-grown man, and I did too, when I filed. The land office clerks weren't too particular in those days. They wanted to get the country settled up."

"The three of us filing together here gave us more than most folks had," Charley said. "So we were better off in that way. Besides, living in Blair and talking to folks who'd been west, we had some idea of what it was like out here. Folks coming from Iowa and Illinois, where 160 acres of land—a quarter-section—is a big place, just didn't realize how different things are here. How dry and rough the country was."

"It was kind of pitiful," Uncle Will said, "a man and his wife with a bunch of children, thinking they could make it here on a quarter-section of land. It wouldn't work in good times, and those were hard times, bad times. Drought [he pronounced it *drouth*, as most western Nebraskans do], grasshoppers, hailstorms—in the 1890s we had 'em all. The stock going into winter is short on feed, you get a blizzard, and they pile up in any little draw, too weak to get up and make it onto their feet and walk to feed."

"The Brittons, of course, had all the work they could do with their sawmill," said Charley. "Everybody needed lumber to build with. There wasn't any money to speak of, but they'd bring something to trade, grain or coffee or a shoat. Father Britton and John felled trees up there in the canyon, everything big enough to make a few boards, and they sawed whatever anybody could snake up to the mill. John was a champion at keeping that old sawmill running."

"Here comes Uncle John now," said Levi.

"Oh dear," said his mother, softly.

A tall, rangy old man with heavy shoulders and arms came striding into the yard. Uncle Will went to the door.

"In here, John," he called. "We're all in here."

Levi's mother introduced me to her brother rather primly.

"How do, young lady," said John Britton. "Somebody was sayin' Levi had him a lady friend, and you're it." It was a statement. "You the new folks have the paper in Crawford?"

I told him yes, we did, and wondered how long it would take to get over being new. Longer than three years, apparently.

Levi's mother fluttered around her brother. "Sit in this rocker, Brother John. Would you like a drink of cool water, John dear?" She seemed nervous.

John Britton was calm and collected. He allowed that Mary and all the children, grandchildren, and great-grandchildren were well.

"Twenty-six of 'em up there right this minute," he said. "Sometimes I get tired of the whole kit and caboodle showing up every blamed Sunday. But Mary likes it, sets the young ones to catching chickens and pulling off the feathers. And the girls all help their ma. All good girls. Bring cakes and pies and stuff. Yeah," he said thoughtfully, "all good girls and boys."

Uncle John settled down comfortably with the glass of cool water his sister had brought him.

"These hills," he went on, as if continuing a conversation with me, "When we come here in '84, was just one mass of varmints: mountain lions, wolves, Indians—my Lord!"

"John dear," Levi's mother said mildly.

"S'truth," Uncle John declared. "Mountain lions was so thick in those days you had to kick 'em out of the way when you went out back. Why, Pa and me, sometimes that first winter, we'd get tired of 'em comin' smellin' around the mill, and we'd just pick up the shotgun and thin 'em out so we could get the work done."

"Brother John," Levi's mother began again, "We . . ."

"Lots of riffraff come out here, too," Uncle John continued. "Not one danged thing on their mind but to make trouble for decent folks. I was a young feller then myself, liked a good time as much as anybody, but, when a bunch of 'em busted into a dance we was havin' up on the Runnin' Water, that was enough!" He paused, his eyes snapping. "I told 'em what I was goin' to do, and I done it." Another pause. "I ordered the women and children out of the hall, and then I threw the men out." He nodded in satisfaction. "That was the end of that bunch."

"John dear," Levi's mother said. "I've made a black walnut cake, your favorite. I've got the lemons all squeezed, and we're going to have cake and lemonade in a little while. Just enough time for Charley and Will to show you the new colt."

All the men left for the barn, and Jenny and I went to the kitchen.

"It's small," she said. "I'd like to have a great big kitchen like we had at home when I was a girl. Of course," she added, "It was the kitchen and the living room and the dining room and everything. The dining room in this house was like that too, when Charley's folks lived here. We added this on, the shed room and the porch, before Levi was born, so we could have a bathroom and a separate kitchen. And, of course, I was glad when Charley got the wind charger so that we could have electricity."

She spoke with some pride; few rural people had bathrooms and refrigerators and electric lights.

"You can help me with the cake and the lemonade," she said, "but first I just want to tell you I tried to talk Levi out of this, this getting married. You're both so young."

"My folks think so too," I told her. "And I know we're young, and it's been only a few weeks. But we've known each other three years, and Levi's . . . he's so . . . We want . . ."

"I know, I know," she said. "But Levi's our baby. We just want you to be sure. You're a long time married."

"Yes," I said, and the words tumbled out, "There was a boy in Lincoln I liked, but it wasn't like this. This is different."

"It always is," she said, a little wryly. "It's always different. But times are so hard right now. Even in a couple of years you'll be only, what, twenty?"

"Yes," I said, "but we're not thinking of getting married now. We're thinking of next summer, almost a year from now. My folks want me to go back to school, one more year, and I'm going. I'm going to stay with my Uncle Charley, my Dad's brother, and his wife, Aunt Ellen. I'll work for my board and help with the kids. The folks think another year might make me change my mind, but it won't. I know it won't."

Jenny sighed. "Well, I've heard that before; it's what Levi said. He says he's not going to change, no matter what. So I guess—" She put a layer cake with swirls of white icing in the middle of the big round table. "All right, you two. I guess you'll manage; people do."

I put a tentative arm around her, and she turned to me with a hug.

I felt lighthearted. It was going to be all right.

CHAPTER EIGHTEEN

When I went back to Lincoln to make good on my promise to "wait" before Levi and I got married, I stayed with my father's brother. Being with Uncle Charley and Aunt Ellen Spence was a lot like being at home but without the pressure. Ellen never told me to do anything and didn't mind if nothing got done. Most of her time was taken up by the new baby. I washed dishes, went to class, hung out clothes when Ellen got around to washing, and went to class.

Once Charley took Ellen to a baseball game, and I stayed with the kids. When they got back, Ellen was visibly glad to get home to her brood.

"I thought it would be a nice change for her," Charley told me, "but I guess it didn't seem natural to her not to have a couple of kids crawling around over her. We've had a kid since six months after we were married, you know."

I'd had a pretty good idea of it. Mother, without being explicit, had always spoken of Ellen with the sniffiness that meant she was a girl who "had to get married." Not that Charley's part in it was any surprise to her; nobody in Dad's family met Mother's standards in the gentility department, and Elizabeth's early arrival was only supplementary, but completely unnecessary, evidence that the Spences' morals were not up to her standards.

Elizabeth's hair had come in since I'd seen her. I could almost brush it over my finger. Her bright blue eyes reminded me of Dad's. I slept in her little bed with her and usually, sometime during the night, made room for her sister Patty.

I'd been there just four weeks when I awoke to find both Charley and Ellen standing by the bed. I knew it was early. It was just getting light, and neither of them was dressed. Charley looked even more like Dad than usual.

"I've been trying to think of some way to tell you," he said, sitting down heavily on the edge of the bed and taking my hand. "Some way that isn't so . . . but I can't. Karl called about an hour ago. Loris died in the night."

A hoarse voice was saying, "No, no, no." It was my voice.

"Went to a night football game in Chadron," said Charley. "Saw everybody, talked to everybody, stayed till the game was over. But, when he got home, he called Karl to help him get his boots off. Said he couldn't get warm. They called the doctor, but in a couple of hours it was over."

Ellen lifted Patty out of the bed and held her on her shoulder. "I wish one of us could go with you," Charley said, "but we can't. We'll get you to the train tonight. There'll be somebody to meet you in Alliance in the morning so you won't have to wait." He stood up looking stooped. "Come on," he said. "Have a cup of coffee with me before you leave. I don't know anything to say, but we can talk."

CHAPTER NINETEEN

Levi and I got married in June 1933, not long after Franklin Delano Roosevelt was inaugurated. Nobody in our part of the country expected much from the new president. It stands to reason, people said, "An easterner, a Harvard graduate, a rich man, shoot!" True, Hoover was rich, but his roots were in Iowa, and he was an engineer, a practical man. He'd earned what he had.

Both our families tried to talk us into waiting, but the urgencies of biology were not to be denied and made waiting intolerable. It didn't seem important to us that we had nothing. Well, not nothing—Levi had ten range cows and a good horse and eighty dollars that he'd earned working on the county roads with a horse-drawn scraper and a team of horses. That wasn't eighty dollars cash, of course; there wasn't any cash in 1933. It was eighty dollars in vouchers that the local merchants discounted when we bartered them for merchandise. I think we spent almost all of it in the hardware store. Levi got a set of harnesses; I got a washtub and a double boiler. I can't think why I wanted a double boiler; there must have been lots of things we needed more.

Levi—oh that man! He was all I'd ever dreamed of: he was a man's man, whatever that is. He looked exactly the way a cowboy should look, and he actually was a cowboy. He could charm a bird out of a tree, and he wasn't a charming womanizer, either. I had the man every red-blooded, right-thinking American girl wanted.

That first summer we lived with Levi's parents, sleeping, the first month, in a tent in the yard because his sisters and their children were home for a visit. All we could think of was having a place of our own. There was a one-room tarpaper shack on the "west place," a ranch Levi bought from his father about four miles west of the "home place," which we all started calling the "east place." The tar paper shack on the west place had been moved down from the hills when some hapless settler got starved out in the 1890s. After the Richardson Brothers—Levi's father and Uncle Will— bought the land, the shack was used for baching by whatever hired man was working on the west place.

The family that had originally occupied the shack had been none too clean, and the male housekeeping by the hired men hadn't improved things. On the walls many layers of newspaper were tacked up, clean newspapers over dirty ones. Even the most recent additions were filthy. There was an ancient, stained, ragged mattress on the iron bedstead. There were so many bedbugs in it that they didn't bother to hide, or perhaps there were so many that there wasn't room for all of them to hide.

Both Dad and Uncle Will Richardson said nobody could live in such a place, that it was too dirty and ramshackle, but we were sure we could clean it up and make it livable. Levi's mother said of course we could; she and Charley had lived in worse places. They'd lived in a dugout in the side of a creek bank when they were first married, as many people had done in the 1890s.

Each morning Jenny fixed a lunch for us, perhaps homemade souse on homemade bread. There were boiled eggs and tea in a thermos. If there was gas for our little Ford roadster or for the old truck the family owned, we drove one of them. If there wasn't, we went to the west place in the wagon with a team of horses, and we went early.

The first thing we did was get rid of that bedbug-infested mattress. Shuddering, we carried it outside, well away from the shack. We poured gasoline over it then put the bedsprings on top of it and set a match to it. What a fine blaze it made! God knows how many bedbugs we incinerated, but the fire cleansed the bedsprings.

Next we tore down all the old newspapers on the bare rough-sawed planks the shack was built of and scrubbed the walls and floors with lye water. The shack sat on a slope and had settled a bit on the downhill side. Levi loosened the lowest planks on that side with a crowbar, so that the water we scrubbed with, and the buckets and buckets of rinse water we threw on the walls, all ran out the lower side. When he nailed the planks back solid, everything looked shipshape. It was only later, when we had company, that we learned how far off level the shack was. Little kids, coming through the door on the high side, picked up speed and ended up running smack against the downhill wall.

After the scrubbing, we made whitewash of slaked lime, adding a good amount of carbolic acid. We took up the mixture in tin cans and slapped it on the cracks, to penetrate every crevice and kill any lurking bugs. Then we brushed it out smooth so that the whole inside was as clean and white as an egg.

It was Levi's idea to put the bed in the rafters to give us more room. He laid planks across the rafters and put the bedsprings on them. His mother gave us an old, clean, mattress-size bag made of ticking, and we filled it with clean straw for our mattress.

Levi's grandfather had made a tall chest of pine boards, and he'd carried that chest out to Valentine on the emigrant train and then to Dawes County by wagon. Levi's mother had given him the dresser, which we climbed on to get to the bed, pulling ourselves up by the crosspieces Levi had nailed between the studs.

The other furniture was a cracked table, an old rocking chair, and three straight chairs, one with a back. I painted it all lemon yellow, including the orange crates Levi tacked up for cupboards. I made curtains for the two small windows and a blue-checked gingham pad for the rocker.

For hot weather Dad gave us an old oil stove to cook on. For cold weather there was a settler's stove, a small wood-burner just one stove lid wide and lids two deep. One section of the stovepipe had a tiny built-in oven—a little drum-shaped double chamber where the smoke would pass by the oven and go on up into the pipe above it, heating the oven as it went. There was a little door in the oven and a shelf inside where a small cake or pie could be baked or meat and potatoes cooked.

For years Levi's mother had kept a shiny, printed linoleum "rug" on the floor of her big dining room. As the pattern wore off, and when she could afford to, she ordered a new one from Montgomery Ward and put it over the old one. For us she rolled back the top one, pulled out the layer beneath, and gave it to us. Most of the flowers and scrolls were gone, but even the smooth brown beneath the pattern looked attractive when freshly washed.

By the time cold weather came, Levi had repaired the cracks in the walls and roof and had banked up earth all around the house to keep the cold out. I was proud of my house. Levi said, "Just wait; someday we'll have a big, beautiful house, and there'll be big front windows looking right out at Crow Butte."

I don't suppose I've ever been so happy, before or since, as I was that first year. Levi had cut down trees on the east place during the year we'd been engaged, to be used for building a log house. By the time we were married, they were well seasoned, and we made trip after trip to haul them to the west place. We used two teams of horses belonging to Dad and Uncle Will. Levi hitched them in tandem, one team behind the other. He took the wagon box off so that logs could be carried on the running gear of the wagon.

Because of its weight, we had to take the load of logs to the west place by way of the county road, about twice the distance of the trip through the canyons.

Going from the west place to the east place without a load, we drove on a rough trail through four deep canyons. Levi stood on the front hounds, a brace on the wagon frame, and I crouched on the bolster with my feet on the rear hounds of the wagon. The lead team, Boots and Pet, was so well trained that the horses would stop when they came to a gate, wait while Levi opened it, go through the gate far enough so that Levi could close it, and move on only when he was back in his place, all without him giving them a command.

The autumn days were bright and sunny. I felt fulfilled and excited, brave and strong, as I hung onto my perch on the wagon.

When we got to the east place, Levi, his father, and Uncle Will loaded the logs onto the wagon, pyramiding them up. Then the men secured the logs with chains. Levi hooked a "boomer," a sort of lever, on the chains and tightened them until the load was secure. We stayed for noon dinner, and, after I'd helped Jenny with the dishes, everybody came to the yard to see us off. I heard Uncle Will say admiringly to his brother, "She's a wiry little thing, ain't she!" and I knew he was referring not to my build but to my scrambling up to straddle the load of logs behind my husband.

"Now lock the wheel when you get to Ball Diamond Hill," Dad always said, but Levi never did. To stop and chain one rear wheel, just to slow the wagon down on the steep grade, took time. He didn't say he would or wouldn't; he just never did, and I wasn't willing to beg him to. If he could hang on, I could hang on, too, and I did, too scared every time to scream and too proud to show my fear.

The worst ride we ever had down that damnable hill was the time we had a green horse in the second team, an unbroke horse, as westerners say. The sharp ends of the logs had been axed to points and were toward the front of the load. As we tore down Ball Diamond Hill, the wagon gained on the horses, and the green horse got poked in the butt by the sharp ends. He went crazy, kicking and bucking and snorting, infecting the other horses with his terror. He even managed to kick himself over the traces; it was fully a half-mile before Levi could bring the horses to a stop and straighten them out. I was scared to death that time, but he laughed, and in no time it seemed a funny adventure even to me, the most cowardly person ever to be near a horse.

We were so much in love anything seemed possible, and I remember, with pride and pain, Levi's saying to me on one of those trips, "You're the best damned company a man ever had." We were poor, I guess, but we were so happy that we were hardly aware of it.

CHAPTER TWENTY

Anderson and Edna Reed came to call on us one evening soon after we moved into the shack. They were our nearest neighbors, and they lived on the bank of West Ash Creek a mile and a half west of us. Their daughter, Burnace, was a year or two younger than I was. Edna was a big, tall, handsome woman, who always wore her hair cut short, with one wide wave carefully set on the right side—finger waves, we called them. Anderson was a small, rather stooped man with a ruddy complexion and hair that got grayer and grayer as the years went by until finally it was snow-white.

Levi had told me about Anderson—the cussingest man he'd ever known, he said, couldn't get a sentence out without cussing, and a famous storyteller in a country famous for its storytellers. That evening, however, Anderson struck me as a quiet, reserved man, pleasant and friendly but not talkative at all. I asked Levi about this after they'd left.

"He didn't say so much as *damn*," I said. "Why did you tell me he talked so rough? He didn't even talk much."

Levi scratched his head. "I don't know," he said. "I've never seen Anderson like that before. He's usually full of stories, and he cusses every other word. Maybe he wasn't feeling good tonight, or maybe he's got religion. He sure wasn't himself."

A week or so later, on our way home from town, we stopped at the Reeds' just about dusk. There was a front door, but in many houses in the West front doors are used only when there's a golden wedding or when family and friends return from a funeral. So we headed up the path that led around the house to the back door. At the squeaking of the gate that opened into the yard, three or four dogs rushed out, barking furiously. Anderson was right behind them.

"Damn your eyes, get to the barn, you sons of bitches!" he bawled.

Then he saw who it was, and he laughed. "Oh hell," he said. "I didn't know it was you folks, damn it to hell. Edna made me promise not to cuss in front of Polly, but I can't keep that up. Come in, come in!"

We went in and stayed until late in the evening, with stories and cussing pouring out of Anderson and gales of laughter out of all of us. That was the end of the quiet, reserved man I'd met the first evening. From then on Anderson was himself in my presence, and a better friend and neighbor never lived. From time to time, knowing it wouldn't make a particle of difference, Edna would say, "Anderson, don't swear so much!"

Anderson and Edna had loved each other since they were kids, and ever since they'd married, at seventeen, they'd spent nearly all their time together. Burnace was their first child, and Marvin came along a year or two later. All of them scrapped and argued continually; it was part of their love.

Cleanliness and order were Edna's passion. Her tiny house was always immaculate, always orderly, yet she never seemed to be in a rush. She was always ready to go with Anderson in the car, as he liked her to do, and she never left beds unmade or dishes unwashed, as I did.

Days start early in the country; still, I was startled to hear Edna say one day, "I'd think it was terrible if I didn't have my work done by seven o'clock." It was clear that she meant seven in the morning. This seemed like a reproach to me, and I tried sporadically to emulate her easy efficiency, but I couldn't do it.

So, when Edna got new linoleum for her kitchen and promptly covered it to the very edge with newspapers, I couldn't resist—I didn't even try— twitting her a bit. I said, "Edna, if you were going to cover it with newspapers, you could have saved the money and just said you had new linoleum." She gave me a sharp look, but we were friends as well as neighbors. She knew my slovenly ways and let it pass.

Edna made as little mess as possible and tried to keep her family from being messy. Burnace once told me that she and Marvin, when they were little, were allowed to have only one toy out at a time. Another time I heard Edna take Anderson to task about his muddy feet, and he answered coolly, "Oh go on, Teddy, you're not tough—you're just big!" as he left the house, with Edna yelling after him. "You're damned right I'm big, and I'm not going to have you tracking mud and cow manure into my clean kitchen!"

Rats thrive and damage buildings in the country, just as they do in cities. Anderson had a particular loathing for them. He cursed them, of course, and he tried trapping and poisoning them. Such methods seldom work against rats, however, because they're too smart to fall for them. He never gave up, though, and he would try any method he heard of, no matter how bizarre, to get rid of the rats. He told us about one endeavor.

"Ed Johnson said a guy in the pool hall was talkin' about it, and he said there's one sure-fire way to get rid of the sons of bitches."

"What's that?" Levi asked.

"Well," said Anderson, "First, you've got to catch one of the damned bastardly things. And you know that ain't easy."

We did know it.

"Worst of it is you gotta catch him alive," he added. "Then you take the son of a bitch, and you give him a good singein' with the blowtorch, and then you turn him loose, and that scares the hell out of the rest of 'em, and the whole damned shootin' match will leave your place!"

Now this was something new, to catch a rat alive.

"I did it," said Anderson. "I sent off for some special wire cage traps and a bottle of the bait you're supposed to use with them. Something that makes the he-rats think there's a damned bitch rat ready and rarin' to go. Well, I did every damned thing the instructions said to do. I used tongs, and I used new gloves right out of the package to handle everything so it wouldn't smell of my hands. I scalded the traps and put them in place with a hay fork and covered them up with straw. I did everything, and I'll bet I worked two months before I got my hands on one. I kept it up and kept it up, and I'd just about decided it couldn't be done, damn it all to hell, when I caught one of the buggers. A big fat son of a bitch with long whiskers and a scaly tail."

Anderson almost gagged as he described the creature.

"Well, sir," he went on. "I got the blowtorch goin', and I hollered at Teddy, and she come on down to the barn, and I started in to singe that miserable, rotten, bastardly son of a bitch."

His eyes were glowing.

"I singed him," he said. "And I singed him. And I just got to havin' so much fun I couldn't stop. And, before I knew it, I'd burnt the bastard all to hell!"

I learned, with some surprise, that the Reeds "rubbered," or listened in on calls on the telephone line. In most households only the women listened in; at the Reed household everybody listened in, and, if they didn't hear all the details of something you'd talked about, they'd ask you the next time you saw them or even ring you up and ask. There were twenty-six subscribers on the party line, and some of the people who lived on East Ash Creek weren't known personally to the Reeds; still, the family was interested in their doings, and they also made inquiries of Levi and me.

The phone line was privately owned by the subscribers, and it was maintained by volunteer work. It had originally been strung up on fence posts or trees. Now it was on poles, but it was frequently down or out of commission. Then somebody had to go looking for the trouble. Sometimes it was no more than a tree branch grounding it; sometimes after a storm it was down in places for several miles, and a crew of neighbors had to get together to rebuild it.

All the phones were wall phones, and during an electrical storm it was well to stay away from them and to be sure that nothing flammable, like a sheer curtain, was within range of the sparks that shot out when a bolt of lightning hit nearby.

The line was connected with the Bell switchboard in town. With one long crank of the ringer, you could reach it to call people in town or other country lines and the outside world. But it was foolish to call long distance from a country line unless you just had to. At the sound of your signal to the operator, so many people picked up their phones that the voices became too faint to be audible.

To call someone else on the same line, you didn't have to go through the switchboard at all. You simply cranked out the correct sequence of long and short rings: two shorts and a long, three longs and two shorts, and so on. In case of a general announcement or in an emergency such as a fire, you cranked a series of short, sharp, urgent-sounding rings, and everybody rushed to the phone.

Everybody but me knew there was a ritual to be observed in telephoning a neighbor. Only later did I learn that my telephone manners were considered abrupt because I said, first thing, "This is Polly Richardson." You weren't supposed to state your name or ask your caller's name. Good form dictated that there should be mutual inquiries about the state of each other's health and the health of the spouse and the children.

When this was taken care of, you went on to a discussion of the weather, the state of the crops and the cattle, and only then, finally and almost offhandedly, you stated the purpose of the call. This was polite procedure even if the caller was someone you saw no more than twice a year. If someone called, courtesy required that you cast wildly about in your mind trying to place the voice, rather than to ask right out who was calling. Sometimes during or after the amenities you might get a clue. "Carl said one of Levi's heifers is in our south pasture"—aha, Lillian Lange!—and you were spared the necessity of exposing your ignorance and perhaps offending the caller. I never did perfect my telephone manners, though, past the point of a perfunctory opening "How are you?"

My neighbors found my telephone habits peculiar in another way: I didn't rubber. They'd say, "Did you hear Jack and Isabelle talking the other evening?" and were surprised to learn that I hadn't picked up the receiver when I heard Isabelle's ring.

"Well, you know he's sweet on her, don't you?" My negative reply was received with laughter and a quick update. And, when I suggested, as I did once or twice, that listening in on other people's conversations was, besides being boring, rather like reading someone else's mail, I was looked at wonderingly. Listening in was so much a part of daily life, a way of keeping in touch with what was going on, that the idea of not listening was odd. Besides, it was known that in the evening, at home, Mrs. McLain, the postmistress, read all the postcards that went through the post office. Who wouldn't?

Marian Lange was an inveterate rubberer, and once, she told Jenny, she was making a lemon pie for Ladies' Aid when the phone rang. Absorbed in what was being said, she let her pie filling scorch. "I'll sure get me a double boiler next time I go to town!" she said.

The switchboard operators in town were the best part of telephoning. They knew everybody, and they recognized hundreds of voices with astonishing accuracy. It was pleasant to pass the time of day with the operator while waiting for your party to answer. After a few rings she might say, "I'll bet he's having coffee at Schwartz's Cafe. Do you want me to ring there?"

Once, when I was trying to call Levi from a friend's house in town, the operator said again and again, "Sorry, that line's still busy." I hadn't identified myself, but presently the phone rang and she told my friend, "Line 110's open now if Polly still wants it."

I remember making an early morning call; as soon as the operator heard my voice, she said, "Did you know Billy Clark died in the night?" because she knew he was my friend.

Sadie Spence, with Loris,
in the "Madonna" pose Polly
jeered at, ca. 1915

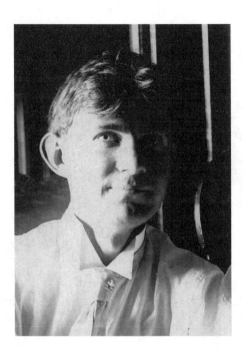

Karl L. Spence, Polly's father, about twenty-five years old, 1914

Polly Spence and Lt. Tony Parks, the man she couldn't bring herself to marry

Levi and Polly's first house, the tarpaper shack, before they fixed it up, 1934

The log house where Levi and Polly lived for twenty years; note the wind charger

Polly Spence, Crawford High
School graduation, 1933

Levi Richardson, Crawford
High School graduation, 1933

Uncle Will Richardson, a
good and gentle man, about
thirty-five years old

Levi Richardson,
about thirty-five years old

Polly Richardson,
thirty-five years old

Left to right: Charley, Bill, and Spence Richardson, 1942

Crow Butte, where Polly's ashes are scattered, from Levi and Polly's front porch

Left to right: Polly, Bill, Spence, Charley, and Levi Richardson, 1942

Polly Spence at her son's home in Caracas, Venezuela, 1965

Once I wanted to speak to the new mechanic at the Ford garage after hours, but I couldn't remember his name. I told the operator, and she said, "Oh yes, that's Joe Acton. He's just moved his family here from Ravenna. They're living in the old Marshall house, and their number is 72-R. I'll ring."

And when somebody was hurt and you gave the doctor's number, saying, "Hurry, Hurry, please," the operator would say, "You go and take care of things. I'll get him there. Do you need the rescue unit?"

CHAPTER TWENTY-ONE

Doors were never locked in ranch country. As a child, Jenny Britton, Levi's mother, had come to Dawes County with her family in 1884, and she told me that in those early days it was taken very poorly if a door was locked, because a neighbor or a wayfarer might need food and shelter. One benighted settler family from the East locked their door because they didn't know any better, the neighbors thought. Jenny said somebody explained local custom and the reasons for it, but still they locked their door when they went out, and it was obvious that they didn't get the point. Accordingly, an armload of firewood and a few matches were laid in front of their door the next time it was found locked. The breach of custom and hospitality was not repeated.

A concomitant unwritten law was that if you needed food and shelter in a house whose owners weren't present, you built a fire and cooked whatever you could find, but you didn't fail to wash whatever pans and dishes you'd used, and you refilled the wood box near the stove from the owner's woodpile.

The Pinneys, who lived on a ranch north of Crawford, gave public notice of their attitude toward neighbor and stranger alike. Old Bailey Pinney had come to the country as a young cowboy in 1887 and had taken up a homestead and built a home and a herd on it. As soon as his roof was on, he put up a crudely lettered sign: HUNT AND FISH ALL YOU DAMN PLEASE, AND WHEN THE BELL RINGS, COME IN TO DINNER.

That first sign had long since weathered to illegibility and been renewed and replaced when necessary; and by the time I saw it, it was a rather large, professionally lettered notice. The message was intended to be taken literally and frequently was, not only at the Pinneys' but also at homes throughout the area. Nobody working on your place or passing by would insult you by bringing along his own lunch; as the British so succinctly put it, it just wasn't done.

One early spring day in 1934, my mother and I set out to spend the day with the Pinneys. Old Bailey's son, Ralph, was now running the ranch, while Bailey, long a widower and now so paunchy he had trouble heaving his bulk into the saddle, lived with Ralph and Bess and their children, surveying life and everybody around him benignly. He loved to sit with friends in the kitchen of the ranch house, bourbon and water in hand, and reminisce about the early days. He talked about the time Crawford had seven saloons and as many or more "sporting houses," some for the white cowboys and some for the black cowboys and the Tenth Cavalrymen, the blacks that the Indians called buffalo soldiers because of their color and their kinky hair. Crawford was known throughout the West, he said, as a rough town, with gamblers and bad men and shoot-outs in the streets, not to mention the intramural knifing of the Tenth Cavalry. A well on the Lake Ranch on White River had God knows how many black bodies stuffed down it, and at the intersection of Second and Main Streets in Crawford, there was a boarded-over well that also held some grisly secrets.

Bailey remembered the incident when the Tenth Cavalry, fed up with the conduct of Town Marshall Moss, hung him in a tree in his own front yard, and nothing was ever done about it.

One day when my mother and I went to the Pinneys', the wind had come up in the night, and by the time the sun rose, the air was so full of dust you could see it only as a dull red ball through the crepuscular haze. I tied one of Levi's red bandannas over my nose and mouth and drove the eight miles to town in the Model A roadster. From there we drove to the Pinneys' in my mother's closed car, groping our way through the clouds of dust that swept across the dirt road, stopping now and then when it was impossible to see beyond the windshield. When we reached the Pinneys', Bess stood on the screened back porch with a scarf tied over her head and lower face, waving us in. We'd started at ten; the eight miles from town had taken us nearly an hour.

Bess's kitchen was warm, and so was her welcome. She said, "Just go in the bedroom and lay your coats on the bed. Never mind the dust on them. It wouldn't do any good to take them outside and shake them now; the dust is everywhere in here anyway."

It was indeed; there were drifts of it under the doors and windows, and you could smell it. We went to the washroom and dipped water out of the pail to wash our hands and arms and faces and to try to comb some of the dirt out of our hair before we sat down in the big kitchen to chat with Bess as she moved around her stove and worktable.

Presently there was a knock at the door; with the howling of the wind, we hadn't heard anybody come into the yard. It was a dusty, grimy cowman, hat in hand. Bess quickly asked him in and closed the door against the wind.

The man told Bess his name was Wade Randall, that he lived near Hat Creek, Wyoming, and that he was trailing a couple hundred head of cattle to Rushville, where he had a buyer. He and the four men with him had been on the road for three and a half days, and the cattle weren't moving well because of the wind and dust—could Bess feed them their noon meal?

"Of course," said Bess, and she put on her coat and scarf to take him to the barn, where Ralph was working on machinery. In a few minutes Ralph led his own saddle horse out of the barn and rode back with Mr. Randall to show him the gate where the herd could be turned into a field and held during the noon stop.

In the meantime Bess had pulled the big round table apart, put in three more leaves, and found extra oilcloth to cover the added length. She had a big beef roast in the oven, and I quickly peeled more potatoes to put in with the others in the big kettle. Bess opened the trapdoor in the kitchen floor and went down into the cellar for jars of home-canned corn and green beans and peaches.

By the time the men had penned the cattle, fed and watered their horses at the barn, and come to the house, the dinner was nearly ready. They filed in silently, nodding acknowledgment as Mr. Randall introduced each of them. They piled their coats and hats on a kitchen chair before going to the washroom to clean up as best they could.

Bailey and Bess and Ralph chatted with Mr. Randall and with Mother and me, but the men with Mr. Randall had little to say beyond "Yes, ma'am" and "No, thank you, ma'am." I thought of the old saying that a cowboy is afraid of just two things: being set afoot by his horse and a good woman. Bess's quiet goodness shone wherever she was, and certainly my mother bristled with goodness, so these men were subdued.

After Bess, Mother, and I had served apple pie and coffee and the men had finished eating, they took their leave, each one thanking Bess for the meal. Mr. Randall thanked us and told us how to reach his place from Hat Creek. He added that he hoped we'd be up his way sometime so he could return the favor. He was a courteous man, so no offer of payment was made.

While we washed the dishes, I asked Bess what she would have done with five unexpected hungry men if she hadn't happened to have a roast in the oven. She said there was always bacon and eggs or canned meat. Of course, the cellar, even at winter's end, always had jars of fruit and vegetables. I could see Bess would have managed a good meal, even on short notice, and by that time I was learning to do it myself.

In the ranch country it is taken for granted that machinery and equipment are for the use of anybody who needs them. Once, when Levi needed his cement mixer, he couldn't remember who'd borrowed it; indeed, he may not have known, since a neighbor, if he found no one at home to ask, might load up what he needed and take it with him, intending but perhaps forgetting to mention it. And, if the borrower knew of somebody else who needed it, he'd pass it on, knowing that nobody would mind. That time, after a good deal of inquiring around, Levi found the mixer not in our neighborhood but south of town at the Raben place, several neighborhoods away. We knew the Rabens, saw them occasionally at bull sales or in the streets of Crawford or Chadron, but they were a bit too far away to neighbor with. There was some kidding about how Lorenz Raben had happened to come into possession of our mixer, but nobody was alarmed or resented the fact that he had it. We all knew we were welcome to use whatever Lorenz Raben had.

In the whole area there was only one exception to the borrowing and lending practices. The Clinton brothers, two old bachelors who lived together, kept everything locked up and never lent or borrowed anything. They neighbored with nobody and suspected everybody. They'd worked hard all their lives, had fallen out with all their neighbors and with their brothers and sisters, and had accumulated a sizable layout, with good buildings and many sheep and cattle.

One time, when they were both away from their place, a fire broke out in the dry cheat grass near the buildings. Somebody saw the smoke and gave the alarm with a general ring on the telephone line. The whole neighborhood turned out with gunnysacks and shovels to put the fire out before it could reach the frame buildings. A day or two later I saw old Joe repairing the fence where we'd driven in to fight the fire, and I stopped to talk.

It's a good thing somebody saw the smoke and gave the alarm," I said. "A few more minutes' start, and all the buildings might have burned."

Ben looked around cautiously. "Oh, we know who started it, all right," he said. "They'll probably try it again."

I was shocked. "Started it?" I said. "Nobody would start a fire against a neighbor! Not any time, but especially in the dry season. Nobody would do that."

Ben shook his head. "You just don't know. We have information. We know who did it."

I started to reason with him, but I could see it was useless to try. His mind was made up.

As it was, they had stopped talking to Levi some months before, because of a remark he'd made when Leonard told him somebody had been stealing from them.

"Then you guys had better start watching each other," Levi had said. "There's nobody else around here who'd steal."

It was true; thievery hardly existed.

Once I forgot my purse at a neighbor's house. She called me the next day and said she was going to town and would bring it along if I'd meet her at the road. I watched the road that went by our place, and when I didn't see her, I assumed her plans had changed. A couple of days later I learned she'd meant the north road, a road we rarely traveled. She'd hung the purse on the gatepost there when she didn't find me waiting. I found it there a day or two later when I drove to Chadron, its thirty or thirty-five dollars, all we had, undisturbed.

CHAPTER TWENTY-TWO

Uncle Will had never married, and he'd lived with Jenny and his brother Charley since the early days of their marriage. In their partnership Charley was the brains and Uncle Will the brawn, an arrangement that seemed to suit both of them.

Charley wore the extra pants to his Sunday suit and an old "good" shirt, and he spent a good deal of everyday lying on the leather couch in the big dining room. Levi said he'd never known his father to do a full day's work in his life, and certainly I never saw him exert himself much.

Uncle Will got up at four o'clock in the morning, winter and summer, and put on his blue chambray work shirt and overalls. He worked steadily all day long, with time out for three big meals, slowly and deliberately eaten. Everything Uncle Will did was done slowly and deliberately.

Uncle Will was gentle and mild-mannered. In addition, he was good, really good, and everyone sensed it. He'd had a disfiguring treatment for skin cancer on his lip. I noticed it the first time I met him and then never thought of it again. It didn't bother kids, either; they'd sit on his lap and talk to him, and sometimes they touched the mutilated place and asked,

"What's that?" Uncle Will would tell them, and they'd ask whether it hurt. He said no, and that was the end of it.

In the years before he went to live with Charley and Jenny, Uncle Will worked for the Chicago & Northwestern Railroad, building fills and, with a team and wagon, freighting goods to Chadron from Valentine, where the railroad ended. He worked as a cowboy on the Pine Ridge Indian Reservation, where white ranchers had preempted grazing rights. Uncle Will worked for a man named Swallow. Most ranges and pastures hadn't been fenced in that early day, so cattle wandered wherever they pleased. This necessitated a roundup, where the cattle were gathered and separated according to their owner. Several years Uncle Will went to the roundup as Mr. Swallow's "rep," the man who took care of Mr. Swallow's interests. Uncle Will told some wonderful stories of those days.

One time at the roundup, Uncle Will said, a cowboy had a terrible toothache.

He was moaning and carrying on something fierce," Uncle Will said. "So we decided the tooth would have to come out, to shut him up."

They had no forceps, of course, and their pliers and wire-pullers were too big, so they decided they'd have to knock the tooth out. They gave the patient several good shots of whiskey to relax him and ease the pain, and they took several good shots themselves to keep him company. Then they stretched him out on the ground, his head between one person's knees, somebody else holding down each arm, and another person sitting on his legs. Somebody else took a chisel and a hammer and knocked the tooth out, while the sufferer thrashed wildly.

As soon as the tooth was out, everybody had another drink and then another and another. In the middle of the night the patient got up and began stumbling around, cursing and moaning, falling over sleeping forms, and lurching against the wagon. The cowpoke on watch quickly rode over to quiet him, lest he run into the water buckets and spook the herd, but he was quite unmanageable until several men got awake enough to help. It was nearly morning before the horrid truth came to light; they'd knocked out the wrong tooth, and the whole thing had to be done over.

Uncle Will's friend Cal Griffith worked on the reservation, too, and he drifted about from one ranch to another, taking his body lice with him.

"He seemed to think it was a credit to him, being lousy," Uncle Will said mildly. "We never let him sleep in the bunkhouse or too near us on the range, and a time or two we made him wash his blankets, but he'd only wash one at a time and put it back in his bedroll, so he never got rid of his lice. I don't know as he wanted to; I guess they were company for him."

I wondered why Uncle Will had never married, and I asked Jenny about it.

"He was sweet on one of the Chaulk girls, really courting her, but his mother made such a fuss that it never went further," Jenny said. "He never got very interested in another girl, but he used to hang around Mrs. Winslow a lot." She sniffed. "There was something going on there all right."

I was dismayed. I thought of Mrs. Winslow as an old harridan. Later I saw a picture of her in her younger days and realized she'd been almost pretty. I hoped they had had something going, and I hoped Uncle Will enjoyed it.

In all the years Charley and Will were partners, Will never begrudged his brother's wife and children anything. The brothers owned everything— land and livestock—as partners, and there was no separating out or dividing up any income. They just split it down the middle.

During the Depression people had no cash, but at least in the country we had plenty to eat. We were never out of potatoes and eggs, because Jenny gave them to us. Levi said we had eggs and potatoes for breakfast, potatoes and eggs for dinner, and eggs and potatoes for supper. At the edge of the highway people sold oranges from the back of a truck at one dollar a heaping bushel, having hauled them all the way from California. We couldn't buy them, though, unless we could find three or four other families with twenty cents, or a quarter, to go in on the purchase with us. Hamburger was five cents a pound, round steak two pounds for a quarter. Still we couldn't buy it very often, and we didn't have to.

Levi's parents sometimes butchered a grass-fat cow or a hog, and then we all had meat for a while. Actually, Uncle Will did the butchering, and Jenny and I helped him. Levi and his dad usually found they had to be somewhere else at butchering time.

Cow or hog, Jenny always cooked the liver first, sometimes for breakfast. She always cooked huge breakfasts of meat and eggs and potatoes and gravy, which Uncle Will ate slowly and steadily, as he did everything. By breakfast time he'd been up for two or three hours, doing the chores and working at the barn. Jenny made just one pancake for Charley, and he sometimes took a bite or two of the meat or the applesauce.

If it was a hog we'd butchered, Jenny made headcheese and souse and sausage, and Charley sometimes smoked the hams and sides of bacon in the little smokehouse, using corncobs for the fuel.

We cut up the layers of thick fat from the hog and "tried out," rendered, the chunks in a cast-iron wash boiler that just fit into the top of Jenny's stove when the lids were lifted out. The house was filled with a greasy smell as the lard melted and bubbled out of the chunks. Cracklings, pieces of crisp brown fat, were left when the lard was drained off, and Jenny made cornbread with cracklings which were so tempting even Charley ate a piece or two.

The sausage came out of the grinder that Uncle Will turned—he was tireless at that and many other tedious household chores—and then we fried it and put it down in great stone jars, with melted lard poured over the patties. It kept for months in the cool cellar house.

Jenny taught me to make lye soap with the leftover cracklings and the bacon grease we saved. She was adept at having everything the right temperature, so that as she poured the lye water into the grease, stirring with a wooden paddle, the mixture became soap before our eyes. Sometimes the soap I made separated and had to be reheated, but not Jenny's. My soap was usually nearly brown; hers was almost white. She lined shallow wooden peach boxes with layers of newspaper and poured the liquid soap into them, where it cured for a couple of weeks. Sometimes she put oil of camphor or essence of roses into her soap, but I liked the earthy lye smell, and I didn't perfume mine.

We canned some of the meat too, in Mason jars with zinc lids and rubber rings that had been boiled. When we butchered an animal, the work took two or three days, and we always felt smug and provident when we had finished and cleaned the kitchen.

The Richardsons had prospered and were considered well-off, but, like everybody else, they had no money in the 1930s. Charley took wheat to the mill and exchanged it for grist, and Jenny taught me to bake bread with a starter that we kept alive for years. She told me to knead the dough until it "had kittens in it"—squeaked—and my very first batch was perfection. I've never lost the pleasure I felt then when I took the loaves out of the oven and rubbed their steaming crusts with butter.

Being poor never kept us from having lots of company. Everybody was in the same boat, so, if we had only potato soup for supper, it was all right, because there was plenty of it. My dad gardened, and Uncle Will gardened, and nothing gave either of them more pleasure than to load us down with garden truck. The first year Dad raised a lot of turnips. Neither Levi or I had ever liked turnips, but we learned to like them. Effie McDowell, famous for her cooking, taught me to taste each turnip as I peeled it, discard the bitter ones, boil the others lightly, and add sour cream and salt and pepper.

My dad thought we ought to have a cow, so he bought a fine Jersey and proudly delivered her to our dooryard. He didn't know, and I didn't either, that Levi, like most ranchers, loathed milking a cow and loathed going out on a horse to get the cow in for milking. He wasn't interested, either, in keeping her in a corral. But there was the cow, and there was Dad, pleased as Punch. For a week we had an abundance of milk, cream, and butter. I tried to make the kind of cottage cheese my mother had made when I was a child, but I never achieved a texture so delicate or a flavor so mild and creamy.

Before long there was no more milk, because, as the cow was milked less and less frequently, her milk dried up. I don't know what became of that cow. She may have wound up as a nurse cow, a wet nurse to some little whiteface whose mother had died. Later on, Levi shut up another cow and milked her for awhile, but he always grew tired of the chore, and he decided he'd rather buy a case of Pet milk, poor taste and all, than milk a cow.

CHAPTER TWENTY-THREE

That first winter we were married, Levi ran a foundation and put up a log house. There was a large living room, a large bedroom, and a small kitchen. Levi had a knack for any kind of construction, and he'd worked one winter in the Black Hills, where an old Norwegian had taught him to fit logs together so that each one fitted the other with hardly any room to insert a knife blade between two logs, even those varying in size as much from butt to tip as Nebraska Pine Ridge trees. He used an axe and an adze to hollow out exactly the right amount of wood, and even the corners were marvels of smooth joining.

In the wide wall of the living room, Levi built a fireplace of native rock, brought down from the hills in a stoneboat—a big land sled—pulled by a team of horses. He'd borrowed a plan for the fireplace and made forms of rough-sawed lumber for the inside. He then poured concrete between the forms and the rocks. The stones over the mouth of the fireplace were supported by a wide band of iron he'd fashioned into a half-circle at the forge and anvil.

As Levi emptied the large paper cement bags, I stuffed them into the fireplace, and, when he'd finished off the top, we both stood admiring our new hearth. The temptation to try the fireplace was irresistible. Levi put a match to the paper sacks, and they began to burn. The fireplace was well made; it drew perfectly, throwing out great heat and no smoke into the room. But suddenly we realized that more than the paper was burning. The wooden forms inside had caught fire. They were pitch pine, and they burned furiously. In a moment the fireplace and the whole house began to vibrate.

I don't think we spoke a word; we grabbed buckets and ran down the hill to the horse tank. We raced back and forth carrying water as fast as we could, running up the ladder and pouring it on the roof all around the chimney. It was all over in a few minutes. The wood had burned itself out, and by some miracle the newly poured concrete had held. It must have been the fastest seasoning a concrete job ever had.

We moved in before the house was finished, before all the windows were installed, and before baseboards had been built around the ragged edges of the flooring. One morning as I was dressing I heard a curious, chilling noise—not a locust, not anything I could put a name to, but instinctively I jumped back. I'd almost stepped on a rattlesnake that had come in through the openings at the edge of the flooring. He was as scared as I was and immediately slipped down into the space beneath the floor. Levi, who'd been filling the boiler so I could wash clothes, came running when he heard me scream and against my horrified protests went down into the tiny crawl space to drive the snake back up. He'd armed me with an adze and told me to pin the snake just behind its head against the logs. Levi got a butcher knife and cut its head off; he didn't want to mar the logs by whacking it off with an axe. I cleaned up the blood and shook all day.

That night I woke up in a cold sweat, convinced there was a rattler in the room. Levi got up, lit the lamp, looked around, and assured me there was nothing there. I finally went back to sleep. The dream came again, though, and night after night I woke him, whispering that I knew there was a snake in the room, scared to have him put his foot on the floor. After four or five nights of this, Levi loaded the shotgun and put it beside the bed. Next time I woke him with my snake dream, he picked the gun up, shot it into the unfinished floor, and told me he'd killed my snake. He had, too; I never had that dream again.

The plains saw some bitter winters in the 1930s, with periods lasting six weeks when the thermometer never got up to zero. During one of those winters Jenny went on the train to visit her daughters in eastern Nebraska and Missouri, and Levi and I went to the east place from time to time during the weeks she was gone and sometimes stayed a night or two. While we were there, I cooked for Charley and Uncle Will and cleaned the house.

One evening we sat around the dining room table playing pitch, a game at which Uncle Will excelled, not because his approach to it was well planned but because he bid wildly and was phenomenally lucky. It was getting late, probably 9:30 or so, as we finished a game. There was some talk of calling it a night and heading for bed. But Levi and I decided we should teach the two old men to play auction bridge. This turned out to be rather more of a problem than we had anticipated, and we were on the point of giving up and going to bed when I smelled wood smoke and, glancing over at the wall, saw a thin curl of smoke coming out of a seam of the wallpaper. Levi jumped up and put his hand on the wall; the whole south wall was hot to the touch. His grandfather had built the house of logs set up vertically, stockade fashion, and it had since been sided with clapboard on the outside and plastered on the inside. It was 37 degrees below zero that night; Levi's dad had been firing the stove to its limit all day, and the whole wall beside the chimney was smoldering inside.

Levi seized his coat and cap and ran outside. He turned the handle of the hydrant to turn on the water and then turned the tap where the hose was attached. Whether by foresight or by great good luck, the hose had been coiled up empty and was not frozen. Levi ran to the cellar house for a ladder and a crowbar and, carrying the hose with him, went up the ladder. The moment he pried away a section of siding, the flames leaped up. The water pressure held, steam rose, and the flames died down.

By this time I was in the yard in my coat, stocking cap, and gloves. I'd grabbed a bucket and filled it with water at the sink. When I thought to look at it a few minutes later, it was frozen in from the side two or three inches.

Levi had always said Uncle Will had just one gear, and that was low. That evening proved it. During most of the commotion he sat on a kitchen chair, getting his overshoes properly adjusted and buckled up, putting on his coat and buttoning it, pulling his Scotch cap's earflaps well down over his ears, and checking his mittens, which were hanging on a wire near the stove, to see if they were dry enough to put on.

Levi went to the barn and got a big tarpaulin to hang in the opening that was burned in the wall. He soaked the walls well on both sides of the chimney, and Charley sat watch the rest of the night. The hole in the wall was boarded up the next day, but rebuilding the chimney properly, with enough concrete around it to prevent another such mishap, had to wait for warmer weather.

If we hadn't stayed up a little later than usual to teach the old men to play bridge, if I hadn't smelled smoke and looked up, if the hose had been blocked with ice, if Levi hadn't acted so quickly—if, if, if. The ancient logs of the house would have burned like tinder the moment air reached them. The telephone was on the south wall near the chimney; all of us but Uncle Will slept upstairs, and he slept way at the back of the house. The Langes lived only a mile away, not far in ranch country but almost impossible to walk in nightclothes at 37 degrees below zero, if indeed anyone escaped the fire.

The next morning Levi thought he should try to go to the west place to see how our cattle were faring. He saddled his cow horse, Bugs, and set out, not once but several times. The wind was so fierce and the cold so bitter that Bugs, the best of cow horses, simply would not face into it. By the following day the weather had moderated a bit, and Levi found all the cattle in good condition except for one. She had drifted into a place where the house formed an L and was frozen stiff, standing on her feet.

CHAPTER TWENTY-FOUR

I was raised in a small-town farming community. When I was a kid, we always had a milk cow, kept in some makeshift corrals Dad had on the other side of town, and Loris had the job of walking over there and milking her twice a day. I don't recall that I was ever urged to learn to milk the cow; if I had been, I'd have fought it because I never much liked anything about domestic animals.

It was different now. I tagged around after Levi. I didn't ride a horse because I was afraid to, but I walked or rode in the wagon or on the tractor. Nothing I learned about cattle raising in the West resembled what I knew of farming in south-central Nebraska. Ranch cattle weren't like milk cows, and ranch practices weren't like farming practices. Herefords—whitefaces—weren't like Jerseys, I learned. They were tough and self-reliant, and Hereford breeders always said that a Hereford cow could pick up a living for herself and her calf where a Black Angus would starve to death.

Herefords, all of them, are red to dark orange, and all have white faces. Aside from the bulls—one bull to twenty-five or thirty cows—there were only a few critters I could recognize, the ones with really distinctive markings. Levi could tell each cow and calf and yearling and steer and heifer from every other one, and there were hundreds of them. I asked how he could tell them apart, and he said, "The same way I tell people apart; they look different."

He had nicknames for some of them. Stumpy had had her tail frozen off in a blizzard; Bally's face looked whiter than the others. Infrequently there were twins. Some calves needed more milk than their mothers could give, so Levi got two nurse cows. There were two Holstein nurse cows, both black-and-white, and I couldn't tell them apart. Levi could, of course; he called one Aggie and the other not-Aggie.

The gestation period for cows is about the same as for humans, and Levi arranged for the calving period to run from mid-February to late March. February is usually a cold, snowy month in northwest Nebraska, but Herefords calve outside, even in temperatures of zero or below, and with this early start the calves that sold as feeders in the fall were big and heavy.

During calving time the cows were put into a large field where wheat or alfalfa was raised in the summer or on the high ground near the windmill, and they were fed extra rations of hay and cotton cake—highly concentrated pellets of cottonseed and binder. On bright winter mornings I'd stand on the tow bar of the tractor with my arms around Levi's waist as he drove toward the feeding ground. He'd begin to cry, "Co-boss, co-boss, co-o-o-bossss!" and we'd see the cows start heading for the feeding ground. Then I'd move to the tractor seat—how the cold bit into my buttocks even through the thick cushions!—and I'd put the tractor into super-low gear and start forward slowly while Levi began stringing cotton cake from the sacks onto the ground.

As the nearest cows reached the feeding ground and began to eat, those on the far hillsides would break into a run, bawling in their eagerness. I might see a couple of golden eagles wheeling overhead and hear the *dee-dee-dee* of a chickadee in the canyon. A doe, heavy with the young that would be born in May, might bound across the slope followed by her almost yearling twins. I knew we'd see them again at dusk as they walked single file down their path toward the meadow, to feed all night on the haystacks.

During calving time Levi circulated every three hours in the daytime, usually on horseback, watching for any cows that might be showing signs that the birthing was near. At night he went out in the pickup two or three times and shined his lights on every cow in her turn.

I learned that when a cow is ready to drop her calf, she goes off by herself. The vulva is swollen by that time. Levi, alert for these signs, was careful to double-check such a cow the next time around. By then she might be back on her feet, with a tiny white-faced calf at her side, still wet from its damp, warm nest and from being licked by its mother's long, raspy tongue as soon as it got to its feet.

I was willing to believe that Herefords were different from the cows I'd known about and that they didn't need to be put into barns to calve.

Certainly, I thought my husband knew his business. Still, knowing those little wet calves were outside in subfreezing temperatures bothered me. I asked Levi if he was sure they'd be all right.

"Just look at that little booger there," he said. "He's not half an hour old, but look at him sucking in that warm milk. Yeah, he's wet, but he'll be all right. No matter how cold it is, once a calf's on his feet—sucking, with his belly full of warm milk—he'll be fine."

I saw the miracle of birth myself many times. I saw the calf come out of its mother, front legs outstretched like a diver, the cow struggling to eject her baby. I watched—from the pickup or at a safe distance—as the little one struggled to its feet and the mother got to hers and began the bonding process with her tongue and nudges and good mother smell. And when the calf had made it to the warm teat and begun filling its little belly with mother's milk, the cow would turn and begin to eat the afterbirth.

Many times I saw what happens when there's trouble during birthing. Every rancher carries a calving chain and knows when and how to use it. The calf may be hind end first, or the legs may be bent back at the knees. When this happens the rancher has to reach in and get the chain around the calf's neck and pull the creature out or else reposition the calf so it can come out by itself.

Sometimes a cow prolapses—turns wrong side out when the uterus is expelled—during or even before the birthing. When that happens, there's nothing to do but, after the calf is out, push everything back in and put a draw wire around the opening until the cow heals and gets back to normal. Most cattle people perform these offices as a matter of course, but, even so, the veterinarian is the busiest person in the country during calving time.

As soon as a few calves are born, the cows set up their system of cooperative baby tending. They take turns, six or eight at a time, making the long trek to the watering tank, but first each mother puts her calf down near the others whose mothers are about to leave. She apparently tells it, "Now don't move, small friend, or you'll catch it when I come back." When a cow puts her calf down, it stays down, not moving even when in danger of being run over by a pickup or stepped on by a horse.

Deer do it too. More than once I've jumped back, startled at seeing a fawn in a brushy canyon hideout, lying ever so still almost under my feet, looking up at me with big, frightened eyes.

Afoot, you'd never get that close to the little clusters of calves Levi called cow nests, because two or three cows always stay near to watch over the young and wait their turn to go in for water. Cows with calves are ready to fight. They're far more dangerous than Hereford bulls, which are mostly good-tempered, unlike milking stock bulls such as Holsteins or Jerseys. All cows hate dogs and will rush a dog fiercely if it gets anywhere near a calf—perhaps an instinct from both species' ancestors.

Cattle had to be branded, and brands had to be registered with the state, registered with a specific location on the critter: right or left hip, right or left shoulder. Each owner chose a brand and a place on the animal's body that was not already registered. A brand inspector was on hand at every auction to check brands.

May or early June was the time to brand, dehorn, vaccinate, and castrate cattle. This was a neighborhood workday. Levi gathered up the cows and calves, putting calves in the corral and cows in the pasture. The cows stood at the fence bawling endlessly for their little ones.

I loved to watch Levi and our neighbors do the cattle cutting, separating the cows from the calves. In the West they say a good cutting horse will turn on a dime and give you a nickel change. None was better than Bugs. Levi had only to cue Bugs by riding up to the critter he wanted cut out and touching Bugs with a toe. From that point the horse took over. Before I understood this, I asked Levi how he reined Bugs back and forth so fast when he was cutting.

"Hell," he said. "I don't rein him. He knows what to do. I'm busy enough, just keeping my ass in the saddle so he doesn't turn out from under me."

On branding day Levi had wood stacked ready in a corner of the corral—scraps of lumber, fence posts, anything that would burn hot. When our neighbor Bus Lemmon got there, he built the fire and set the branding irons to heating. Our brand was "R mill iron": an R with the mill iron, a U with long ears, under the R.

When the crew was ready, Levi roped the calves and dragged them in. He scoffed when I called it trick roping, but I thought there had to be a trick to roping running calves for hours, almost always by the left hind leg, seldom missing one.

When the calf was dragged up to the men waiting at the fire, Bugs, without being signaled, would back up to keep the rope taut then slack off just enough to let the men slip the rope off. While two men held the calf, another man pressed the red-hot iron to its shoulder, another stuck it with the vaccinating needle, and, if the calf was male, another slit its scrotum and took out its testicles with a razor-sharp knife. The testicles, one of the West's great delicacies, were carefully put in a nearby empty coffee can.

Early cowboys used to roast the testicles, membrane and all, over the branding fire and eat them on the spot. Now, when calves' nuts are cooked, it's an occasion to invite company to share the feast. Calves' testicles are small; you dip them whole in beaten egg, then in fine cracker crumbs, then fry them in a shallow mixture of lard and butter. Big critters have big nuts, and these you cut into slices before you dip and fry them. Big or little, the flavor is delicate and the texture tender. I used to make escalloped potatoes and a big green salad to go with them. If there were any left after everybody had eaten as much as they could, I put them on a pie tin in a cool place and heated them in the oven the next morning for breakfast.

CHAPTER TWENTY-FIVE

We lived on that land eight years, working hard and trying our damnedest, before we made a crop. Each year there were a few more cattle, but each year we went deeper into debt.

It was the same with everyone. In rural Nebraska there was no money and no way to get any, no jobs and no prospect of jobs. There were no crops because of drought and grasshoppers. Even if there had been good crops, they wouldn't have been worth much because farm prices were so low. Still, in Northwest Nebraska there was almost no idea of the suffering in the cities of the nation and the world. Able-bodied men drifting through our end of Nebraska offered to work for their room and board and were glad to find a job on those terms. Local people saw the dirty, discouraged people riding the trains and felt sorry for them, and they wondered why they didn't settle down someplace—some other place—and make a living.

In one of those mid-1930s years Uncle Jim and Aunt Lottie McBride moved to Chadron, a town twenty-five miles east of Crawford. Like many another small-town bank, the one in Cowles, Nebraska, which Uncle Jim managed, had failed. Uncle Jim got a job as appraiser for the government program that was intended to ease the money pinch for farmers and ranchers by buying up submarginal land. Aunt Lottie closed up the big square house in Cowles, stored some household goods, and got rid of the rest.

"We don't need all that room anymore, with all the kids gone from home but Betty," she said. "I'm glad to be shut of all that work."

Aunt Lottie had always worked—cooking, cleaning, and taking care of a big family. No matter what she said, she loved to work. She'd never taken a job before, but she took one now as manager of the faculty apartment building at Chadron Teachers College, where her daughter Betty was in her first year of college. Being manager meant she cleaned corridors, washed windows, and mopped the laundry room. The building had never been so clean and comfortable as it was when Aunt Lottie took hold of it. If she felt a pang for the big house that had been her home so many years, she never let on.

Aunt Marg and my little cousin Mary Marg moved in with my folks. Marg had a job at Durant Hospital, but almost everything about it except the fact that she had a paying job enraged her.

"Hospital!" she cried. "How can she get away with calling it a hospital? Gags me when I have to answer the phone, 'Durant Hospital.' If you could see the way she runs that place!"

"The care's good, though, isn't it?" Mother asked. "I know Madge is easygoing, but people say she's good to the patients."

"Care! Patients!" Marg gritted her teeth. "You get a few hospital beds and some sick people who don't know any better, and you call yourself a hospital! I'm the first R.N. she's ever had in the place, and she wouldn't know a chart if one came up and bit her."

Marg had no patience with sloppiness, and there was no denying Madge Durant was a sloppy woman. She was a workhorse, though. She cooked and cleaned and tended sick people cheerfully, no matter how many messes she had to clean up.

Mother wasn't having an easy time herself. After Loris died, she and Dad huddled together. She started working at the shop, learning to sell advertising, covering local news, filling in wherever she could.

Dunc, a printer who had been with Dad a long time, left Crawford, and the Spence twins, Leland and Leslie, came from Bladen to work in the shop. They lived in the house too, and Grandmother, from Arkansas, would be along in June, to spend the summer, as she always had since Granddad Charley Spence died. I don't know what the family would have done without Lucille.

Lucille cooked and cleaned and washed and ironed. She liked all of us and didn't care how often Levi and I stopped in for a meal. People were critical of Mother for paying Lucille $3.50 a week with the going wage at $2, but Mother felt it was worth it, not having to worry about a thing at the house. Meals were always ready, nothing was wasted, and Lucille planned to can a lot of food in the summer. Dad's garden would supply a lot of it, and there'd be chokecherries and wild grapes and plums in the canyons and on the hillsides.

The cities were hungry, but in Dawes County people had cattle and hogs and chickens. With bartering and neighboring, people managed to have something to eat.

Dawes County was Republican. Dad was; I was; *all* the Richardsons were.

Almost everybody denounced FDR and the New Deal. Nobody wanted to go on relief—relief was charity. To accept charity was a disgrace. Almost everybody opposed government meddling, but nobody balked at working for the Works Projects Administration, or WPA, a government-sponsored program to give people employment. Although the WPA did some useful public works, in some ways it was make-work. Still, people were glad to do it and to get the checks that meant they could pay off the grocery store and get coats and shoes for the kids.

During the winter of 1934–35 Levi worked as supervisor of a WPA timber crew that cut down trees for firewood, cleared brush, and made trails through the canyons. We felt rich; Levi's pay was, I believe, one hundred dollars a month. I got a fine wood-burning cook stove from Montgomery Ward. Not only was it enameled beige and green; it had a thermometer—not a thermostat—in the oven. I became very cunning in feeding just the right amount of wood into its maw to keep the baking temperature right. No more having to put my hand and forearm into the oven to guess at the temperature.

The WPA money made it possible for Levi to hire his cousin, Arthur Hoevet, to work for him that summer. This was the year we were going to make it for sure. It was July, the rye was thick and tall, and the corn was "knee-high by the Fourth of July," as corn is supposed to be. Levi and Arthur were cultivating it for the last time.

I'd driven into town, and Aunt Lottie and I were downtown shopping. We heard a little thunder and noticed that a heavy, dark cloud moved across the eastern sky, but there was no rain. I was nearly home, toward evening, when I saw the signs of disaster. Within a mile of home I saw there'd been rain, and I noticed Anderson Reed's cornfield looked ragged. By the time I crossed the canyon and reached our cornfield, I saw only shredded stumps perhaps four or five inches high, where waving dark green leaves and stalks had stood at noon. The rye had been pounded into the ground so thoroughly you couldn't have guessed what, if anything, had been growing there. We'd had a garden too, and I burst into tears when I saw it—and then thought how stupid I was to weep over tomatoes when all the grain was gone.

Levi laughed and showed me the shirt he'd been wearing when the storm hit—a few tatters of faded blue cloth hanging from the yoke. His back and shoulders were beginning to show the black and blue and green and yellow bruises that would last for weeks.

He and Arthur had been cultivating corn with horse-drawn cultivators. It was a long field. The cornrows were a mile long. Levi said Arthur was a hundred yards or so in the lead when he saw him jump off the cultivator, unhitch the horses, snap the traces onto the harness, and hit his team with the lines.

"For a minute there I thought he'd gone crazy," Levi said. "The sun was still shining when the first hailstone hit me, and when I looked around I knew why Arthur had unhitched. It was all I could do to hold the horses long enough to unhitch, and I knew we were in for it."

There's nowhere to hide under a corn cultivator. Levi and Arthur took a frightful beating. The hailstones, large as walnuts and jagged, had come with a driving wind. That's the way hailstorms come to the hail belt— almost literally out of a clear blue sky. Just across the road it didn't even rain until about eight that evening.

There were huge banks of ice in the field; it was several blistering days before it melted away. The day after the storm Levi rode a horse down to the north end of the field. At one point, when he was riding through a gully washed in the banks of hail, I could see just his head and shoulders.

Anderson and Edna Reed drove over the next day and got a tubful of ice for their hand-cranked freezer. And on Monday, when the rye harvest was to have begun, Levi rode Bugs into the hills and brought in the horses that had been running loose, harness and all, since Saturday.

There were the grasshoppers too. I used to put my washing out on sunflowers to dry, but, when the grasshoppers came and ate things full of holes, I had to start drying clothes inside. One year the fence posts and even the wires between the posts were green with grasshoppers. They ate the crops and the fence posts, and, liking the taste of salt from men's hands, they ate the handles of tools left outside.

I was pregnant that summer. The first three months I was hungry all the time, but whatever I ate unfailingly came up within a few minutes. I got so thin I had to tape my wedding ring on, and my pumps clacked noisily as I walked.

It was the summer of Crawford's golden anniversary, and the men grew beards to create a pioneer atmosphere. Levi washed his hair and beard every evening, and still I had to turn my head away from the smell of that beard as we lay together in bed.

My parents, Levi's parents, and Levi all tried to find something I could keep down. I was so hungry I would eat anything, sure that this time it would stay with me. It didn't, though, and I cursed the fools who wrote that morning sickness was purely psychological in origin and that a woman who'd never heard of it wouldn't suffer from it.

By August the morning-noon-and-night sickness was gone as completely as if it had never been, and I grew and bloomed. WPA work, mostly abandoned during the summer while people farmed, began again, and we were happy to have the WPA check. We prepaid the doctor's fee and the seventy-dollar charge to Mrs. Durant, who provided ten days' lying-in care in her home. We had a snug, provident feeling about ourselves as a family.

Levi liked working with the WPA crew again. The men were neighbors, and Levi was used to working and joshing with them. Most of the work the crew did was useful, and everybody wanted to earn his money. The crew felled trees and trimmed them up and snaked them into a pile for sawing, and always by noon they were hungry and ready for the lunches they'd brought. They built a fire near the creek and boiled coffee in a tin bucket. As they ate, they'd kid about who'd worked the hardest and who'd slacked off and who'd done the dumbest thing.

One day when Levi came home I found his food almost untouched in his lunch bucket. "What's wrong?" I asked. "Weren't you hungry?"

"I was to start with," he said. "But I lost my appetite. Joe Griffith brought some cold biscuits," he said. "Some cold bacon and a glass of jelly."

"Yes?" I prompted.

"He started eating them, the biscuits," Levi said. "Put jelly or bacon on them and was eating away, drinking coffee and everything. I'd have to be pretty hungry to go for cold bacon, but he seemed to like it. Then he put his spoon in the jelly glass and found something and pulled it up."

"And . . . ?"

"It was a mouse," said Levi. "Not a very big mouse, but a mouse. And, would you believe it, that son of a bitch just tossed it out into the weeds and took some more jelly out of the glass and put it on his biscuit and ate it. Just went right ahead and ate it."

I stared at him. The Griffiths were known to be "dirty," but this was a bit much, even for Joe Griffith, who'd been raised dirty.

"Ate it?" I asked. "The jelly he'd pulled the mouse out of?"

"Yeah," said Levi. "He ate it all right. Never even hesitated. Went right ahead and ate the jelly. He was about the only guy eating. I went around the truck, and what little I'd eaten came up. Some of the other guys tried to stick it out, but they kind of wandered off too."

He paused.

"Damn!" he said. "I guess that's the way you felt all summer."

After the nausea had gone away, being pregnant was delicious. I'd never enjoyed food more. Both families pampered me, my husband was proud, and I was joyously certain we'd have a son, a circumstance considered as desirable in Nebraska as in China for a first baby.

I fell into a phase I'd despised in my mother when she was photographed with my brother as a baby, the two of them swathed in chiffon, Mother gazing down at him with an expression of vapid adoration which I thought idiotic. I became the quintessential Madonna and decided I must make all my baby's clothes by hand. The only problem was I hardly knew how to sew. In college my roommate had sat me down and taught me to darn my stockings when she caught me wadding the heels up with adhesive tape that stuck to my feet and my shoes. Beyond darning, I knew nothing; Mother had loathed needles all her life, and any sewing she did was straight seams and hems, done at furious speed on an old FREE treadle sewing machine.

Beautiful baby dresses, hand-made and embroidered in the Philippines, could be bought for eighty-five cents each, but that wasn't good enough for me. I'd have been sunk if it hadn't been for Aunt Lottie. She wanted me to buy nainsook and dimity and lace and God knows what all. She had sharp dressmaker's scissors, and she cut the sheer materials without a pattern, never basting anything. Her fine needle darted through the fabric like a glittering snake, leaving behind, to my everlasting astonishment, a straight track of stitches, each one the same size as each of the others. She made exquisite rosebuds with embroidery thread and edged and hemmed and scalloped. And when she was finished there were enough little dresses to satisfy my absurd fantasy. I believe I even imagined that I had made them.

Our first son, Bill, was born on Valentine's Day in 1937 while Mother was at Sunday School playing the piano. Levi, almost incoherent, leaned out the window where our baby lay squirming between my legs and shouted to a passing friend, "Come in and see my son!"

He recovered enough to call his parents and then mine. Dad ran the four blocks to the church and, I was told later, walked down the center aisle beaming and bowing right and left in the middle of the service, to reach Mother at the piano. The following week every newspaper in the western half of Nebraska, and many in the eastern half, carried a headline: "KARL L. SPENCE BECOMES A GRANDFATHER."

The two first winters after Bill was born were bitterly cold, and, to make sure our baby wouldn't get uncovered during the night, Levi and I used to lay him on one corner of his blanket and roll him up into a little bundle like a cocoon. One morning when I checked the thermometer near his crib in the tarpaper shack, I found it at 14 degrees below zero. The baby was snug, however. In the kitchen, water was frozen solid in the pail, and the teakettle, sitting on the cold stove, was half-full of glittering ice. Even our chamber pot had a rime of ice around the edge.

When Bill was nine months old I was pregnant again, so Levi decided we needed more room. The new log house we lived in was on a slope, and with a slip—a horse-drawn scraper—he moved earth away all around the house, leaving it sitting on a small knoll. He burrowed like a badger until he got far enough under the foundation to put in heavy posts and jackscrews as support. Finally, there was a space big enough for him to use a team of horses and a slip to dig out from under the house. In a few days there was room enough for a large kitchen, pantry, dining room, and small bedroom. Levi left space for the closets and bathroom we'd have someday.

That summer of 1938 was a hot one, and we moved into the lower rooms as soon as the concrete floors and walls were dry enough. There were no windows yet, but Levi tacked screen across the window openings. The worst part of that summer was having no refrigerator or icebox. Whenever we went to town we bought a block of ice the last thing before heading home. I kept it in a washtub, covered with old blankets and a tarp, setting the food in the tub around the ice and bailing out the melted water.

It was a time of give-away contests by all sorts of manufacturers, particularly the soap makers. I'd never entered a contest, but, when Proctor & Gamble offered refrigerators as prizes, I knew I wanted to have a crack at it. I'd never used P&G soap, but I bought twenty-four bars and unwrapped them all to get the wrappers, four for each of my six entries. I liked the earthy smell of it, almost like my own homemade soap, and six times, in twenty-five words or less, I wrote an ode to the efficacy of P&G soap.

I mailed my entries in March, and I'd almost forgotten the whole thing, except when the ice was gone or the melt water in the tub didn't get bailed out soon enough and ran over into the food. In August 1938 I won a refrigerator, the best-designed refrigerator I've ever seen. Our new refrigerator came a month before our second son, Spence, was born, and it meant luxury and pleasure and comfort to us. It ran on kerosene, and later, when bottled gas became available, we had it converted to propane. We used that refrigerator for twenty-five years, until it died and couldn't be revived.

CHAPTER TWENTY-SIX

Dad died in late August of 1938. I don't think it soaked in for a week or two. I stayed at my mother's house and talked to all the people who called and brought food. I ate when people told me to. I slept when somebody noticed the weariness of my swollen, eight-and-a-half-month pregnant body and led me to my bed.

It wasn't possible that Dad, so exuberantly, eagerly, unquenchably alive, could be dead. He was only forty-nine, and he'd never been sick; I said to Mother, "How can he be dead? He's never been sick." We wept together after the funeral, and she recalled the flu epidemic of 1918, when he had been sick, very sick. Of that I remembered only myself, age four, lying feverish in the Morris chair in the living room, and seeing the Congregational preacher trot from house to house, taking out ashes and building up fires, emptying slops and sponging people's hands and faces.

I remembered my father in front of the base burner on Sunday mornings shaking me down into my long-legged underwear, always a little stiff and shrunken from washing. I remembered riding on his back as we all returned, late in the evening, from a visit to friends clear across town, Mother and my older brother hurrying to keep up. I remembered Dad's clear tenor voice soaring above all the others in the church choir. I remembered my mortification when I was entertaining my friends by imitating a visiting preacher's gestures. Dad saw me and left the choir loft to sit beside me in the pew for the rest of the service. I was bitterly ashamed of myself, but he took my hand in his, and I leaned my face against his arm. I remembered the good scratchy feel of his Sunday coat sleeve.

I remembered thunderstorms; I love them to this day. They were times of love and warmth and welling happiness, because Dad took Loris and me to the front porch to watch the show, sitting between us on the swing, singing, holding us close, and shouting, at any especially loud clap, that the Old Man was rolling his potato wagon across the sky.

My grandmother came from Arkansas after Dad died. She and I sat on the side porch together, and she told me, as she had before, what a funny, loving, absurd little boy Dad had been. His brother Fred was a year and a half older, and the two were inseparable. One day, as they played near the woodpile, Karl laid his middle finger on the block and said, "Chop 'er off, Fred!"

Fred chopped 'er off, and the blood spurted, just as it did when a chicken's head was chopped off. The two ran screaming to the house and, said Grandmother, "I tore a strip off my petticoat and tied that finger back on. It was hanging by a bit of skin, and I pushed it together and tied it up, good and tight. I took those little boys on my lap in the rocking chair, and I rocked and sang and held them tight—they weren't much more than babies—and pretty soon they stopped sobbing, and after a while they went to sleep. I guess I did too, because when Charley came in he found us all right there, with blood all over the floor. That finger grew back on; you've seen it."

I had seen it; I'd seen the welted scar all the way around that finger, and

Dad had told me the story himself, laughing, "Chop 'er off, Fred—that's what I told him, and that's what he did. Chopped 'er off, and look at her now! I've never had a minute's trouble with that finger."

As we sat there with my baby son Bill playing at our feet, Grandmother told me the tragedy of Dad's life. I'd heard only a bit of it before, from Mother. Two little girls, Katie and Minnie, were born after Fred and Karl.

"We were walking down the road to church one Sunday, all of us," Grandmother said. "I watched them running on ahead, the two boys and the two little girls. I got the feeling—you know that feeling of bliss, just bliss you can't express. I said to Charley, 'We must be the luckiest people in the world.' And he looked at me and said yes, just breathed yes. He felt it too. It was something I remembered later."

I waited while her mind went back to Williamson County, Illinois, back to a century that was gone, back to children that were gone, all but two of them. Gone from their mother, this old woman who'd lost them one after another.

"It was the last Sunday of that good time," she said. "By another Sunday Minnie was in her grave, and Karl was gone to some far place we didn't know if he'd ever come back from. His body was with us, but his spirit had wandered away." She paused heavily. "Minnie was dead because he'd shot her."

I waited, hardly daring to breathe.

"We had a shotgun," Grandmother said. "Everybody had a shotgun. There were varmints that got after the chickens—'coons and foxes and bobcats. We kept the shotgun in the corner of the kitchen, same as everybody else, so it would be handy. The boys knew how to use it. Boys in southern Illinois in those days were used to guns; everybody shot squirrels and rabbits to eat."

My baby son Bill toddled over and leaned against my knee.

"The girls washed dishes every evening, and sometimes they got the boys to wipe them. Minnie'd helped Karl carry wood that day. He was supposed to wipe the dishes, but he wanted to wash. They argued and scuffled over the dishpan, and Minnie tipped it over both of them.

"Karl was laughing; he said, 'I'll fix you for that!' He grabbed the shotgun and whirled around, and it went off. Minnie lay there in her blood looking up at us, and Charley kept saying, 'She'll be all right; it's only a scratch.' 'A scratch!' I said. 'I guess I know death when I see it. She's gone.' I knew she was gone. Karl knew it too. He knelt over her a minute, and then he ran out of the house. I ran after him. I saw him in the corn stubble. He'd run a ways and fall down, get up and start running, fall down again."

Tears were pouring down Grandmother's cheeks and mine too.

"I ran after him," she said. "I was heavy, about six months pregnant, but I ran. He fell down so often I finally caught him, and I held him down until the neighbors came and got us. The Perkins had come when they heard the gun go off in the house, and somebody got the Chamnesses. The preacher came and prayed, of course, and I prayed, but Minnie was gone, and Karl was gone away, and for a while I wondered where God had been when all of it happened. My sisters and Erna Day washed Minnie and laid her out with her good dress covering her little bloody breast, and they washed the blood off the floor, but there was always a stain."

"And Dad?" I asked. "How long was he gone?"

"A long time," Grandmother said. "A long time. We never left him alone, night or day. The neighbors came and took turns sitting up with him at night. My sister Ellen came and stayed, and we never left him alone. I don't know how long it was, weeks and weeks, that he just wasn't there, and we didn't dare leave him alone for fear of what he'd do to himself. Finally, I looked into his eyes one day, and I saw that he was back. I watched him for an hour, looking into his eyes, and I saw that he was back for good. Then I could thank God again."

We sat there looking across the garden Dad had planted, thinking of that time he'd been far away and knowing without really believing it that he'd gone away again.

"And do you know," Grandmother said, "in all those years he's mentioned Minnie to me just twice? The first time was when he fell in love with your mother and asked her to marry him. He told her there was something she'd have to know, and he came to me and said, 'Mama, you've got to tell Sadie about Minnie. I can't. She may not want to marry me when she knows about Minnie.' So I told Sadie. I told her all that had happened and that it was a burden on his heart that she had to know about. We wept together, Sadie and I. We wept then, and we wept today. I wish we hadn't pulled and hauled at Karl so; he loved us both.

"The second time was this last Sunday, when we kept this baby while you and Levi went to the picnic. Karl sat out on the lawn and played with him, and Mary Margaret played with him too. They had him staggering around from one to the other. After Mary Margaret went in the house, Karl said to me, 'That child always puts me in mind of Minnie.' And, once he'd mentioned it, I could see what he meant. Those were the only two times in more than forty years."

My grandmother had seven children, and of the seven only two were still alive, the two youngest, Charley and Fred. The baby she was carrying that terrible day had died at six weeks old, and Katie had died less than two years after her sister Minnie.

"I went to pieces completely," Grandmother told me. "I'd stood everything till then, and I took care of my husband and my children, but when Katie died I thought of nobody but myself. I took her clothes out of the chest and held them in my lap and wept over them. My sisters came and helped me, and they tried to talk to me, but I didn't want to think of anything but my grief. We had just one picture of Katie, and I held that in my arms at night and cried. My neighbors and my sisters cooked whatever we ate, and they did whatever washing was done.

"I didn't eat much, and I didn't change my clothes. The neighbors and my sisters had their own families, of course. One day I looked up and saw Fred and Karl standing at the door, looking at me while I rocked and cried. They looked lost and lonesome. I got up and caught a glimpse of myself in the glass, hair straggling, face yellow and sick looking, dirty, bedraggled. It came to me, 'What would Katie think of her mama now?' Well, I cleaned myself up. I combed my hair. I went out in the garden and found some late string beans, and I put them on to cook.

"I swept the floor and set the table. I made up my mind to live again and I did."

"I don't know how you stood it," I said. "I really don't know how you stood it. And then Fred dying when you and Granddad were already old. And then Granddad."

"Well," Grandmother said. "I really don't know either. If anybody had come and asked me if I could stand all that had happened, I'd have said, 'No, certainly not.' But nobody did come and ask. It just happened. You don't get a chance to decide what you can stand."

We went into the house.

Some Indians came to call. Dad had been absorbed in archaeology and history for as long as I could remember, not superficially as a dilettante but as a devoted amateur. He was fascinated by a chance to meet real-live Indians and horrified by the events that had reduced them to indigence and begging. Some sensed his real interest, and they became his friends and talked to him of their lives and their history, and all the Indians knew that Karl Spence was always good for a small touch. When they learned that he was dead, they came to pay their respects.

Eight days after Dad's death, our second son was born, as skinny and wizened a little wretch as his brother had been plump and smooth. I named him Karl Spence for my Dad and hoped he'd have Dad's blazing blue eyes and black hair.

It took a long time to get used to Dad's absence, and that's all I ever did. I never got over it. A hundred times, when something struck me as funny or interesting, I thought, wait until I tell Dad—he'll get a kick out of this.

I'd always thought Dad would live with me in his old age and tend a garden and we'd laugh together. As the new baby waxed fat and lively, I thought of what he'd miss, not having his grandfather around.

I was happy about the first two pregnancies, but when, with my second baby only three months old, I found myself pregnant again, I was furious. I always got huge when I was pregnant. To find out I was pregnant again while I was toting my second son, Spence, a tiny baby, around on my hip, with his not-quite-two-year-old older brother, Bill, clinging to my skirts, seemed an intolerable burden.

The burden lifted abruptly when an insufferable woman, a DAR friend of Mother's, attempted to commiserate with me one day about having so many babies so fast. I was appalled. Did I look pathetic? Did she think I wanted sympathy? Had I been feeling sorry for myself? The answer could only be yes. How ghastly. I lifted my chin, just as I'd seen my mother lift hers.

"We're very happy about this baby," I said. "We want our children close together."

This time I didn't want to leave my two small boys in somebody else's care while I went to the hospital. It wasn't a hospital, anyway—only a big old house with many bedrooms, a sort of nursing home with a practical nurse in charge. So, with the approval of my young doctor and with directions from a pamphlet published, appropriately enough, by the Department of Labor, I made plans to have the baby at home. I got everything ready—dressings sewed into tight bundles and sterilized on a rack in the wash boiler, blocks made by Levi to raise the bed, and a practical nurse engaged to come out from Chadron to take care of the new baby and me. We hired a girl, Dena, a couple of months before my due date.

Only weeks before that date my doctor, practicing medicine with his uncle, told me he had a chance at a better job that would take him away but that his uncle would take care of me just as he would have done.

On a day near my appointed time I was seized with a fit of energy. Dena and I washed all the dirty clothes in the gasoline-powered washing machine, ironed them, and cleaned the house thoroughly.

"Sure," Mother said, when she heard about it later. "You've noticed how an old sow will make a nest when she's about to have a litter of pigs."

I bathed in the zinc tub and put on a freshly ironed maternity dress. How ugly maternity clothes were in those days—all made on the wraparound principle, with room for expansion in the overlapping fronts. At least this one was made of a pretty material, pale green Swiss with white dots. As I leaned over to pick up my shoe, the waters broke. Levi was just coming in on a horse from the hilly pastures south of the house, and Dena ran out to tell him. He tied his horse to the fence and came running as if, his mother would have said, "his shirttail was afire."

Levi wanted to call the doctor at once, but I wouldn't have it. I knew everyone on the line would listen, and word of it would get to my mother. It wasn't that she'd be unsympathetic; she would, in fact, cluck over me, and I didn't want that. So, we drove to town, and I, with a bath towel between my legs to absorb the flood of water that was still coming, went into the drugstore and called the doctor.

"Okay," he said. "Go on up to the hospital, and I'll look in on you later."

"I'm not going to the hospital," I said. "I'm having this baby at home. You remember. Jack told you."

"Nonsense," said the doctor. "I'm not going to drive way out in the country on your whim." He wouldn't budge, but I was going to have my baby at home, where everything was ready and where I could be with my other children, and I told him so.

Barley and Ardith, our friends from high school, went to Chadron to fetch the practical nurse, and not long after we reached home they brought her. She was a large, motherly woman who'd had ten children of her own, but she told me she'd never seen a baby born.

"That's okay," I said. "I have all the books, and everything's ready."

Everyone insisted that I go to bed, although I hadn't had even the first twinge of labor pains. Barley and Ardie sat beside me, and we chatted a while. It was about seven when they left, and Ardie said, "Wouldn't it be funny if you'd have this all over by midnight?" It would be funny, I thought, and they'd hardly driven out of the yard when the first pain hit.

Levi called the doctor, who took the message calmly, not to say indifferently. The pains began to come thick and fast, and Levi frantically called the doctor's "nurse," a wholly untrained woman known to dispense medicines and advice as widely and confidently as if she herself were a physician. By the time they arrived our new son was about forty minutes old.

Before the birth the pains had been almost continuous but by no means unbearable, and I felt the baby moving along the birth canal. Levi and Dena were shocked and helpless, and Levi begged me to wait until the doctor came. "Can't wait," I gasped. "He's coming along. Dena, boil the scissors and some No. 8 white thread. Levi, get the book."

Levi, usually so ruddy, was pale as milk, and great beads of sweat stood out on his nose and forehead. Having midwifed the birth of hundreds of calves didn't help him now. After much rummaging in the dining room bookcase, he found the book, but his eyes were glazed, and he thumbed through it aimlessly, as if he'd never heard of an index. At last I said impatiently, "Give it to me!" and I found the right pages and read the directions aloud. Just as I finished, the baby popped out, and I raised myself on my elbow.

"It's another boy," I said, disappointed.

"Yes," said Levi. "I wasn't going to tell you. I know you wanted a girl."

I laughed and laughed, and Levi turned away, bewildered. As I looked at this little new one now, it seemed to me that having three little boys so close together was a stroke of wonderful luck, and before long I was sure that the whole thing had been my own idea.

Again I read from the book, and Levi tied the umbilical cord tightly in two places and cut it between the knots. But when I suggested that he could help me rid myself of the placenta, he flatly refused and went out to the kitchen to pour himself a jolt of whiskey.

The baby was washed and dressed by the time the doctor and his "nurse" arrived. He put drops of silver nitrate in the baby's eyes, gave my belly a gentle push to expel the afterbirth, and remarked, rather patronizingly, "Well, Polly, having babies in a hurry doesn't seem to hurt you a bit. You're really built for childbearing."

This doctor never called on me afterward, nor did he ever telephone to see how we were doing, but he sent his bill—the usual fifty dollars—for the full course of prenatal and postnatal care his nephew would have given me. There were, and sadly still are, besides the many dedicated, concerned, and compassionate country doctors one has read about, physicians like this one, who was egotistical, indifferent, autocratic, and completely self-absorbed.

There's no way to describe the blissful sense of having done something wonderful that filled me after this nearly painless, perfectly natural childbirth. I was so relaxed and euphoric I didn't want to be bothered with much cleaning up; I barely let Dena attend to the minimum of washing me. I lay awake, high and happy, for a while. Then I went to sleep as gently as my new baby. I didn't wake until eight or nine o'clock, finally hungry for breakfast. As soon as he was allowed to enter my room, Bill, my two-and-a-half-year-old, came to the side of the bed and said in a peremptory tone, "Dit up!"

We had a beautiful baby. We named him Charles after his grandfather and called him Charley. The other children had been the victims of the prevailing advice that infants must be kept on a strict schedule, that they must not be held and fondled much, and that, if anything distressed them, they must be allowed to "cry it out." Milk was boiled and dispensed to my first two sons in sterilized bottles, propped up on a pillow, so they would not be spoiled by being held in their mother's arms while feeding. Both Jenny, Levi's mother, and my grandmother protested against this barbaric treatment, but my mother, who always believed whatever she had read last, encouraged me to do it.

By the time Charley came along, however, I had so much to do and so little prospect of getting it done that I was ready to relax and enjoy this baby. I held him and cuddled him a lot. He always woke up mad from his afternoon nap, and I'd take him on my lap and rock him and sing to him and kiss him and talk to him for about an hour. I'm glad I did; those quiet times are among my most precious memories.

CHAPTER TWENTY-SEVEN

We made our first wheat crop in 1941, and it was a good one. I remember jumping into the truck and wallowing in the wheat, running it through my fingers, and exulting in the new feeling of having something that would bring us money, freedom from debt, solvency at last, after going a little deeper into debt each year for so long.

It did, too. Just making a start on paying off the debts made us feel prosperous, and, when the Japanese bombed Pearl Harbor in December, prices and demand leaped up, and restrictions on production were summarily dropped. All through the war we worked hard, and there was never any possibility of Levi being called up because he was too valuable as a producer of food. I planted and hoed a victory garden each of those war years, and I canned thousands of quarts of food. One year it was 648 quarts. I got sick and tired of picking and washing and peeling, but I did it because I thought it was my duty.

It was a wild fruit year too, so I tramped up and down the canyons picking chokecherries and wild grapes and plums, and, when, with every jar full, I looked up the hillside and saw the wild plum trees red with fruit, I gathered up my kids and my buckets and went picking again.

Cows had made the plum thicket a work of topiary art; they'd eaten every plum and neatly cropped the leaves as high as they could reach. Coyote scats showed that cunning, agile beast had eaten its share of plums as well; let the fox say sour grapes, the coyote manages to get what it wants, however

high it hangs. We picked so many plums that at last the teacups were full
of jelly, with only our two favorites, Levi's and mine, saved back for coffee.

The years when we had those three little boys one right after the other
were the good years, and I knew it even in the midst of breaking up a
fight, cleaning up a bloody nose, and trying to answer the phone while
something boiled over on the stove. I snarled at my mother for saying,
with a sentimental sigh, "You'll look back on this as the happiest time of
your life." It sounded so like the words of a sentimental author. Besides, I'd
always say black if Mother said white. But I knew she was right.

From the first Levi helped me take care of our babies. His mother was
shocked the first time she saw him matter-of-factly change a dirty diaper
and rinse it out in the slop jar. That wasn't men's work. Levi said, "This
is my baby too, Ma, and somebody's got to do it. You changed my shitty
pants, didn't you?"

His mother shook her head, but by this time there were three baby boys,
the oldest only two and a half, so she didn't worry about it anymore. In
fact, she thought it a good thing for all concerned that I'd had to give up
my notion that the sky would fall if every one of them weren't bathed every
day.

"It isn't natural," she said. "It isn't good for a baby to be bathed too
much. You'll make his skin dry."

"Ha! What did she know?" The book said bathe the baby every day before
the ten A.M. feeding. The book didn't say put a freshly ironed petticoat and
dress and pretty bootees on the baby every day; that was my idea, and
Bill, my firstborn, caught the brunt of it. He was washed and oiled and
powdered and dressed up every day, like the prize calf at a 4-H show. His
brothers had it easier; by the time the two of them were born, I was lucky
to get them bathed twice a week.

We worked out a routine. On winter bath nights we heated water on
the stove, poured it into the washtub, added enough cold to cool it down
a bit, and popped them all in. Levi washed, and I dried, and then the boys
ran wildly through the house until they were out of breath. And when we'd
caught them and pajamaed them and put them to bed, if I had any energy
left, I'd wash the kitchen floor with the water left in the tub.

We often were out of water at the house, but it was always ten or twelve
degrees cooler up in West Ash Creek Canyon, and Barker's spring never
played out, even in the hottest, driest years. It ran unfailingly out of a pipe
at the road, where a tin cup hung on a wire twisted around the pipe. I'd
load the car with kids and cream cans and drive up there to get that cold,

delicious water. We'd play in the creek across the road from the spring and have a bath before filling up the cream cans.

The best times were when Levi could get out of the field a little early and we'd grab whatever we had to eat, the kids' sleepers, and a blanket and make a picnic of it. As it got dark, we lay on the blanket with our babies crawling over us, watching the smoke rise straight up through the trees of the canyon, while the stars and the fireflies came out.

I guess you could have a dozen children and no two really alike. Our three were in some ways wildly unlike, yet they clung together in a tight little band, except for the times they fought one another or two ganged up on the other one. There weren't children nearby for them to play with; even the Lemmon kids were a couple of miles away, and visits were infrequent.

Bill, like Levi, could see what made things work. Before he was three he'd taught himself to tie a double bowknot and insisted on tying his own shoes. I tried to force Spence to do that too, but it was no use.

Bill, like me, was a born patsy; he'd believe anything. Spence, from the time he could talk, would maneuver you into saying something you hadn't meant to say and didn't mean at all.

Charley was tough, loving, and independent. One day in 1942 I heard the others designate him the Japanese enemy and start work on a deadfall for his entrapment. The next thing I heard was a crash as a rock fell on them and Charley's cry, "Now, God damn you, who's a Jap?"

His bravery, however, was a sometime thing. Dynamite, the kids' tiny Welsh pony, did pretty much as he pleased, carrying Bill home, crying in frustration, after going only halfway on a planned trip to the mailbox.

"You've got to show him who's boss," I said. "Make him go where you want him to go."

"I'd show him!" Charley boasted. "I'd get on him, and I'd kick da hell out of him!"

Yet at the moment of mounting this little beast, when I lifted him up and promised to walk all the way with him, holding the bridle, Charley would clap his legs together and moan, "Oh no, I am just a teeny boy!"

All that changed the day Levi rode Big Red, the sorrel gelding, into the yard and "tied" him by dropping the reins onto the ground, since in the pasture there's usually nothing to tie the reins to. Cow horses stand when their reins are dropped, moving only to browse a bit.

The towering sorrel was different from the other horses that often stood near the house waiting. He was a "cut-proud" horse, gelded so late in his maturity that he would never lose the stallion's nervous, fiery disposition. A fine horse but a handful, even for a good horseman. But it was only for a minute, Levi told himself, just long enough to make a phone call, and besides the kids were taking their nap.

Charley wasn't. Levi's minute stretched out a bit, and as he started out the door he saw Charley, wearing only his underpants, sitting on Big Red. Levi moved carefully, talking gently, and when Charley saw him he shouted, "Daddy! Look at me!"

"I see you, baby. Sit tight, baby. Good Red."

"Daddy!" Charley cried reproachfully. "I'm not a baby! I'm a cowboy!"

"Yes, my darling," Levi said softly. "Sit tight, darling. Good Red." He moved carefully, holding out his hand as the horse looked around.

It was over in a moment.

"How did you get up there, baby?" Levi asked, holding him tight. "How?"

"I got up on the tank, Daddy," Charley said. "Daddy, I'm a cowboy. Daddy, put me down."

"That goddamned Red," Levi said, telling me about it as he poured himself a shot of whiskey. "Gentle as a dog. Walking around like he was on eggs. Looked up at me like, 'What's all the fuss about? Me and that baby were getting along all right.'"

Those times, that life, that place, were a different world. Then, as now, there was beauty, and there was menace; the trick, then as now, was to tell them apart.

Old-timers told of wolves and bear and mountain lions people had seen occasionally in the early day. Dad and Uncle Will remembered an ornery old longhorn that had strayed away from a trail herd and wandered around for years. When he was a kid, Levi said, walking through the canyon on his way home from school, he'd seen a gray wolf. "Nobody believed me," he said, "but by God it was a wolf, and I saw it as plain as I see you. Ran all the way home and told everybody, and nobody believed me. I saw it, all the same."

Those wild animals were gone, but one wild animal remains to this day: the rattlesnake. In spite of the ranch country maxim that you never let a rattler get away, the rattler survives. Communities organized extermination parties when the rattlers emerged from the dens they had wintered in, tangled together for warmth; hundreds were shot and stomped, but the rattlesnake survives.

Our little boys learned, as all ranch children do, that you don't fool with a snake; you go and get help. A ranch kid doesn't deal with a snake by himself until he's nine or ten, and by then he knows one snake from another. Indeed, the rankest tenderfoot, people say—and I believe—knows the chilling sound of the rattler, even if he's never heard it before. You hear it, and you jump back; it's a primordial reaction.

Charley had to learn, without getting scared again, that he wasn't quite a cowboy and that Big Red was really a little too much horse for him. Yet it never occurred to us to warn our kids against talking to strangers or getting into a car with somebody they didn't know. Westerners like talking to somebody new; in a small community strangers are a treat. And, of course, rides were offered or accepted as needed, whether or not you'd ever seen the other person.

This way of living, this freedom and openness, we'd found when my family moved west had felt right from the first. Falling in love with Levi had been the rightest thing I ever did; everything proved it. Our kids were smart and good-looking; I determined they'd grow up the western way: easy with their surroundings, easy with people, responsible for themselves and for others. I'd been right to dream my dreams; all I had to do now was to make them keep on coming true.

CHAPTER TWENTY-EIGHT

When I was about five, my aunt Carolyn gave me a kaleidoscope. It was only a cardboard tube I could turn toward the light and peep through, but it was enchanting. The bits of colored glass moved as I moved the kaleidoscope, and each pattern was more beautiful than the last. But each time, just as I had the ideal pattern, a tiny movement, hardly more than a breath, changed everything, no matter how carefully I tried to hold onto perfection.

I've done a lot of that in my time: seeing perfection, trying to hold onto it. With all my might I've clung to patterns that have fallen into place, each one seemingly the loveliest, the best of all. Each time, when the pattern was exactly right and all I'd dreamed of, a small, internal shift would occur to change it. I thought that hanging on was a sign of being strong; it took me a long time to learn about letting go.

One of the first things I had to let go of was the idea that Levi would absorb the boys into his life outside the house, teach them about cattle and horses and machinery and fences, teach them to be the kind of man he was. He'd loved being with them when they were babies, but once they were old enough to tag around outside there was always some reason he couldn't have them with him. I knew he loved them. I told myself it was all right that he didn't want to be bothered with them. Later he'd have time for them, after they'd learned how to do all those things. I kept them from pestering him, and even when they noticed that the Lemmon kids were always with their dad, following him around, learning how machinery works and how calves are born, all the wonderful things there are to know about ranch life, I shushed them and didn't make an issue of it.

I didn't make an issue of anything. I couldn't risk jarring the perfect dream. I made a life for myself and for my children. I went about it calmly and matter-of-factly. I had no idea that inside I was frantically trying to hold my illusions together.

Wanting to be as unlike my mother as possible, I grew to be like her. I knew exactly what children needed to grow up to be the right kind of people, and by God my children were going to get it. My notions were somewhat different from Mother's, but they were no less rigid. If they were not to have what their father could teach them, most certainly they would have what I could give them.

I read to them from the time they were able to understand words. Before that we'd browse through picture books, the boys cuddling on my lap. As they grew, I proceeded from Mother Goose and fairy tales to *Wind in the Willows, Gulliver's Travels, Tom Sawyer, Huckleberry Finn*, the *New Testament, David Copperfield, Crazy Horse*, and God knows what all. It wasn't only that reading is one of life's great pleasures which I didn't want my kids to miss. This was culture; they were to have the best of all worlds.

My kids had to have Sunday school. They had to know the glorious stories of Abraham, Isaac and Jacob, Joseph, David and Solomon, Queen Esther, Ruth and Naomi, about the God who talked to Moses and the people who wandered for forty years through the wilderness. They had to hear about Jesus and the fishermen who dropped their nets and followed him, the stories he told, the rich man, the prostitute, the people he fed on loaves and fishes on a hillside overlooking the Sea of Galilee. They had to color the pictures and learn the memory verses; I couldn't let them miss it.

I dressed them in identical little suits; I loved people's admiration of my three little stair-step sons. I learned to dress Spence first. If I got the right size clothes on him, the middleman, the others were easy. The flaw in this system was that Spence was the least likely to stay put and clean, the most likely to start a fight, to tip over a pail of eggs his Grandmother Richardson had brought, to open the petcock on the cream separator, or to coax Gus the dog into the house. Threats had little effect on Spence; he knew perfectly well I wouldn't cut him into little pieces and feed him to the hogs, as I threatened to do one time. The occasional blow struck in anger bounced harmlessly off his cool amusement.

Sometimes I felt bitter when I thought of all that my kids were missing with their father; I remembered how Dad had filled my childhood with love and warmth. I didn't want my children to sense their loss and feel bitter. As for how Levi remembered his parents, I really didn't know much about it. To hear his mother and sisters tell it, you'd think he'd been everybody's darling. But, no matter what anybody said, I sensed a deep, unspoken emptiness in him.

I got an inkling about it the Christmas before we were married. Levi had spent Christmas Eve, Christmas Day, all of it, with my family. When he left he thanked Mother for inviting him, and he thanked us all for a wonderful time. Later he said to me, "That's the way Christmas should be. Christmas was always the lonesomest time of the year for me, till now."

I was shocked. Christmas was just about the best time of the year for my family.

Levi went on. "We didn't have a tree or presents or anything," he said. "All the other kids did, but we didn't. Dad would give me ten dollars if he thought of it, and I'd wind up having Christmas dinner with the McDowells or the Gortons." He laughed a little. "I guess they felt sorry for me. I was kind of a stray dog at Christmas."

A stray dog at Christmas! I couldn't imagine it. How could it happen? One thing was for sure: it would never happen again, I'd see to that. I'd make it up to that lonesome kid. We'd have the happiest Christmases of all. We'd have each other, and someday we'd have our children. He'd never be lonesome again.

In our first years of marriage there was almost no cash. One year we sent off to Montgomery Ward for a kerosene lamp with a reflector as our Christmas present to each other. Another year it was outing flannel pajamas for both of us and a pair of fuzzy flannel sheets for our bed. I wrapped them in holly paper and put them under the tree. I got a toy truck for nineteen cents at the dime store, and we filled it with twigs cut to represent the load of firewood my parents would get as their gift.

From the first, Levi was in charge of the tree, and it was always a Ponderosa pine, cut from our own hills. We loved the Ponderosa for filling our house with the heavenly scent of Christmas and for its bright green needles.

I don't remember how or when we started the Christmas tree picnic. By then there were our kids and the Lemmon kids, and we may have had one of those irresistibly mild and beautiful spells of weather Northwest Nebraska can produce, even in December. After that first year it was just a matter of Florence Lemmon and me deciding which Sunday it would be—a Sunday near Christmas, of course, but not too near; the kids couldn't be put off that long, and I could hardly wait myself. In Nebraska nobody waits until Christmas Eve to put up the tree, as they do in New England; I've heard mothers and fathers there decorate the tree after the children have gone to bed.

You also don't wait until you see stacks of Christmas trees trucked in for sale. If you live on a ranch or know somebody who does, you go out and cut your own tree. With all those pines and cedars growing on the hillsides and in the canyons, you don't pay money for a tree. It's free for the taking, like soil for your flowerpots or a yardstick from the hardware store.

The weather wasn't always mild and bright for the Christmas tree picnics. Some years it was cold and snowy. Then Bus Lemmon would uncover the bobsled, smooth its runners, hitch up the mules, and drive us through the snow, harness bells jingling and everybody shouting and singing. The snow picnics were a joy; the Lemmons had a toboggan, and there were ice skates and a half-dozen Flexible Flyer sleds.

Over the years other families joined us from time to time; we might be twenty or thirty people altogether. Every year the food was always the same: I made a huge kettle of mulligan stew, and Florence and the other women brought everything else. Florence always made her apple spice cake. She gave me her recipe, but I never could get it just right. Besides, it couldn't be so good, even when Florence made it, as it was when you ate it with coffee boiled in the big smoky pot over the campfire, standing bundled and mittened, stamping your feet to try to keep warm.

It takes imagination to pick out a Ponderosa for a Christmas tree. You could search through hundreds all over the hillsides and never find one neatly cone-shaped Ponderosa. There are gaps; branches spread too far or not far enough. Levi was good at sizing up possibilities. When he had set it up in the living room, best side out, wired it this way and that and wired extra boughs in the gaps, we could see his vision.

Levi was usually impatient with any kind of tedious work, but he became a painstaking perfectionist with the Christmas tree. Each light, each ornament, was placed to guide the eye to the star on the top. To me using the foil icicles that came after the war took too much time. If it had been up to me, I'd have stepped back and tossed them by handfuls at the tree. I wasn't allowed to do it. Levi hung hundreds of them one by one, each one vertical, until the tree was a shimmering miracle. I think a lonely kid made that miracle.

CHAPTER TWENTY-NINE

Bill planted a garden the summer he was six—a three-foot row of radishes and a three-foot row of lettuce—in the hard, baked earth north of the house. He got manure from the corral and worked it in, he carried water and pulled weeds, and he watched eagerly for the seeds to sprout. It was slow going for a while; then, after a June rain the plants sprang up, and he began to think of the harvest.

One day he burst into the kitchen, livid and almost crying with rage. "Spence peed on my radishes!" he shouted. "They'll taste of pee!"

"Oh, I doubt it," Levi said mildly. "They may be a little pithy."

My laughter made Bill more furious, but he'd been doing some unauthorized peeing himself, and so had they all. I smelled urine one day when I was in their room and found a streak of it across the windowsill. They'd been standing on the bed spraying out through the screen, and they'd been doing it quite a while too, judging from the dried yellow crystals on the logs beneath. I made them wash the logs and carry buckets of clean sand to put under the window. I tried to shame them for being so dirty.

"Now, now," said Levi. "Don't you know every little boy has to see how high he can make it go? Most natural thing in the world."

Bill was gullible. Uncle Jason, the host of a weekly children's program on the radio, would ask, "How many are ready for breakfast this morning? All you boys and girls who brushed your teeth and combed your hair hold up your hands!" When he did, Bill held up his hand.

Spence said, "What are you doing that for, dummy? He can't see you!"

Bill's faith was unfazed. Would Uncle Jason ask to see hands if he couldn't see them? Of course not.

Charley sided sometimes with one, sometimes with the other, depending on whom he was mad at.

One morning Bill went out to feed his snake and shrieked; it was twice the size it had been the night before. He came running in to tell us; everybody had to go see this marvel. All the grasshoppers he'd gathered, all the baby mice he'd caught—it had paid off.

"Just like a 4-H calf," said Spence, "only quicker."

When Bill's joy turned to complacency, Spence couldn't bear it. Nobody had a right to be that trusting.

"You think Willie's the only snake in the world?" he demanded. "You want to know where Willie is? He's in the empty oil barrel in the shed. Dummy."

I had to move fast; Spence deserved whatever he got, but there'd been enough bloody noses and, once, a broken tooth. I caught up with them at the edge of the alfalfa field, tumbling over and over. I flailed with my broom until they broke it up.

I suppose those eruptions were inevitable. Bill, equable by nature, could be goaded to murderous rage. Spence, unable to tolerate much tranquillity, enjoyed pushing him to the brink; once Bill was past the edge, Spence knew enough to head for the brush. It wasn't only his brothers; he did it to Levi and me. From the time he could form a sentence, he'd lead us to take indefensible positions so he could invite us to defend them.

"My God!" said Levi. "A Philadelphia lawyer. What are we going to do with this kid?"

I really didn't know. Urging Bill to ignore his needling was not only ineffective; it was hypocritical. Too often I'd hit him. It was vain to remonstrate with Spence. He liked watching the storm build, and, if it spilled over, well, that was fun too. A bloody nose was a small price to pay for so much satisfaction.

The one person he really didn't want to push too far was his father, but at times he managed even that. I was aghast one day to see Levi, hammer in hand, chasing Spence, who was running like a scared rabbit. Levi didn't catch him; God knows what he'd have done. Spence didn't show up until supper was half-over.

Still, temptation always lay in wait.

In the summer workdays start at four in the morning, and sometimes don't end until nine or ten at night. If Levi could grab a twenty-minute nap once in a while, it was sheer luxury. He was not to be disturbed for any reason—this was understood: no horseplay on the days when Daddy took a nap, no fighting, no nothing.

Spence, however, had found an old alarm clock in the junkpile. It wouldn't keep time, but a tortured ding could be coaxed out of its rusty innards. One warning from Levi was usually enough; this naptime there were two. In the silence as we drifted off into delicious first sleep, there was a single strident boing. In two leaps Levi was up the stairs. All I heard were the sounds of the thrashing—nothing else, not a whimper, not a squeak. When Levi came downstairs there was silence, but sleep was gone for that day. I never heard that clock again; the whaling may have taken the edge off Spence's pleasure in it.

The fall Bill was six he started to school in District 23. District 23 was simply an area where somebody had drawn lines on a map in the county superintendent's office. The schoolhouse was a small one-room building a little less than a mile from our house. It had been built before World War

I and was as innocent of plumbing as were our houses. There were two privies, one for girls, one for boys. The first few years the parents brought water to the school in cream cans, week in and week out. Sometime in the 1920s they hired a "water witch," a person of special talents who could allegedly locate underground water by the way a willow twig turned in his or her hands. The school board had a well drilled where the witch's dowser tipped. The witching certainly worked in this instance. We drilled to water and found a good well. An iron hand pump was set in concrete over it. The water bench, the bucket, and the dipper all the children used were in the entrance hall, along with a wood box and hooks for coats.

Like most rural schools of the period, most of the windows were on the south side of the building, and all the desks were bolted to the floor facing west. This was in accordance with the received wisdom of the period: daylight must come to the pupils over their left shoulders. For gloomy winter days and the occasional evening program there was a Coleman kerosene lantern.

The annual meeting of District 23 was held in June and gave the patrons—parents and landowners—a chance to inspect the premises and equipment. The teacher always left a list of needed books and school supplies. Parents tended to favor the purchase of whatever the teacher thought necessary; nonparents tended to resist. Every year the two Clinton brothers, old bachelors, voted nay on books.

"We've got books," Leonard would say. "Just look at them shelves! Must be fifty, sixty, books on them shelves and only six school kids in the district. Nine or ten books per kid, and we need more books?"

During the war good teachers were scarcer than ever, and standards, never high for rural teachers, dropped further. A district looking for a teacher could get a real lemon—a half-baked seventeen-year-old girl putting in time until she could get married or a housewife so long out of teaching she'd forgotten most of what she ever knew. We were lucky. We got Mary Prieshoff.

Mary was a large, homely woman about my mother's age. She'd gone to Chadron Normal, taught school all her life, and never married. She taught children to read; what's more, she made them want to read. Dick and Jane got short shrift from Mary Prieshoff; in a world full of fascinating books why bother with those tedious texts? Horseplay was out; there was too much to learn and see and do. Projects abounded; history was people and action, not dates and lines of succession. A new word? Look it up. A new idea? Run it down. A news item? Find out about it. So much was going on in Mary's schoolroom that the kids had to be reminded when it was time to go home so Mary could start up her elderly Ford sedan and head back to town.

With six kids and maybe four or five grades in one room, a lot of unscheduled learning went on. The little kids couldn't help hearing what the older kids were learning. Ripples spread.

They spread at home too. Spence and Charley longed for four o'clock and Bill's return. Waiting for him, they'd hound me: "What time is it?" I taught them to tell time, but I didn't have to teach the boys' dog, Gus; a few days of Bill's absence and four o'clock found him at his post, nose on his paws, looking across the fields at the schoolhouse. All three lay on their bellies in the upper yard watching. Every day Bill had something new to tell them; every day they had something new to show him. In the evening they all piled together in the big chair like a heap of puppies.

Charley had a tonsillectomy in November. When Bill and Spence had had theirs in May the doctor decided to postpone Charley's because he had a little cold. "Just a precaution," he said.

We took the boys to the hospital in Chadron a little early so there'd be time to walk around a bit and get used to the place. I knew a couple of the nurses there, and I knew the cook. We saw two babies in the nursery, peeked into the kitchen, said hello to Dr. Leo Hoevet in the hallway, and went to a room where the two beds had sides that could be raised and lowered. Charley thought he'd like to stay too; he hated to miss anything.

"No," I said. "You'll have a good time at Grandmother's, and tomorrow you and Daddy can come get us."

The superintendent of nurses came into the room as I was talking.

"You're staying here in Chadron tonight?" she asked me.

"I'm staying here with the boys," I said. "Didn't Dr. Hoevet tell you?"

"No, he didn't," she said. "And it's completely unnecessary. This is a routine childhood operation. Why make a big thing of it?

"It *is* a big thing to us," I said a little apologetically. "They've never been in a hospital before. I just want to be with them."

"There's no place for you to stay," said the lady, in the tone some people might take toward a rather backward child who was being a nuisance. "You'd just be in the way. The staff is excellent, and I don't propose to let staff routine be disrupted."

"I know the staff is excellent," I said. "I will sit on that chair and be in nobody's way. The only disruption you may expect is if you attempt to keep me from staying in this room tonight." My voice wasn't even trembling, and I looked at her steadily.

Her uniform crackled as she left the room.

It really was rather routine. The boys were uncomfortable, I was uncomfortable, but that was all. Sometime near midnight a nurse brought in a high-backed rocking chair, a pillow, and a blanket for my knees. The boys slept, I slept some, and we were home by noon the next day.

When Charley went into the hospital for his tonsillectomy, a cot for me had been placed in his room. "Dr. Hoevet's orders," said the nurse who settled us in. She winked.

"I'll go downtown and have a sandwich while you're with the doctor," I told Charley. "What shall I get you?"

"A sailor hat," he said. "I want a sailor hat."

The afternoon wasn't bad; the evening wasn't bad. Sponge the little face, push the damp hair back, and feel relief when real sleep ended the restless tossing.

The croupy sound started about 11:00 P.M., a hideous harsh sound—we'd never had that. Never mind, Leo Hoevet would do something. He came at once. He stayed too, on and on; the breathing didn't ease. I came close to screaming, "DO SOMETHING! YOU'RE A DOCTOR, DO SOMETHING!"

Does God pay any attention to prayers that rise from abject, squalid panic? I meant to tell you, God, how much I thank you for this kid. I just forgot. I won't forget anymore. Just help me hold down the fear, God; that's enough for now.

I almost shrieked "NO!" when Dr. Hoevet put his arm around my shoulder and said, "I think you'd better call Levi and tell him to come in."

I made the call. A half-dozen neighbors heard the ring before Levi got awake. It's okay, Polly, we'll keep trying; I'll drive over there and get him up, don't worry; oh, there he is. Thank you, God, for those neighbors who listen in to every ring.

It was all over by 5:00 A.M. Charley was gone. Levi and I looked at each other and couldn't think of anything to say. I got my bag and the sailor hat, and we went home.

CHAPTER THIRTY

Levi's parents were waiting for us in the kitchen when we got home. They'd driven over as soon as Levi called, to be with the children while he went to the hospital. I'd never seen Levi's dad without his false teeth.

They didn't have to be told. But Bill and Spence had to be told when they got up. They looked at me gravely, and Bill said, "You mean we won't see Charley anymore?"

I nodded, "That's right," I said. "We won't see him anymore."

I didn't believe it, of course, and they didn't believe it either. Spence didn't say a word.

My mother came. The neighbors came. Shorty, our hired man, was visiting the Lindeman brothers. When he heard what had happened, he came home. He didn't say anything; he just went outside after a few minutes and started working.

In the days that followed I mostly did what people told me to do. I ate the food that was put before me; I lay down when I was told that it was time to rest. When Levi and I drove into town to make arrangements for the funeral, we looked at our child's body lying in a coffin and agreed that it didn't look much like Charley. We didn't say anything else; we didn't put our arms around each other and weep. We didn't put our arms around Bill and Spence and weep. We didn't know how.

As I dressed for Charley's funeral, I thought of a game we'd played. It always started when I was putting powder and lipstick on. He'd say, "I think you're a pretty mama." I'd say, "Oh no you don't," and he'd say, "Oh yes I do," and it always ended up in a flurry of hugs and kisses. We liked that game.

I dressed with care. I didn't want to look bereaved or bedraggled. I wanted anyone who looked at me to see that I was proud, both of myself and of the little boy who thought I was a pretty mama. I wore my big black hat, the one that made people look twice, and held my head up high—I had to, with that hat. The pain mustn't show, only the pride.

After a loss like that, people don't know what the hell to do with you. They want to help, of course, but they don't know how. A week or two after the funeral I ran into an acquaintance on the street, a woman I knew only slightly. I said hello. Her mouth worked, and she tried to respond, her face contorted in a look of absolute anguish, and she was unable to speak. Others, instead of being tongue-tied, babbled relentlessly, scared, I guess, that there'd be a reference to Charley's death. Maybe they felt they could divert us, entertain us, stop us from thinking of Charley.

A man came by to look at feeder cattle a month or so after Charley's death, someone I'd not met before. Levi brought him to the house. He tarried a moment after the other men had started for the corral. "I was told you lost your boy a while back, Miz Richardson," he said.

I looked up, a little startled that he'd speak of it when so many others had shied away.

"I know what it's like," the man said. "I been there."

"You lost a child too?" I asked.

"Yes," he said. "Prettiest little girl you ever saw. It was sudden," he added, "like yours. Four years old she was, like yours." He paused. "I run over her and crushed her. Playin' there in the yard, and I backed over her."

"Oh . . ." It was all I could say.

"Yeah," the man said. "A thing like that comes hard. You think your baby's safe, and a thing happens, and . . ."

"Yes," I said, "And if you could just . . . but you can't. And I think every day . . . but it doesn't . . ."

"No," he said. "It doesn't. It's like an itch you cain't scratch. My little girl would be twenty-four now." He laughed. "I might be a grandpappy by now. Well, I'd best go. Them guys will be lookin' for me. Goodbye, Miz Richardson."

"Goodbye, Mr. . . . , Mr. . . . ."

"Mason," he said. "I'll be thinkin' of you and Levi."

"Thank you, Mr. Mason," I said. "Thank you."

Mr. Mason must have spoken to Levi as he spoke to me, but Levi didn't mention it, and neither did I. We didn't say anything to each other, and we didn't say anything to our little boys.

I cooked and cleaned. I did what had to be done, I guess, and I did it in a stupor. I thought about myself. I suppose Levi thought about himself.

I thought of the downy little head I'd cupped in my hand the day Charley was born, the unfocused eyes blinking, searching. For what? For my eyes, so he could look straight at me and find out how things were going to be for us in this strange new place I'd thrust him into?

I remembered the after-nap times that came later, when I held him, grumpy from waking up, in the rocking chair, humming, half-asleep, both of us. Does the tiger mother love the smell of her cub as I loved the sleep-warmed little boy smell of mine? Sometimes it was almost too much; I longed to take his nape in my teeth as the tiger mother does, and not gently either. One day, when he was awake and before he squirmed off my lap to go find his brothers, I said, squeezing him, "Can I bite your neck?" and he answered gravely, "No, but you can pinch me."

I don't know if I thought about my other children. I don't remember much about that time. Once I got away from everybody and walked up to the top of the hill by myself and howled aloud.

Somehow we got through Christmas. I guess we had the Christmas tree picnic. I don't know.

Sometime in January I woke up. I heard somebody snarl at my child. It was a harsh, exasperated voice I heard. It was my voice.

I looked at Spence. There were tears in his eyes and an angry curl to his mouth. I couldn't remember what he'd said, but as he turned away I wanted to know. I called him back. "Wait a minute," I said. "It's past two. Let's go visit school and walk home with Bill."

I got our coats and caps and mittens. He walked beside me, but he wouldn't hold my hand. We didn't talk. He didn't have anything to say to me, and I couldn't think of anything to say to him.

The fifth grade—Kenneth Barker and Sue Wohlers—were in geography class when we got to the schoolhouse. So, unofficially, were all four other kids, and so, in a few minutes, was Spence.

We had a tiny world globe at home, so small the place names were mostly just the countries and their capitals. The school had a small globe too, but it was much larger than ours, and it was on a pedestal. That day the subject was the Pyrenees Mountains.

"Who can tell us," asked Miss Prieshoff, "what people live in the western part of the Pyrenees?"

"The Basques," said Sue Wohlers. She was the only one with the answer, but the Barker kids actually knew a Basque sheepherder; he was married to their mother's cousin. They'd visited the family in Idaho; they'd eaten Basque bread and heard Basque songs. The Barkers bubbled over with all they'd heard about the Basques. "Best sheepherders in the country," their dad said. "Nobody like a Basque to hold a flock together and bring them to market." Sue had a book about the Basques; the talk moved on to ethnic groups and race and language. We all knew sheepherders out in the gumbo; were the Wasserburgers Basques?

Miss Prieshoff assigned the fifth-graders sections of the text. Did anybody have an atlas at home? My boys' hands went up. The big atlas in the Crawford City Library had more on the Basques, Miss Prieshoff said. Could anybody get to the library? All the hands went up.

She was apologetic when she told us it was four o'clock.

"I have a dental appointment with Dr. Freimuth," she said. "Last one of the day. I wish I'd made it for another day, so we could talk," she told me. "I'd like to know how you're getting on. You'll come for another visit, won't you?"

We would, I told her. Except for the Christmas program, I hadn't been in the school since October, when Spence, Charley, and I had visited. We knew, because Bill told us, what was going on at school, but I hadn't been paying much attention.

We started home. Spence, like a demented puppy, raced ahead of us, behind us, round and round us. He wasn't the angry, bewildered child I'd seen that afternoon.

Until November Spence had never known life without two brothers. The three of them had been tight as peas in a pod. Now, when Bill was at school, Spence was alone in a way he couldn't have imagined. I thought I knew about loneliness. I had a lot to learn.

I could make a case for myself, of course: I wasn't a monster mother, not really. I loved my child. He had been dogging my heels, wanting my attention every minute. No wonder I was irritable. I'd do anything in the world for Spence—except pay attention to him, listen to him, talk about Charley, weep with him, give him the love he longed for.

I remembered an exchange we'd had. He'd been walking on the wooden gate of the hog pen when I looked out the window and saw him. He jumped to the outside when he saw me coming. I was almost crying in exasperation. "Spence! You know better than to do that. How many times has Daddy told you about that boar? If you fell into that pen he might kill you!" I was almost sobbing. "You could be killed, and then what would we do?" I grabbed him and held him tight. "How could we get along without our Spence?"

He pulled away and looked at me levelly.

"You said how could we get along without Charley, but we're doing it."

It was true. I'd said it, while we still had him. I'd caught him up and said, "What would we do without our Charley?" as we all laughed at something funny he'd done. It was an entirely different, frightening thing when I'd said it about Spence, and yet I left it at that; I forgot it.

I thought of my grandmother and her two lonely, bewildered little boys, Karl and Fred. She knew she'd wallowed in her grief and been self-indulgent when she had her great loss. I thought I was different because I cooked and cleaned and washed clothes.

That evening we read all we could find in the old encyclopedia about the Basques. We went to town on Saturday so we could go to the library. Spence felt a proprietary interest in the Basques because he'd been at school when the study began. Bill told us about new things as they came up in school. We looked things up, I read aloud once more. Two kids in the big chair now instead of three.

A couple of weeks later I sent a note to Mary Prieshoff; could I come over and talk to her? By the rules Spence wasn't old enough to go to school, but Miss Prieshoff took him anyway. I couldn't wipe out what he'd been feeling. I couldn't wipe out what I felt—everything was different now. Nothing would ever be the same.

CHAPTER THIRTY-ONE

The home place, where Levi was born and raised, and where his parents and Uncle Will still lived, was part of the neighborhood that built Bethel Church in the early day and buried its dead in the little cemetery there. People had homesteaded and were living on almost every quarter-section of land, 160 acres, in the early 1890s. They were still optimistic about the new country. They still believed you could make a living on a quarter-section, as people did in Iowa and Illinois.

They wanted a church, and they wanted a center for the community. The land for the church was donated, and the cemetery was fenced and plotted first. Grandfather Britton sawed the lumber, and the men of the neighborhood raised the church. Only later, when the small building was painted white, did people realize that it could be seen from all over the country, even from the gumbo—an area of sticky clay hundreds of square miles in area which extends from north of Crawford into South Dakota— some forty miles away.

As drought and grasshoppers took the crops, family after family starved out and went back east. There wasn't any money; these families had a hard time making it back at all. Levi's Dad and Uncle Will traded a sack of flour for the deed to a quarter-section that was being abandoned.

"We'd have paid them something besides flour if we'd had it," said Levi's dad. "The land adjoined ours, and we wanted it, but we didn't have money to pay for it, only some flour."

The Richardsons and a few others managed to hang on. In 1933, when Levi and I got married, there'd been no regular services at Bethel Church for a long time. Occasionally, a preacher came from Whitney or Chadron, or a traveling evangelist made an appearance, and that was all; still, Bethel Church was the social focus of the community. The school Christmas program was held at Bethel, and the Bethel Ladies Aid raised money with suppers and box socials to maintain the building. There were funerals at the church, even for people who'd long ago moved away from the neighborhood and weren't even to be buried in the churchyard. People had a special feeling for Bethel. We did too, although, living on the west place, West Ash was our real neighborhood.

The Bethel Ladies Aid had a life of its own. It met in members' homes, it made quilts for missionaries, it performed good works, and it bored me stiff. I squeaked out of that. But I went to club—that's all it was ever called, club—because Levi's mother went, I guess.

It was the county extension club, and mostly the same women who went to Ladies Aid went to club. It also met in members' homes, and the hostess served refreshments ranging from Marian Lange's spectacular gold-and-silver tube cake to Mrs. Betson's Kool-Aid and canned raspberries.

West Ash was a good neighborhood, and it was different from Bethel. Nobody was noticeably religious; we had card parties in one home or another, and sometimes we danced after a program at the schoolhouse. That couldn't have happened in the Bethel community, where most families didn't dance or play cards. We got Edgar Seegrist to fiddle when we danced. He'd lost his right arm in a shooting accident when he was just a kid, but he tied the bow to his stump and played as if he didn't miss it. He made his living painting and paperhanging too.

The card game everybody liked best was pitch. It's a fast game, not complicated like bridge. I like the conversation and conviviality of card parties, but after a few hands of cards my mind tends to wander. With pitch it didn't seem to matter much. The kids all played, everybody played, and Uncle Will, who seemed to me to have even less grasp of the game than I had, was a whiz at it. Good cards or bad, he bid like a maniac, gave the table two smart raps when, infrequently, he passed the bid, and played by snapping his cards down on the table exactly as if he knew what he was doing. He almost invariably came out ahead.

Revilo McDerby and I tried to get up dances. Revilo liked dancing as much as I did. She was a large, good-looking, vigorous woman who spoke with a wheeze and always found something to laugh about. Floyd McDerby was a small, self-effacing man, and his wife's exuberance put him in the shade. They had three daughters about my age, and FloyDeen, a flaming redhead, a year older than Bill.

"Wouldn't you think I'd have a boy after all those girls and getting pregnant at this time of life?" Revilo asked. "But FloyDeen's like her ma, I guess. I was supposed to be a boy myself, but I fooled 'em. That's where I got my name," she explained. "From Oliver," she said. "I was supposed to be named Oliver. *Revilo* is *Oliver* spelled backwards, see. Oh well, they liked me well enough once they had me and," pinching FloyDeen's arm, "this one suits us just fine too."

Revilo danced as she did everything else—energetically, stamping her feet, bouncing and sweating, smiling with pleasure. At home she worked all the time, in the house or outside, doing whatever needed to be done.

Revilo was of a practical turn of mind. I realized it most fully when she told me about her mother's death. Tears welled up in her eyes as she told me how her mother's health had failed. "Mama was just like me," she said, "always doing something. It just didn't seem possible she could go downhill so fast."

Revilo took care of her mother in her own home for several months, but when winter came on, with bad roads, a decision had to be made. "I wanted to keep her," Revilo said. "It was night and day care, and I could have managed that, I know I could have, but the doctor said he couldn't guarantee he'd make it out here in time if she got one of her bad spells and the road drifted."

Reluctantly, she and her two brothers decided that their mother must be cared for in a nursing home in Alliance, some sixty miles south of Crawford.

"I stayed down there as much as I could," Revilo said. "But wouldn't you know, when the end got close, I happened to be here at home. When they called me, I picked up my brothers in Crawford, and we drove down there." The tears came fast now.

"I had the feeling she knew me, just at the last," said Revilo. "She couldn't say anything, but . . ."

After the doctor had signed the death certificate and gone, Revilo packed up her mother's belongings, and her brother Maurice said he'd call Junior Houston's funeral home in Crawford.

"No," said Revilo. "No use having Junior Houston driving down here in the middle of the night. We're going anyway; we'll just take Mama with us."

She had her brothers carry her mama's body out to the car and seat her in the back. When they were all ready, Maurice was unwilling to sit there with their mother's body.

"He wouldn't do it," Revilo said. "Absolutely wouldn't do it. I said, 'Why Maurice Abel, I'm surprised at you! Your own mother! But he wouldn't sit in the back with Mama. I gave him the keys. He drove, and I sat with her and held her hand all the way." She was thoughtful, remembering it. "Junior Houston acted kind of funny about it too," she said. "We had the death certificate and everything, all signed up proper by the doctor. But Junior had to write up some kind of report or other and send it to the State of Nebraska. Quite a lot of red tape. I never did find out why anybody would make a fuss over us taking Mama home in the car."

CHAPTER THIRTY-TWO

From the time our boys were big enough to walk, Uncle Will periodically gave them bib overalls—stout blue-and-white hickory-striped ones, the kind railroad men and Uncle Will wore. He never asked me if it was time for new ones; he just bought them. He never asked me about size either; he got them plenty big, as he did his own. Levi said Uncle Will felt he came closer to getting his money's worth by buying overalls a couple of sizes too large.

Uncle Will remembered the hard times he'd seen; the ones we knew in the first few years of marriage paled in comparison, and we knew it.

"These gosh-dang fellers," he'd say sometimes. "They just want too much for their stuff. Why, I remember when you could buy a good pair of shoes for two dollars." After a trip to get a prescription filled at the drugstore, he complained, "I remember when you could buy a whole handful of pills for a quarter."

He admitted, when pressed, that in those days hogs and cattle brought very little by the time you'd paid the freight, but he still thought the gosh-dang fellers nowadays wanted too much for what they sold. I often thought so myself, and I knew Uncle Will approved of my patching and makeshifts. We both thought there was a special virtue in making do and making things last.

Certainly, the kind of sewing I did—patching and mending—I considered virtuous. I had an old FREE sewing machine my mother had bought secondhand in 1907, and I sewed miles on it, turning the cloth this way and that, treadling away. One of the lessons I learned at club was of a way to get about a third more wear out of sheets. As soon as they began to show wear, you tore them down the middle, sewed the finished sides together, and hemmed the new sides. This was a lot of work, but I did it. And overalls— I might work an hour on a pair that was nearly worn-out, but I did it, even if they burst out in a new place the first time they were worn again. I felt superior because I didn't waste time on embroidering dishtowels or crocheting potholders, but I sewed miles on overalls that should have been thrown away.

I ought to have known those bib overalls would be a thorn in my kids' flesh after they started school. Their dad wore Levi's, Kenneth and Dale Barker wore Levi's, all ranchers wore Levi's. Bib overalls were for farmers, I knew that. I also knew the boys wanted to be ranchers rather than farmers. I suppose the boys protested to me, and, if they did, I'm sure I said, "Nonsense, there's nothing wrong with these overalls; Uncle Will gave them to you. Of course you'll wear them." It was my virtuous make-do pioneer spirit at work. It was also my mother's detested Calvinism visited on my children. Whatever it was, it made them miserable.

To conceal the bib of the overalls, they wore their knit shirts over the top of the hated garment, but hope of fooling anybody vanished the day Spence lost his shirt down the privy hole. He was gone so long Miss Prieshoff began to wonder what was wrong. He was seen, shirtless, running back to the school from the canyon with a tree branch he'd found, and Bill was sent to see what had happened. He found his brother fishing desperately with the branch in the hole of the privy. God knows what Spence thought he could do with the shirt if he managed to retrieve it, yet he couldn't reappear with his underwear showing. Bill took Spence's jacket to him, and he wore it zipped up all afternoon. He was still seething when he got home. All adults have been kids, yet, by the time they have children of their own, they've forgotten how it feels to be a kid. I detested my lumpy, long underwear when I was a kid. I'd fought with my mother over it, and I'd sneaked into the Sargents's lilac bushes and rolled the legs up above my knees. Still I was adamant about the bib overalls. My kids wore them as long as they were in grade school.

CHAPTER THIRTY-THREE

By the time the war was over Levi was itching to build a barn. When we'd moved to the west place, where we lived now, there was only a tumble-down shed, thatched with bundles of wheat straw and set halfway into the bank of the canyon, to serve as a barn. With steel available once more and a four years' shortage to fill, Levi began to sell Quonset buildings—steel, prefabricated structures—on commission. The demand was there. Farmers and ranchers hadn't had any money in the 1930s, but now they were prosperous.

In a few months Levi sold enough buildings to pay for the Quonsets he wanted. The big one was to be the upper story of the barn; the slope of the canyon, rising gently to the east, provided a perfect place for a lower story to be set into the hillside, so that machinery and animals could be driven into either level.

Lumber was needed for the foundation forms and for the stalls and other framing in the lower story. Levi bought an old sawmill and set it up. Neighbors helped fell trees and snake them out of the deep canyons. In ranch country neighbors help one another without keeping track of time; an offer to pay a neighbor would be taken as an insult. Besides, Levi's project fired people up.

Levi's dad said, "I thought John Britton took every tree out of those hills in the 1880s and '90s that was big enough to put through a mill."

"He did," said Uncle Will. "But Levi's going in where nobody but a damned fool would try to take logs out."

It was up to me to get food to the men at noon. Dad had given me a cast-iron pot that was perfect. There'd been scores of those three-legged cooking pots with bails—iron teakettles and old cavalry saddles too—stored away some place at Fort Robinson from the days when it was one of the last frontier posts in the country. Somebody ran across the cache, and the items were put up at an auction of equipment that had been "inspected and condemned." Dad bought them all. He paid ten cents apiece for the pots and teakettles, a dollar apiece for the saddles. Mother groaned in dismay when she saw Dad unloading them into the garage, but it was soon cleared out. He gave the stuff away to anyone who was interested and sold the rest as antiques at a tidy profit.

Each day that the logging crew worked I cooked meat and vegetables—boiled beef, hamburger, ham, and sometimes chicken in the cast-iron pot. I made noodles for the chicken and cooked potatoes besides. I always made plenty of potatoes, no matter what else I cooked.

The crew worked only three or four miles from our house as the crow flies, but it was over the highest of the hills and through the deepest of the canyons. I loaded the grub into the truck, drove five or six miles up West Ash Creek Canyon road, and walked another mile and a half, carrying the kettle in one hand and a flour sack of bread, butter, tin cups, pie pans, and tableware in the other. The coffeepot was kept at the work site, where the men kept a fire going all day.

I liked to start early so I could try one route and then another. My favorite was across one of the West Ash Creek fords. I liked to tarry awhile and look at the tracks in the snow and mud left by those that had been there to have a drink of water: the wild turkey, the deer, the bobcat, the coyote, and always the raccoon, which leaves a print like a tiny baby's hand. If the food cooled while I took my time, the iron kettle went into the glowing coals raked out of the campfire and began to bubble in no time.

The weather that January was clear and bright, and the men were in high spirits. There was laughter and joshing as they dipped their food out of the pot and squatted on their heels to eat it or perhaps stretched out on a dry spot in the sun, their hats over their eyes, to rest their backs.

The trees were felled with axes and two-man handsaws. With a cant hook—a lumbering tool for rolling logs, called a "peavey" in some lumbering areas—one man positioned each downed tree so that it could be trimmed of its branches and chopped off at the point where it tapered past usefulness for sawing into boards and two-by-fours, the smallest lumber Levi sawed. He and the other men would back the team of horses in, throw a chain around the butt end of the log, and snake it out onto a high meadow, to be hauled down to the sawmill later.

When the logs had been hauled out of the canyons and hills where they had been cut, Levi moved his tractor to the end of the sawmill and blocked its tires so that the tractor's pulley could be used for power. A long belt ran from the pulley on the tractor to a larger pulley on the sawmill. I could watch it all from my kitchen window.

The neighbors crewed the sawmill. Two or three men carried each log to the carriage, lowered the dogs that held it in place, and, when all was ready, Levi threw the gear that started the blade whining through the log. The first cut took off the outside layer, mostly bark, and the log was turned again and again to get it square and free of bark.

Now the mill was set to move the carriage for the logs sideways after each cut. The boards and planks came off in a steady rhythm. They were seized and stacked by the off-bearers, a layer this way, a layer the other way, with space for the air to move through and make them dry and seasoned.

Levi built the barn in five months—excavation, concrete foundations, and all—with the help of the neighbors. Except for one railroad car of thirty-six-foot stringers and three-by-twelve planks from Canada, all the lumber came from our own hills.

CHAPTER THIRTY-FOUR

Uncle Will had come to live with us after his eightieth birthday. The whole Bethel neighborhood had given him a party at the church. Ruth got the word out to people who'd moved away, and they came from all over to help us celebrate. That afternoon Levi said impulsively, "Let's ask Uncle Will to come live with us—what do you say?"

I said, "Yes! What a good idea!"

Uncle Will had rented a room at a boardinghouse in Crawford. He thought he would play pitch and pinochle with the other old men in town, but after two days he was desperately unhappy. Levi could sense this, and asked Uncle Will to come out to our ranch, where a small apartment awaited in a Quonset. Uncle Will didn't want to bother us but was so bored by not having work to do that he accepted. The only problem was, he said, that his rent was paid until the end of the week, another three days. Not staying and using what he'd paid for bothered his thrifty soul, but he finally agreed to move that day, an arrangement that was wonderful for him, for Levi and me, and especially for the boys.

The first day of 1949 dawned bright and mild. About ten o'clock, while hanging dish towels on the clothesline, I saw that the whole western sky had turned dark. Great bluish-purple clouds boiled up over Soldier Buttes, advancing as I watched. Within forty minutes, snow, driven by a high wind, was so thick you couldn't see anything.

Uncle Will had been with us about a year when the blizzard—it later got its own name, the blizzard of '49—hit that January day. He moved from window to window, trying to see out. "Levi calculatin' on bringin' them cows in from the wheat stubble?" he asked.

I didn't know. My mind was on beef soup and oatmeal cookies. Being snug inside while the weather rages always makes me feel like cooking and talking.

By noon, cookies baked, beef simmering, boys and Uncle Will fed, I was beginning to catch the old man's uneasiness. The thermometer stood at 18°F, the snow still fell, and the wind still blew furiously.

"He's just making sure everything's fastened down and the stock's okay," I said. "He'll be in anytime now."

At one o'clock Uncle Will said, "Believe I'll just go see what's holdin' Levi up."

"No!" I said sharply, then, trying to keep my voice steady, "Please no, Uncle Will. He'll be in soon. You'll see." I didn't want to say, You're eighty-one, your legs are numb half the time; it won't help for you to be wandering out there too.

Wandering around too? Dear God, what was I thinking?

It was 2:30 when we heard Levi at the door. "Thank you, God," I said to myself. "Anytime I can do anything for you, God, just let me know."

His eyebrows were plastered with snow; his nose and cheeks were like ice.

"Just about froze, ain't you?" said Uncle Will, reaching to help him get his coat off.

"No," said Levi, a little shortly. "I was too busy to get cold."

"I'll help you with the chores," said Uncle Will.

"No!" Levi almost shouted. "You're not going to set foot out of this house! Or you kids either! Get it?"

The kids got it. They were startled, and Uncle Will stood openmouthed.

"It's a goddamned rough day out there," Levi went on in a more normal tone. "I've got everything snugged down, enough feed in the bunks till tomorrow. Nobody's going out of this house anymore today." He turned away. "I'm going to get in the bathtub," he said. "I didn't know how cold I was till I got here in the warm."

I took a tray of soup and crackers to the bedroom and sat while he ate it.

"It's a bugger out there," he said, between gulps of soup. "Nobody's going out of this house. I couldn't tell you how—" He pushed the tray to me and was asleep before he could finish his sentence.

It was nearly six when I heard him stirring. I went in and sat on the edge of the bed. I kissed him and put my head down on his chest." Boy, am I glad you're back in!" I said. "You had us worried there for a while."

"Had me worried too," he said, holding me tight. "I really was wondering—" He pushed me back and looked me in the eyes. "I'm going to tell you something I don't want Uncle Will and the kids to know: I lost my bearings for a while out there, and I was scared. I mean, *scared*." He rubbed his eyes and looked away.

"I never . . . ," he said, "never in my life . . . I mean, I really didn't know where I was. I was no more than twenty or thirty feet from the barn, our own barn, I was sure of it, and I didn't know where the hell I was. Spookiest goddamned feeling. . . . I wasn't even sure which way was up." He laughed a little. "Like to scared the shit out of me," he said. "I went forward a ways, back a ways, and sideways, trying to figure out where I was, and I couldn't find anything to take hold of. I had all I could do to keep from yelling. I just didn't know what the hell was going on." He swung his legs around and sat up, still holding me tight. "When I finally put my hand out, my God, there was a fence post. I was so relieved I was shaking when I got back to the barn. I got inside and just stood there for a while, getting things straight in my mind."

"Uncle Will knew right away it was a bad one," I said. "I thought it was just a stormy day, but he knew."

"Yeah," said Levi. "Probably thinking of that first winter, '84, the die-up. People got lost and froze to death that winter, just a few feet from the house. Yeah, he knows, he remembers."

"Well," he said, heading for the bathroom, "I don't know how it happened, but it's not going to happen again. When I came out of the barn I took a spool of wire with me and fastened it to the barn good and tight. I hung onto that wire and paid it out as I felt my way along the fence to the tractor. Took a dally around the tractor wheel, twenty-seven steps south-southwest, and here I am. I hung onto that wire all the way, and I'll hang onto it tomorrow if this keeps up.

It kept up and kept up and kept up. It began to feel as if the snow and wind and cold were never going to stop.

The telephone line held, and it worked. It's a wonder those high winds didn't bring it down. With fourteen-foot drifts everywhere, it would have been lucky to find a break if there'd been one and almost impossible to get out and repair it. But we were lucky; it held.

The trouble was everybody wanted to talk about the storm; everybody wanted to know how other folks were making it. There wasn't much to do but hang on the phone, talking or listening. There was even more rubbering than usual. As each receiver was lifted the sound became fainter, so that sometimes you could hardly hear your party at all.

News reports from KLZ Denver, KOLT Scottsbluff, and KOTA Rapid City told of motorists stranded in their cars, rail passengers stranded in the *California Zephyr* on the tracks at Kimball, sick people stranded in their homes without medical care, cattle stranded without feed. Until the weather cleared, planes—the kind used in rescues or food and medicine drops—couldn't fly, and snowplows couldn't make any headway against the drifts that constantly formed and reformed. Western Nebraska, eastern Wyoming, southwest South Dakota, and part of Colorado were locked up tight.

After ten days of an unremitting, impenetrable storm, a bright, clear day dawned. A general ring—seven or eight short, sharp rings, which was the signal for everybody to pick up the telephone and let everyone know that this was the day to bring tractors and clear the trail to town. Most people kept good stocks of supplies on hand, but now everybody was short of groceries, feed, medicine, and other necessities. Ten days of storm without any warning—and there'd been none from the weather bureau—had caught people unprepared.

The boys were wild to get out of the house; they tore into the drifts, whooping. Uncle Will and I walked out and looked around at a world I'd never seen and Uncle Will hadn't seen since 1884. There were enormous drifts over familiar landmarks. Fences had disappeared, and even one of the smaller Quonsets was covered with a snowdrift. Levi had managed to keep the cattle fed, those that were in, but some had been out in the hills, and we could only hope they had survived.

The trail the men made that day, Levi told me, went through pastures and fields because the road was drifted in. They had gone on the high spots, where the wind had blown away much of the snow, everywhere they could. It took a long time to dig that trail out, and it was a good deal farther than the usual eight miles to town because of the zigzagging.

It was getting toward dusk when Levi got home with the tractor and trailer.

"It's drifting back in already," he said. "All the places we cleared, they're going to be full again by morning."

I'd always kept a big stock of supplies on hand. With plenty of storage space, there was no reason to let yourself run out of things. The pantry, back against the earth bank, had shelves with hundreds of quarts of home-canned vegetables and meat, and for years I'd bought coffee by the three-pound case and flour and sugar in fifty-pound muslin bags. This trip I doubled everything on my list, just to be sure. We loaded the big trailer with feed and minerals for the cattle and boxes and boxes of supplies from the grocery store. Levi lifted his eyebrows when he saw what I'd bought; he told me that one neighbor brought home only a couple of boxes of food from the store. They were more optimistic, I guess, than I was.

Optimism took a dive for a lot of people that year. The storm continued, and the trail, renewed whenever the weather cleared a bit, promptly filled back up each time the wind blew. There wasn't much new snow, but the old snow never got a chance to melt and run off. The wind whipped fiercely during most of those seven or eight weeks, blowing from one direction and then another, and each time it drifted the snow into new and unexpected places.

News reports told about real hardship and enormous loss. Thousands and thousands of cattle and sheep didn't make it. The horror stories mounted. Near Van Tassel, Wyoming, sixty miles to the west, five thousand head of sheep had wandered up against a fence then drifted over with snow and died. Ben Norman, out in the gumbo, had huge losses.

Bales of hay and cottonseed concentrate were dropped when possible to starving cattle in all the affected states. Sometimes it wasn't dropped in the right place; sometimes nobody could reach the bales to spread the hay out. One man sourly asked, "What are them critters supposed to do, bite the balin' wire off with their teeth?"

Rescue planes, when they could fly at all, carried some sick people out of the area. Some people froze in their cars.

After that rough first day we were safe, and we were all together. We found out about cabin fever. The kids drove us nearly crazy; often I sent them into the cold upstairs, where they banged on the piano in the upper living room until I'd let them come downstairs again. Even Uncle Will, that most equable of men, at times admitted that he was tired of being cooped up. We played so much Monopoly, I've never enjoyed it since. I cooked and baked and gained twelve pounds.

One bright day we arranged a trade with Phyllis and Lawrence Wohlers—cigarettes for aspirin, I think it was. The walk to the canyon where Lawrence and I were to meet was exhilarating, and I told myself I'd do more walking when the storm was over. I saw Lawrence, we waved, and I began to run toward him. Everything looked so different covered in snow. I fell into a deep drop-off that looked like level ground and couldn't get out by myself. Lawrence pulled me out, like he was hauling a cow out of quicksand.

Not everybody was so lucky. A young couple we knew headed for Scottsbluff one bright, white day with their child on her mother's lap in the cab of their pickup. The mother and child were found a couple of days later, huddled, cold, and hungry, in the cab of a big semitrailer along with the driver, who'd taken them in.

The young husband wasn't found for a week. He'd fallen into a snowdrift covering a deep draw, a quarter-mile from a ranch house where he could have found the help he was after.

CHAPTER THIRTY-FIVE

Looking back, I can see a lot of things that should have alerted me to the fact that Levi was unhappy in our marriage. Not bitterly, desperately unhappy—just trapped and restless and dissatisfied.

It was strange, his feeling trapped. I'd gone into marriage with a full set of theories, chief of which was that if I didn't do anything to make Levi feel constrained or crowded, he'd feel free and happy and would love me for it. It was a point of pride with me never to ask him where he was going or when he'd be home and, when he did get home, never to say, "Where have you been?" "What kept you?" and, most of all, "But what about me?" I urged him to go out with the boys, to go to dances alone, and he did, and I hated it, every minute of it. But I felt proud and enlightened when Levi's friends commented enviously on how free he was to go where he pleased and to do what he liked.

It never crossed my mind that Levi hadn't demanded or even asked for this kind of freedom and that he might not want it. My mind was made up; I even had some aphorisms to justify my notions: "The only way to hold a man is to set him free," "Love can't be forced," and "I want him to be with me because he wants to be, not because I nag him into it or make him feel it's his duty."

That was decades before I'd even heard the word *machismo*. I knew, of course, that men felt threatened by a brainy woman; every woman knew that, if not from her own observation, then from the articles in every one of the women's magazines that inveighed against letting your brains show. If you did, you might fail to attract a man or, having attracted him, lose him.

Our best friends were Barley and Ardith McDowell. Barley and Levi had been friends since childhood, getting acquainted on the Saturday trips the Richardsons made to Crawford. In high school they'd boozed and chased girls together. Barley never did finish high school. Barley was a charmer. He seduced girls right and left, but even the mothers, who'd heard of his exploits, found him appealing because he was so sweet and charming and eager to please.

Ardith was a girl from a nearby town, attractive and charming herself and just as much in love with Barley as I was with Levi. Barley had one scheme after another which was going to make him rich, and he used these projects as excuses to postpone marriage. Ardie was careful not to push him. I was stunned when she went with him on one of his trips to try to borrow money, openly traveling together, sharing a room, even in the homes of Barley's friends, to whom he introduced her as "my fiancé, Miss Kloppel." I shuddered at the thought of my parents' reaction had I told them, as Ardie told hers, that I was going on an unchaperoned trip with a man.

Finally, it seemed almost offhandedly, Barley married Ardie. They dropped in at the courthouse for the license and then to the judge's office for the ceremony.

From the first Barley and Ardie lived a sort of hand-to-mouth existence, moving often, to Crawford or to Chadron for a while, with Ardie taking part-time work as a drugstore clerk to pay the rent and buy food. She was always cheerful, always warmly welcoming, always sure that the latest scheme was going to work, and she never complained.

After our first three or four years of marriage Levi was away from home more and more, and I was home with the kids day after day, not knowing where he was or when he'd be back or even if he'd be back. It was my job; I was sure of it. I must be there, with food and love and the eager interested attention that the *Ladies' Home Journal* said was essential if a woman wanted to hold onto her man. And, of course, I never once questioned the dictum that holding one's man was the be-all and end-all of a woman's existence. Indeed, for me it really was; Levi was the center and focus of my life, even after the boys were born.

My house was pretty messy between sporadic bouts of housecleaning, whereas some others, like Ardie's, were always neat and orderly. I told myself that my house was cleaner, much cleaner, than Ardie's when I cleaned. It was true that when I cleaned I did a thorough job, but it didn't change the fact that her house was always fit to be seen, and mine seldom was.

And I was fat, very fat, between bouts of dieting, when I'd take off twenty, thirty, once seventy, pounds. Ardie helped me with advice about clothes, but nothing looks like much when you're grossly overweight.

I'd also get migraines, with pain and despair and nausea that lasted for an average of two days out of every week. Everyone felt sorry for me when I had a migraine, and I felt sorry for myself, and then, when it had ended, I'd be exuberant and twice as alive, confident that I'd do better and that everything would be all right.

I had a dream that came once or twice a year: I was walking on a high scaffolding in a huge, cavernous building and was scared to death I'd fall.

We'd had little "social life" in the first few years of our marriage, only suppers with family and friends and activities in the West Ash neighborhood. But after the war we were prosperous, and we began to be included in the dinners and bridge parties and outings of a group of married people our own age who lived in Crawford. We met in someone's house for drinking, quite a lot of drinking, and then we either had dinner there or went out to a restaurant. Best of all for me, we sometimes went to dances in a group. I'd always loved dancing, like my mother and all her family. Levi was a smooth dancer but without any real sense of rhythm or pleasure in the dancing. Dances had been, for him, a place to drink and pick up girls, a place for horseplay and laughter and sometimes fights outside the dance hall. Now he danced dutifully with each woman in the group, beginning with me and then his hostess.

For me dancing was sheer joy when I had a good partner. It was the best part of socializing with the group, far better than the bridge parties, which I barely endured. And, when I noticed, as I finally did, that flirtations and even affairs went on within the group, I'd arrived at the conclusion that other people's sexual peccadilloes were none of my business.

I learned suddenly that Levi had decided to build a house. He'd made all his plans in one afternoon when he was waiting for a cow about to calve. I didn't ask about the financial feasibility of it; Levi was already getting his building materials together, and in any case I'd never known where we stood financially, except that for a long time we'd been terribly hard up and now we seemed to be prosperous.

We were caught up in the excitement of building a new house. Levi's plans seemed grandiose to me, but I did talk him down from a fifty-foot living room to one thirty-six by eighteen feet and, feeling a little grandiose myself, asked for a fireplace in our bedroom and a dressing room off it. It was only at night that I'd wake up suddenly from a sound sleep, with heaviness in the pit of my belly, thinking, "No, I can't leave this good house. This is my home." But by morning I'd be less panicked, and I'd go along, as I'd always gone along.

Levi did most of the work himself, between May 31 and Christmas Day 1949, when we moved in. He did the regular work of tending crops and cattle too, and he fell in love with Eleanor Avery.

CHAPTER THIRTY-SIX

George and Eleanor Avery had moved to Crawford that summer. George worked as a car salesman with Eleanor's brother, Clyde Moore, in the Ford agency. The Averys were immediately included in the dinners, bridge parties, and dances.

Eleanor was tall and thin and beautifully dressed, and she had a sharp wit. George was small and aggressive in the way small men sometimes are. He turned almost every remark into something leeringly sexual, but people laughed, and nobody seemed to mind. Eleanor minded, though; she was openly contemptuous of George, and it was obvious that she was miserable in her marriage.

We became friends at once, Eleanor and I. She was stimulating intellectually. She'd been in one of the stable of Betty Crockers who conducted cooking schools all over the country to promote General Foods products, and all this traveling about, staying at good hotels, seemed glamorous and exciting to me. I pictured her meeting new men, dating and having fun, being taken out for dinner and dancing. But one day one of my ingenuous, half-envying remarks brought a sour rejoinder from Eleanor that it hadn't been that way at all.

It all fell together: this glamorous woman, with the stunning clothes and the thin figure to make the clothes look good, this woman who was so different from me, who'd had what I imagined had been an exciting life of travel and fun, had actually had very few dates. Finally, at age thirty, she had married George Avery not because she loved him but because she was afraid of winding up an old maid. This explained her announcement, made when her guard was down and after she'd had a few drinks, that she was frigid. It explained her unwillingness to let George have the credit for giving her a new fur coat: "He didn't give it to me. My General Motors stock bought me this coat."

It explained a lot of things, and it made me feel luckier than ever to have found the right man and to have fallen in love with him and smart to have married him instead of going after the "career" my mother had urged on me. What a lucky woman I was!

I went to a hospital in Denver that fall and stayed for three weeks, to get started on a weight loss program. I stayed on the program until I had lost seventy pounds, and I knew that at last I was going to be all right. Even the migraines were coming less frequently, and I hadn't had the bad dream for almost a year.

The house was shaping up, and I plunged into the finishing work. I stained and waxed the paneling in the living room, cleaned all the windows, and sealed and waxed the red stone floor in the kitchen. Bess Pinney organized a drapery-making "bee." Seven women came to spend the day and make pale yellow corduroy draperies for the two huge windows in the living room which, as Levi had promised twenty-five years earlier, we'd eventually have.

My plan was to get everything finished in the new house and then move in methodically, cleaning and waxing each piece of furniture before it was carried over. After all, it was just across the yard; there was no reason everything shouldn't be newly polished and glistening and orderly as we made the transition. But I'd left Levi's habits and preferences out of my plan. Of course I knew he loved big building projects and that he never quite finished anything. Hadn't the steps in the entryway of the log house been a "temporary" job, and hadn't they been there for thirteen years? Of course I knew that nothing was ever repaired or taken care of or put away, that machinery sat rusting in the wind and rain until it was urgently needed and then pulled out of the weeds and somehow made to work. Still, I was shocked when on Christmas morning he mobilized Shorty and Uncle Will and the boys and started carrying furniture over to the new house.

"Aren't we going to finish the painting first?" I cried. "Things are still in a mess over there," I protested. "Let's not do it this way, let's get things finished and cleaned up," I said. "Christmas is no day to move," I moaned.

It was no use. Beds, sofas, tables, and chests of drawers were picked up and carried to the new house, where they were set down every which way. I was angry, but it was done.

"Hell, we wouldn't be moved in by the Fourth of July if we'd done it your way," Levi said.

I knew there was some truth in this.

"Besides," he added, "you know you can't stay mad at me, so forget it."

I did put it out of my mind, and I made the beds and searched for the pots and pans and dishes I needed most. Day by day I achieved a little more order, and in a few days the house began to look settled and comfortable. Carpets were put down in the living room and the big bedroom, curtains went up at all the windows, and the missing parts of the household appliances turned up.

New Year's Eve we were to go to Ruth and Bill Hudson's house for drinks and then on to the City Park Pavilion for the annual Firemen's Ball. The kids were openly admiring as Levi and I came out dressed for the party. I felt slim and sexy in my new dress and my three-inch heels and my cloud of Arpege. I hadn't had a drink, but, as I looked around the beautiful living room, at Levi, so handsome and poised, and at the two tall sons who looked like him, a wave of blissful intoxication flooded over me. My God, I thought, I've got it all, I've really got it all.

At Hudsons we all got happily, noisily drunk, and by the time we got to the dance intermission was over, and the band was beginning to play again. We trooped into the drafty pavilion, shouting greetings to everybody. It was near zero outside, and the two coal stoves glowing on one side of the big dance floor didn't make much of a dent in the cold, but nobody felt it. We were all warm and loose and happy. First dance was with Levi, then with Bill Hudson, and then with Rex Hagemeister, the best dancer of all.

Dancing with Rex you just couldn't make a mistake. He looked down at me and smiled. "I don't know how you do it," he said. "I mean, I don't know what I'm going to do when I start dancing. I don't see how you always know."

Lovely, I thought, lovely. Rex likes dancing with me as much as I like dancing with him. I knew he'd be back for another dance as soon as he'd danced with everybody else in the group. I don't know whom I was dancing with when "Auld Lang Syne" began, but Levi was at my side in a moment, kissing me, and everybody kissed everybody else, and I was dancing again, and I couldn't believe it when the band began to play "Good Night, Ladies." Damn, I thought, that's what happens when we go to somebody's house and start drinking. You can't get people rounded up to go to the dance, and by the time you get there it's nearly over. Already people were getting into their coats and heading up to Bishops' house for bacon and eggs.

It was much later, after the food and coffee, that I realized I was sleepy and wanted to go home, but I couldn't find Levi. I told Ben Bishop, and he said, "Mary Ellen and Bill Hudson went up to Simmons' for more scotch; maybe Levi went with them."

I thought that was unlikely; Levi didn't like either of the Simmons much, and he and Bill Hudson weren't that fond of each other either. Still, it was an idea, so I took Ben's car keys when he offered them and drove slowly up the icy hill to Simmons'. I rang and rang, and presently Jim Simmons, looking rumpled, came to the door and said hurriedly that no, no, Levi wasn't there.

I drove around. No cars at McDowells', no cars at Gues', no cars at Hudsons', and I remembered Ruth Hudson had been in the Bishops' kitchen when I left. I saw our car when I headed down the street where the Parks lived, and, when I stopped, the headlights showed Levi and Eleanor sitting in it.

I walked over and yanked the car door open.

"Am I interrupting something?" I demanded in my haughtiest tone, feeling angry and bewildered.

I don't remember what either Levi or Eleanor said; I know he escorted her up to her door, "as if he were her date," I thought angrily. He came back to the car and said, "I'll pick you up at Bishops's."

At Bishops' we gave Ben his keys and said goodbye to the few people who remained. Then we started the long, silent ride home. I didn't sleep much after we went to bed, and I felt Levi, awake and silent, staring into the darkness too. He'd told me, in the car heading for home, that he and Eleanor had gotten to talking and that she'd asked him to take her home.

But things I'd resolutely overlooked before came back to me now: Levi and Eleanor sitting together almost all one evening at a party, talking in low tones. The day I'd brought Eleanor home with me from a trip doing errands; George would come after her, she'd said, but he didn't, and Levi drove her in and was late getting back and said without my asking that he'd been in the bar, playing pool and talking to the guys.

I finally dropped off to sleep. I don't know when Levi got up, but I woke suddenly about nine with the sound of our ring on the phone. It was George Avery.

"Tell Levi I want to see him in here right away," he said abruptly.

Still dazed with sleep and with all last night's drinking and with all the doubts that had been rolling around in my mind, I poured myself a cup of coffee just as Levi came in the back door. The message didn't seem to come as a surprise to him. He said, "I'm going in."

"What do you mean, you're going in?" I said. "George Avery summons you, and you go? What's this about?"

"George and Eleanor are having problems," Levi said. "That's what Eleanor and I were talking about last night."

"What in hell has that got to do with you?" I demanded. "What's this all about?"

"I don't know, I don't know," he muttered.

"I'm going with you," I said, and started getting my clothes on. "If that nasty little creep thinks he's going to involve you in their troubles, he's got another thing coming."

Levi had to go to the barn to give the boys instructions about a cow he'd penned up for observation, and that gave me time to brush my teeth and hair and get some makeup on. I reached the car just as Levi did, but he didn't say a word when I got in. All the way to Crawford I seethed with anger at the nerve of that unpleasant, tiresome little George, thinking he was somehow going to involve Levi and me in the failure of his marriage. I'd soon set him straight on that.

But when we reached Crawford, Levi drove to McDowells' house and told me to get out, to go have coffee with Ardie. He said that I simply could not go with him. As he drove off, I stood stunned for a moment; then I walked up to the door. Ardie was having coffee, and she got a cup for me. I told her contemptuously, "The Averys are having some kind of trouble, and George called Levi to come in and talk to them."

For nearly two hours I sat with Ardie, and she kept up the light talk she was so good at. At first I tried to talk about the Averys and find out if Ardie knew anything about what had been going on between them, but she avoided answering directly.

When Levi picked me up and we started home, I demanded, "What happened? What did he have to say?" We were halfway home before he finally answered. "You have to know. It's not just George's imagination. Eleanor and I have been . . . Well, I asked her to marry me, and she said she would. George has known about it for a couple of months. Eleanor told him right away, and she's been wanting to tell you. She feels you ought to know."

My mouth was dry. "Marry you?" I whispered at last. "Marry you? How . . . ?" I couldn't get it out.

Levi was hurting and sweating, I could see that, but as yet I felt nothing—no pain, no anger, nothing but bewilderment.

"It's not going to happen. It's over," he said.

Two or three more times on the way home I tried to understand what he had said. I started to ask a question and found my voice coming out as a hoarse whisper and trailing off. I still felt nothing when we got home and I saw the boys coming from the barn. I got out of the car, feeling lame and awkward and unwieldy, and I went into the house and started making escalloped oysters. We always had escalloped oysters on New Year's Day.

We were still at the table facing the window when Levi noticed a car coming down the road. "Oh Jesus," he said.

I didn't know who it was and felt no interest in knowing. I didn't know until I saw them on the porch that it was the Averys.

Now I could feel something: blazing anger. Levi was right behind me as I closed the door on the kids and Uncle Will in the kitchen and marched to the front door. I yanked it open and said, "To what do we owe this honor?"

Tears welled up in Eleanor's eyes. "I want to talk to you," she said. "May we come in?"

"By all means come in," I said. "What do you want to talk about?"

"About what's happened," she said, taking off her fur coat and sitting down in my chair. "Has Levi told you . . . about us?"

"Us?" I asked. "You and George?"

"No. No," Eleanor said. "Levi and me. Has he told you?" She looked at Levi. "Didn't you tell her?" she asked.

"I told her," he answered shortly.

"Well," she began. "I just want you to know that I'm going to California for a while and get myself straightened out. I just want you to know how sorry I am that I did this to you. It just happened. We couldn't help it."

"Bigger than both of you?" I asked.

"Really," she began, "I wouldn't have hurt you for the world. I told George quite a while ago, and I've been wanting to tell you. I really thought you ought to know, but Levi . . ."

My God, I thought, she was afraid Levi wouldn't tell me about it. That's why she's here and why she dragged that poor bastard George along. Of course, George and I both had to know. George had known, everybody had known, but Levi had balked at telling me. It was no good for her that way. She had to be sure I knew, and that's why they'd driven out this sunny New Year's Day.

I looked out the window at Crow Butte soaring up from the wide plain, at the white clouds drifting in the blue sky behind it. I saw two cars heading up West Ash. Uhls must be having company, I thought. A winter fly droned and bumped against the window, and the pain hit me, a sick, heavy feeling in my belly.

"Well," Eleanor said again. "I just wanted to tell you. How sorry I am, I mean."

"Okay," I said. "You've told me."

"Well, I'd really . . ." Eleanor said. She seemed to be having trouble, and nobody was helping her. George and Levi sat silent, looking at the floor. "I'd really like to do something for you," she burst out at last. "I feel so . . . What can I do for you?"

"I believe you've done enough," I said.

It was as if I were standing off somewhere outside, watching myself, listening to everything.

Nobody said anything more, and finally Eleanor rose and started putting on her coat.

"We'd better go, George," she said. "We're supposed to pick Clyde and Louise up at five." She turned to me. "Are you going to the Houstons' New Year's party tonight?" she asked.

"Oh yes. We're going," I answered. "We always go to the Houstons' New Year's party."

We saw the Averys to the door as we always saw callers to the door, Levi and Polly, side by side as always. He turned an anguished face to me when they had gone.

"Do we have to go to Houstons'?" he asked.

"Yes," I said. "Yes, we have to go." I guess that was the first time Levi did something he really didn't want to do. This was the first time there was no mention of a sick cow that couldn't be left untended, no sudden indisposition, no bland excuse to cover Levi's refusal to go somewhere he didn't want to go, do something he didn't want to do. Me, I was like iron; it was only much, much later that I realized how like my mother I was that ghastly day—strong, unwavering, filled with righteousness and rectitude, contemptuous of the frailty that made me want to hide myself like a sick animal.

I dressed carefully, glad for my good, slender figure so newly won back from layers of fat. We went to the Houstons' party, and I smiled and chatted and laughed and drank without getting a glow and longed for the lapse of enough time so that we could leave. I knew everyone knew; I knew I was the classic spouse, the last to learn. I imagined that everyone was watching for weakness, so I lifted my chin and sucked in my belly and fought to seem relaxed and natural and composed. My cheeks burned at the fatuous parade I'd made of my happiness, my joy in being married to Levi, my complete fulfillment in just being his wife. "Fool, Fool," I said to myself and, "Don't let it show, Fool."

That was only the first day, though. For months nothing had any reality for me except the pain and fear, the abject, sweaty fear of losing Levi to Eleanor after all. She'd said she was going to California, but she didn't go, not yet. This was, after all, her first taste of being wanted by two men, even if one of them was only George, for whom her scorn had not abated. We were invited to the same parties, and her complacent enjoyment of being the other woman made me feel clumsy and gauche. To see Levi and Eleanor together at parties was exquisitely painful, and I knew they were meeting privately too.

Even then, if I could have pulled myself together, if I could have brought myself to confront Levi with a choice, with an ultimatum, I might have salvaged something for both of us. But I'd prided myself on being above ultimatums, and I'd had no practice in saying, "You son of a bitch, how could you do this to us?" I couldn't have done it anyway. I was too scared of losing him.

I moved about in a fog, doing all the usual things during the day, longing for night so I could go to bed and hide myself, waking suddenly at two in the morning and longing for it to be six o'clock so I could get up and begin to work. Levi's absences were agony because I knew he was with Eleanor, and his presence was scarcely better because I felt stiff and speechless. He didn't tell me how he felt, and I was afraid to ask him.

I grew thin, really thin, for the first time since the early days of my first pregnancy. I tried eating to comfort myself, as I'd done all the years of my vague unease, but I could swallow very little, and most of that came up so suddenly that I was lucky to make it to the toilet, and I was left weak and gasping.

When, after a couple of months, somebody told me Eleanor had gone to California, I thought Levi might turn to me, but he didn't. I guess he didn't know how, and I think he'd have considered it a weakness. Only once did he suddenly put his head down in his hands and mutter, "Can you ever forgive me?"

My heart leaped up. He *did* care; he did want to stay with me and the kids. I assured him I'd forgiven him. I suppose I gushed. I think I even said, "Someday we'll laugh about all this."

What happened, however, was that he regathered himself almost at once and pulled back into that distant place beyond my reach, and again I was left dumb and bereft, not knowing what to do or how to do it.

CHAPTER THIRTY-SEVEN

When I fell in love with Levi, I went from being emotionally dependent on a mother for whom I had never measured up. I told myself I didn't want to measure up. I couldn't wait to get married and become utterly dependent on my husband for the way I felt about myself. It was an unsolicited burden, a heavy load he never asked for, didn't want, and couldn't handle.

I had changed. From being a smart girl, a girl who flirted and had flip answers and made good grades, I became a Perfect Wife, a woman who concealed her brains and native opinionatedness. I had the effrontery to imagine that I knew, without asking him, what my husband's needs and wants were. I choked down any questions he might not want to answer; I ripped out every tendril that reached out toward being myself. I permitted myself no real existence apart from what I told myself he wanted. I invested all I had into building and maintaining the perfect facade.

I became a nothing. There was no reality or truth in me. When my pose worked, or seemed to, I felt vindicated. How right we'd been, the *Ladies' Home Journal* and I! When it didn't, there was the grinding, gnawing fear inside that put me at the edge of the great emptiness I'd known all along was out there.

Often enough the facade slipped. Occasionally, I made a monumental miscalculation. One of the worst was because of a marvelous idea that popped into my head. I could hardly wait to tell Levi about it. When he came into the house I said, "You'll never guess what I'm going to do when the kids are grown up? I'm going to run for the legislature." I was bubbling, eager for his reaction.

He looked at me coldly. "When you do," he said evenly, "just be sure you find yourself another place to room and board." He turned and left the house.

It's useless to say to someone as benighted as I was, "You shouldn't have taken it from him! You should have stood up on your hind legs and said, 'Look, Buster, I'm me. I'll do what I think is right for me to do. And who the hell do you think you are, telling me I'll lose my home if I run for the legislature?' "

I did nothing of the sort. I took it. I wept but privately. I would not, of course, do anything that would upset this man I loved. His wish was my wish. This was the nature of love.

I really thought it was love. I had no idea it was abject, squalid fear. I told myself the tears were pure selfishness. I didn't allow myself to examine

my feelings. I didn't merely hide my pain; I denied its very existence, even
to myself.

By now I know that in this, as in so many other things, Levi was afraid
of being diminished. I still don't know why, but he was. The man had
everything: intelligence, personality, appearance, and love from others—
overwhelming evidence of love and admiration from every side. I still don't
understand it. I wanted him to think as well of himself as I thought of him.
I was aiming, I suppose, not only at reassuring my husband of his worth
but perhaps also reassuring myself. I didn't want anything to diminish him;
after all, he was my idol too.

I remember a story in one of the women's magazines about a woman
who had it all figured out: how to create the perfect marriage. Her way was
somehow, each day, to anticipate—it must have absorbed all her time—
what her husband's mood would be on his return each evening and to meet it
with the perfect persona to intrigue or comfort him according to his varying
needs. Some way, God knows how, she knew that tonight he'd feel an itch
for the exotic; she was ready with soft, rosy light, perfume of musk and
sandalwood, a costume alluring in its mystery. Another day she sensed that
he'd need help with an office problem; she got out the white-collared Kitty
Foyle dress she'd worn for business before she got married. She sharpened
pencils and perched reading glasses on her nose. For another homecoming
there'd be homemade bread and bean soup and a wife in cotton print and
braids, for a man turned homesick boy.

I was overcome with admiration for this fictional woman's insight, her
art in divining and meeting the needs of the man she loved. Mystery, heady
perfume, and seduction weren't my style, of course, and, besides, they
might be somewhat awkward with the boys in the house. I'd have to settle
for homemade bread and bean soup. I'd be the Kathleen Norris woman,
the one with tawny, sun-streaked hair and a wholesome earthy fragrance.
She waited too, that woman; she also knew that selflessness and constancy
and devotion resulted unfailingly in a happy marriage. No demands, no
requirements, no discussion. Her love and self-abnegation kept the pieces
from slipping out of place, kept the dream from getting lost. The notion
that one person, working by herself, can create happiness for two people
now seems so grotesque I can hardly imagine how I could be so sure of it.

Still, it was all around us, all of us, then. Ministers and educators
proclaimed it; women's clubs promoted it; every magazine confirmed it, in
articles and in fiction: marriage was the only real fulfillment for a woman.
To build a happy marriage was to build America, and it was the woman's

responsibility. The way to do it was to acquiesce in everything, to question nothing, to ask for nothing for herself. To build her marriage was to build the home, the foundation of civilization. To fail in marriage was to fail in everything that mattered.

Grotesque as it was, it was what I believed. Mostly we live by ideas; this one was mine. It wasn't logic that moved me out; it was deciding to live.

CHAPTER THIRTY-EIGHT

I don't give up easily, so it took me a long time. For five years I tiptoed around, terrified lest I say something, do something, that would upset Levi, the source of my existence, and thereby lose him after all. I never even thought of how ghastly it was for Bill and Spence. All I thought about was how much I was hurting. All I wanted was to keep from hurting any more than I already was.

Twenty-five years had passed when I found out how it had been for the boys. I was in Spence's home in Fukuoka, Japan, where he was the American consul, and we'd both been drinking enough to open up and express the pain we'd kept inside us for so long.

"How do you think it was for Bill and me?" he demanded. "Nobody saying anything to anybody, nobody telling us anything. Why in Christ's sweet name didn't you put us in an orphanage and be done with it?"

I couldn't say, "Good mothers don't put their children in orphanages, Spence." I couldn't say anything. I put my head down and wept. We both wept.

Uncle Will had died, Levi's parents had died, Bill was in college, and Spence was in the Marine Corps when I decided I couldn't stand the iciness of life alone anymore. My husband was there, of course. He ate the food I cooked, he slept with me in our bed, and he did his work outside. But after it was over—the affair, the tears, and the brief spurt of remorse—we picked up and went on as if nothing had happened. And in all those years we didn't exchange a personal word, not one. It was as if we'd never known good times or bad times or pain or loss or love.

He backed off. Any time I approached anything personal, he backed way off. I don't know how to explain it. On the face of it, and looking back, it does seem there should have been some way to reach him. I shared a house and meals and a bed with someone I'd loved a long, long time. It doesn't seem reasonable that once he'd withdrawn I could never get close enough to him to know how he felt about me or the way we lived or any of the internal, important things.

It was like groping in a thick fog. I was sure he was in there someplace, but I couldn't find him. I tried; I really tried. Even now I wonder if I could have done something different to reach him. It made me sick and furious, but he could leave. He had a horse and a pickup and a hat to put on his head as he left, a big black hat like the man in the Marlboro ad.

So I left. I couldn't stand it anymore, and I left.

I found a job as housekeeper-factotum to Elmer Rice, a Pulitzer prize–winning playwright whose work I knew and admired and who lived in New York. The job was perfect for me. I loved that big, beautiful, dirty city. I made new friends and a life and a living for myself. I stayed eighteen months and was happy, and then I returned to my husband and the ranch in Nebraska. Partly it was because he told me he loved me and pleaded with me to come back. Partly it was being courted that moved me back—the newness, the excitement of being courted by the man I'd loved so long. Levi had never courted me before—he'd never had to—before or after our marriage. And the promises—they moved me too. I believed them, that everything would be different, that we'd go back to being happy, talking, sharing. I wanted to believe it.

Mostly, though, I went back because I still loved the man. I couldn't give up on my love. It was the force that had made my whole life important to me.

I didn't impose any conditions. When you love someone, it isn't necessary, is it? It's squalid to say, "You Must Do This. It Must Be Understood . . ." I did, in short, what I'd always done. It was what I wanted to do; it was the way I wanted to live.

I guess I thought things would change by themselves, because of the promises. I certainly didn't want to force anything; it wouldn't be any good that way, would it? Yet I found the barriers were still there; the fog that had hidden us from each other drifted in again.

One day I sat in my living room looking out for forty miles across the land, thinking of the years since I'd first seen the Pine Ridge in 1929. I'd seen it a million times since then and never lost my wonder—my astonishment—that this too was Nebraska. I'd grown up on the Republican River near the flatlands of Kansas, seeing corn and alfalfa fields, smelling river and feedlots. Here with one sweep of the eyes I saw desert, hills and prairie, the great buttes soaring up from the plains, and the pine-covered hills sloping down to the cool deep canyons. Here breezes brought the scent of sun-warmed pine needles.

From my window I could see the buttes Sugar Loaf and Roundtop on the horizon. I could see Toadstool Park, named for the great sandstone shapes whose bases have been eaten by the wind into the shape of wine glasses. There, at first glance, you think it's a weird and barren and inhospitable part of the earth, but as you look around you find it's full of life—rock wrens, rattlesnakes, and scorpions. In the spring flowers bloom in every crevice in which they can make a roothold. The coyote, that cheerful, raffish, inextinguishable gamin of the West, trots through this land, alert for the small, unwary creature he can snap up on his way to the prairie dog town. Now and then the meadowlark breaks the silence with her sweet, piercing, gurgling song; overhead a golden eagle wheels, and a vulture sails, tipping this way and that.

After thirty-five years, the Big Dream came to me; the makings of it had been there all along. In the dream there we were, Levi and I, before the blazing fireplace with our guests, drinks in hand—Levi lean, handsome, windburned, charming as always, the perfect host. I would be slimmed down, dressed casually but smartly, with everything in the kitchen under control for the dinner I'd serve a little later.

The house would be in perfect repair, glitteringly clean. The log house would be restored and repolished. Outside, the weeds would be cut and the trash picked up; the cattle would be fenced out so they could no longer walk onto the stone porch and look into the living room windows or tear down the trees and flowers I'd planted.

Best of all, Levi and I, in the Big Dream, would be working together at something we both loved, having company. We would take paying guests for a few months of the year, and in time someone else would be doing the heavy work of raising the cattle and the wheat, while for at least half the year we'd be free to do whatever we pleased.

The Big Dream grew and I knew that if I worked hard enough and believed hard enough I could make it come true.

CHAPTER THIRTY-NINE

Indirectly, my Big Dream was because of the deer. We'd seen them occasionally, beginning in the 1940s. In the 1950s the deer had increased in number. They fed in the fields and from the haystacks. Their evening trek to the hayfields brought them by the dozens. Later we saw more than a hundred deer going to the hayfields as dusk fell, then back into the hills as the sky lightened.

They were inquisitive, like cattle, and not much more fearful. One warm autumn evening I sat in the living room looking at Crow Butte against the glowing sunset, listening to Brahms. As the lead doe reached a point opposite the open door, she stopped and listened. The whole herd stopped, cocking their heads this way and that until the record was finished and I turned on the lights.

As the deer became more numerous, people began to complain of their depredations. They tore at the stacks and consumed a lot of hay, and the pleasure of seeing them had begun to be a rather expensive pleasure. Local people poached them—we poached them—because we liked venison, and the meat helped with the grocery bill. Once Levi brought in an old eight-point buck whose scarred hide bore traces of a full and vigorous life. I thought he'd be too gamy to eat, but the meat turned out tender and delicious. Later the meat of a two-year-old came up rank in the cooking pot, and I made him into mincemeat, eighty-six quarts of it. I chopped apples and washed raisins and messed around tasting that mincemeat so long before I canned it that it was four or five years before I really liked mincemeat pie again.

Poaching wasn't enough to thin the deer to a manageable number, and, when the game and fish commission announced a controlled hunting season, the ranchers were glad. A few local people began to offer room and board and hunting privileges for money. We were a little shocked; as long as anyone could remember, no ranchers had taken money for food and a bed. Almost anyone who came to the door and asked politely could hunt freely on private land—though it was fiercely resented if a person assumed the privilege without such amenities.

Hunting season became a festive time for us; there were friends and friends of friends and relatives from all over the state. Dozens of people stopped in to ask directions or permission to hunt and stayed for coffee or a meal or maybe overnight. Levi was in top form with these people, and I loved cooking and having company.

Only our kids didn't like it. When Nebraska started having a hunting season, they were still going to the one-room grade school across the fields and through the canyon. During the hunting season I made them wear red caps and walk around by the road because some hunters blazed away at anything that moved. Cattle and horses were occasionally shot dead by trigger-happy tenderfeet.

As time went by, my ideas changed. In a few years it seemed we were the only ones not cashing in on the bonanza. I heard people were getting ten dollars a day for room and board and hunting privileges and that hunters gladly slept on the floor in their sleeping bags. Mima Lu Moody had made enough money from one hunting season to carpet her whole house, and I began to think of the warm red wool carpet I'd put over the cold gray-painted floors of the two big back bedrooms if I had the money. After all, times had changed; taking money for food and lodging in 1963 was hardly the breach of decency and hospitality it had been in 1884, when the wayfarer was at the mercy of settlers for his very life. My brother urged us to get in on it; people who stayed with us offered money and couldn't understand why we didn't take it when everyone else did. But Levi said no.

I was thinking of it one day when Cecil Avey, the game warden, stopped in for coffee a few weeks before hunting season. He said, "Polly, the Gate City Hotel and the Hilltop Motel are all booked up, and I've got ten hunters from Omaha who need a place to stay. I know what Levi says, but that's silly. Times are changing. You're cooking and cleaning all through hunting season anyway; surely you can use a little extra money. I know Levi likes Chivas Regal, but you do the work, and how many electric carving knives can you use?"

Cecil stayed, drinking coffee and chatting, until Levi came in and, almost as if he'd never opposed the idea, agreed that we'd take the hunters and the money they'd bring in.

I got Robyn, a neighbor's daughter, to help me, and we waded into the log house, so long unused; as we cleaned it, I thought what a good little house it still was. We set up makeshift beds, I borrowed blankets and pillows, and we laid wood ready for lighting in the fireplace. We cleaned the big house too, and I planned meals and went to town for boxes and boxes of groceries and supplies.

Everything worked according to plan. Our guests arrived late in the afternoon before the opening day of the season and were as appreciative of the beauty and comfort of the place as I'd imagined they'd be. Levi was affable, mixing drinks and telling hunters where to find deer.

I don't suppose our hunters were all rightists and drunks and members of the National Rifle Association; however, they were, to a man, males of the great American middle class, who are uneasy until they've established themselves, in much the same way the dog lifts his leg to the tree or the lamppost.

It began in the living room as soon as they had settled down and had drinks in hand; I overheard some of it. They traded stories about the big deals they'd handled, the money they'd made, and the important people they'd met. Those who hadn't handled big deals or met important people boasted about the huge rigs they drove or the bulldozers they operated, all in the self-deprecating way of the good ol' boy. The rich ones had been to Africa and Alaska big game hunting, and nearly everybody had been fishing or hunting in Canada. And, just to be sure there was no doubt about anybody's masculinity, they joked about homosexuals and penis size.

I made rib roast for dinner, along with the bread I'd baked earlier, a green salad, and apple pie with cheese.

The hunters ate hugely and praised my cooking extravagantly. Robyn and I had our dinner after they'd finished. She said as we sat down, "They're like a bunch of kids, aren't they?" They were; they really were. They had come to Northwest Nebraska on a hunting trip to get away from the little women and to be with the boys, and they really were like kids.

Some of the hunters left for bed before we were through washing dishes and getting things ready for breakfast; they wanted to leave the house before five, they said. "Great, breakfast would be ready at a quarter past four," I said. "No, no, too much trouble for you," they said; they'd come in later for breakfast. "Nonsense," I said, "no trouble at all."

When my alarm sounded at 3:30 I hit the floor, and by the time the hunters stumbled into the kitchen there were sausages and scrambled eggs and baking powder biscuits.

There were no deer on the trail as the light grew this morning, only a fusillade of rifle fire that we heard off and on all day. Some hunters bagged a buck deer at once, some a few days later. I had to come out and admire the gutted carcasses hanging in the garage. Why not? I asked myself. You eat meat, don't you? You're making money from the slaughter, and it's necessary to thin the herds out. Don't be a hypocrite just because you'd rather not look at all the sightless, staring eyes and the blood that's dripped onto the concrete floor.

Some of the hunters came in for a hot lunch. For those who wanted to stay out to hunt, I made brown-bag lunches. That evening they gathered before the fireplace and drank and talked of the present hunt and of other hunts they'd been on, told and retold in tedious detail.

These first hunters were all pleasant, courteous men, and I had things to watch in the kitchen, with my own bourbon and water and the current Double-Crostic puzzle, kept handy near the stove. The hunters didn't miss my company and didn't consider my staying in the kitchen standoffish; after all, hunting is a time for drinking and being with the boys, a time to get away from women, and the men who kill animals for fun are more likely than not to look on the kitchen as the proper place for a woman.

This party stayed four days, and when they'd paid and gone, leaving liquor just as the earlier nonpaying ones had done, it seemed to me I'd made a good deal of easy money, even after paying the household account for the food and liquor out of my own, new account. It hadn't been that easy, of course; I'd worked my head off, but it had been exciting and stimulating, and the good green bills and crisp traveler's checks made me feel rich.

After hunting season the beautiful canyons of West Ash, East Ash, and Dead Horse were garbage dumps. Robyn and I drove up the roads in all three canyons, as I'd done each year after the season was over, to clean up the mess. I stopped the pickup every few hundred yards or so, and we walked up and down the road with our gunnysacks, gathering up beer cans and food wrappers. At a favorite picnic place on East Ash Creek we got bushels of garbage and trash: broken glass and clay target pigeons, paper and plastic plates and tumblers, beer cans and whiskey bottles. We started a fire with the driest of the paper and cooked hot dogs. Before I dropped her off at her home on Dead Horse Creek, we were both beginning to bog down and feel discouraged by the senselessness of having to clean up the junk after every hunting season. When I got home and unloaded at our own junk pile behind the hill, I told myself, " Someday I'm going to get a bulldozer and at least cover this mess over with dirt."

After the season local people found animals that had been wounded and had escaped to drag themselves around or die. Even people who disliked deer hated seeing an animal suffer needlessly.

CHAPTER FORTY

By January after that first hunting guest season, with the holidays over and three cold months of little to do looming ahead, I'd done a lot of thinking and a lot of estimating. It was obvious that hunters were easy to please and didn't mind makeshift accommodations, so the deer seasons and the wild turkey seasons would be a reliable source of income. But I had other ideas of what could be done over the long range if we were to take paying guests during the spring and summer and autumn.

I could put the ranch—so beautiful, so beautiful!—into the kind of order I admired when I saw the places on the tableland. I could get fences repaired so the cattle couldn't walk through the yard and tear down the little trees I'd set out—twenty-seven of them one time, of which only three survived—or leave deep hoof prints in the grass I cut from sod on the creek and flops of dung on our stone porch.

The log house could be weatherproofed, the window glass replaced. It could be made into two units, one upstairs and one down, for housekeeping guests. And, with only the two of us living in the big new house, there were the back bedrooms, empty most of the time and in winter closed off entirely to save heat.

I didn't want a dude ranch. I didn't want people who needed to be organized or entertained. I wanted guests who'd like us for exactly what we had: a working cattle and wheat ranch in a remote area of superb natural beauty, horses to ride, real cowboys and real Indians, nothing hoked-up or touristy. I'd have the hunters, and I'd have my "real" guests. Already in my dream were these real guests, who would like to walk or explore or loaf or go sightseeing. They wouldn't need or want to be entertained. I knew the kind of people I wanted, and I thought I knew where to find them: through the classified section of the *Saturday Review of Literature.*

And, when the guests had gone and the weather got dreary and the money was in the bank, we could have a neighbor or someone look after the place for a while. Then we could see the world, and, when we got tired of traveling, we could come home to our own place, which we both loved.

When we first moved to the west place in 1933, I'd found a wilderness of rubbish around the one-room tarpaper shack—bottles, rusty tin cans, bits of crockery and broken glass turned purple by the sun, half-rotted gunnysacks embedded in the earth, bleached animal bones, scraps of lumber, fence posts and unidentifiable metal, and at least a million bent and rusty nails. Some were the old handmade square nails used in the early day; some were scattered widely, and others were concentrated in spots where old buildings had been torn down.

I took a bucket and began picking up, picking up, picking up. I carried my haul over the hill to the big junk pile, where it would be out of sight. I stacked boards that could be used or burned in the stove, and I had bonfires when I'd raked up enough dry weeds and paper and cardboard and rags together. I started around the shack, and as I moved my circle out toward the old tumbledown shed, thatched with barley straw, there were times when the place took on a look of neatness and prosperity. But always after a hard rain or a high wind more rubbish turned up, and I'd begin again with my rake and bucket.

I'd long since lost the battle, except for an area of about fifty yards around the house we lived in, the new house. Levi built and built and built, and, as the new barn and garage and shop and dwellings rose, the trash grew all around them and threatened to engulf us. It simply wasn't in Levi's nature to put anything away. He got around to repairing a piece of machinery only when it was urgently needed, and debris dropped from his hand wherever he was through with it. Unless somebody else picked it up, it stayed there.

My attacks on the accumulation were sporadic. Still, at the back of my mind there was always a vision of the place as it could be: swept and varnished, repaired and freshly painted, like the farmsteads of the descendants of the Germans who lived up on the tableland.

Wind, rain, snow, hail, and dust had wasted the log house for ten years. At first, after we'd abandoned it to the mice and the weather, I'd go over after a storm and sweep out the snow that had sifted in or swab up the water under doors and windows. Then some of the windowpanes were broken by hail, and it became more and more depressing to see what neglect and disuse were doing. Finally, it had come to be only a storage place for junk I wasn't ready either to use or to dispose of. When I went into that house for any reason, I got out as quickly as possible. Like many other things I'd cherished, it had been lost to discouragement and apathy.

I was sure Levi would see the possibilities as soon as the money began to come in, so I went ahead with my plans. I used the few thousand dollars my mother had left me, I borrowed money, and I ran up bills at the lumberyard and the hardware store and the furniture store. I worked early and late, I hired high school kids to help me, and I hired an old man who could do carpentry and plumbing and wiring. I carpeted the back bedrooms of the big house. I cleared the rural slum that had grown up from a fifty-yard perimeter around the big house, and I even got a big fourteen-year-old boy to load and haul out the knee-deep manure from the barn.

In the log house, fired by ideas of what I could do, I got rid of the junk. I sanded and refinished floors, washed and waxed the logs and the paneling, installed a bathroom and a kitchen upstairs, and refurnished the downstairs rooms. I bought new beds and made curtains. I painted and papered; I stained and refinished old chairs and tables. During those first years guests often arrived to the smell of new paint and a welcome from a hostess who'd worked until one and gotten up at five.

Some of my ads were overly lyrical; I realized it when I saw them in print. Those paeans, besides costing a dollar a word, probably put some people on their guard. A vacation in Nebraska? For anyone who'd ever smelled Omaha's stockyards or traversed the dreariness of Highway 30, Nebraska was a place to be gotten through, not a place to stay for a period of weeks that might amount to the whole year's vacation. And it wasn't cheap. I charged the real guests half again as much as I did the hunters. Partly, that was because I thought that what was too cheap might not be valued; mostly, it was because it took a lot of work to surround my guests with the kind of order and comfort and beauty I wanted them to have.

I had letterheads printed on fine paper, and every inquiry was answered with a personal letter and color snapshots. Even after a good deal of correspondence, it was a leap of faith for those people to embark by train to Crawford or on Frontier Airlines to Chadron, where we picked them up. The guests were mostly from eastern and midwestern cities. They'd been moved by my ads to ask for more information and finally to pay the deposit and come to our ranch.

But they came.

I'd cleaned the house for the hunters; I buffed it to a high gloss for the real guests. As fast as towels were used they were replaced with fresh ones for guests and hunters alike, but for the guests there were fresh wildflowers in the rooms every day and a bowl of fruit beside the bed. The table was set with place mats and cloth napkins for the guests; for the hunters it was the bare clean board and paper napkins. Food was good and plentiful for hunters and guests alike; for guests I took the time and trouble to make it look beautiful. Uncle Will's house—he had died a few years earlier—would do only for hunters, who didn't seem to mind the mice running in and out and their acrid stench. The real guests were lodged only in the log house and the big house.

By the time guests arrived, everything was at its best. I was tired from all the work of preparation, but I was ready to relax and pay them the compliment of making it all seem easy and effortless.

The first ad brought us Emma, a librarian at a great university in New Jersey. She was small and shy and charming, and she loved everything about the ranch. She'd been amazed, as she rode through the Sandhills on the train, to see scores of miles of rolling hills dotted with little lakes. Only occasionally did she see a moving vehicle on the highway that paralleled the tracks.

All the guests were openly astonished at the beauty of the countryside; who ever dreamed Nebraska had such glorious land and sky? And, if there was some surprise at finding the house so spacious and beautiful, with hundreds of books, a grand piano, and music, it was lost in their pleasure at all they saw.

Emma said she'd like to see the local flora and fauna. I called Doris Gates, a professor of biology at our little college. Together with a bunch of her students we trooped up West Ash and down Dead Horse Canyons.

I'd always loved walking in the hills and canyons; I thought I knew them. I'd always thought myself observant, but that day, as Doris parted the grasses to reveal tiny wild orchids growing at the foot of a clump of hackberry trees, as I watched the cliff swallows shoot like little rockets, each into her own nest on the overhanging creek bank, and saw, actually *saw,* a brilliant western tanager, I began to realize I'd seen but never observed the world that lay about me, the beauty at my doorstep. Except for the broad sweep of the countryside, I hadn't had my eyes open.

My eyes began to open that day. When we went back to the house and sat at the big table with coffee and fruitcake, I asked Doris where I could get a book like the green-backed one she'd carried all day which showed us what to watch for.

"Why, that's Roger Tory Peterson's *Field Guide to Western Birds,*" Doris said. "You can get it at the college bookstore, or any bookstore, but I'll trade you this one for a fruitcake."

That day I began to be a birder, and the next Christmas, to signify my status, my daughter-in-law gave me a disreputable pair of old sneakers and a hairnet.

Our guests' privacy was carefully maintained; if they wanted to go with Levi or me, they were welcome. If they wanted to rest or take a solitary walk, they were left alone. Our privacy was not quite so assured, of course. We had to be available to answer requests and possibly to talk when we'd really rather read or be silent.

One of our guests was Dorothy, a schoolteacher who talked without ceasing from the time she opened her eyes in the morning until she went to bed at night. She confided to me, "Floyd, my husband, may he rest in peace, used to say, 'Dorothy, you talk too much. Why don't you let somebody else talk once in awhile? Why don't you just shut up for awhile?' But," she said, "I just love to talk."

I murmured something, checking the thermostat on the oven. Dorothy really didn't expect any response. As I heard the washing machine click off, I went to the utility room to put the towels in the drier. Ah, I thought, the sun's bright, and there's a good breeze—I'll just hang the sheets and tea towels out on the line. I started the bath towels in the dryer and went outside with the sheets in a basket. I hung them out on the line, enjoying the sun and the wind, and all the time I could hear Dorothy in the kitchen, talking, talking, talking. She didn't pause when I came in and began to clean celery under the tap. I don't know whether she knew I'd been out of the house or not; it really didn't matter to Dorothy.

Almost all our guests offered to help with the housework, but almost all gladly stopped offering as soon as I told them I preferred to do it myself, at my own gait and in my own time. Not Betty. She insisted on helping me in the kitchen.

I went to class three times a week at our little college in Chadron, twenty-five miles away. Since I finished at eleven, I had plenty of time to do my errands and get home to fix lunch at 12:30. But Betty thought I was brave and overworked. She urged me not to change the towels in the bathroom each time they were used and not to iron sheets, and on class days she said, "Don't worry about a thing, I'll just wash up these few dishes, and they'll be out of the way."

I wanted the butter on a clean dish at room temperature. Betty put it in its messy dish into the refrigerator. I liked to do most of my dinner preparation in the morning, but I couldn't with Betty messing around at the sink and the cabinets. Worst of all, Betty thought once she'd got the dishes wet they were washed. I told her what had worked with all the others: I prefer to do things my own way at my own time. I tried tact, I tried mock severity, I bit my tongue so as not to be rude, and in the end I left the kitchen while she did all the things she thought would help me, and later I rewashed the dishes and put things back my way. Except for that, Betty was a perfect guest.

The most effective help I got were the local girls I got in from time to time, as I needed them. Robyn, who lived up in Dead Horse Canyon, and my grandniece Mary, who lived on East Ash—each had a squad of younger brothers and sisters. They were used to working hard and could do anything, from saddling a horse to scouring a skillet.

I wondered a little when Jo Struempler, a birding friend, asked if I could use Bobbi, her thirteen-year-old daughter, as a helper. Her father was a professor at the college; her mother was an R.N. Would the kid work as Robyn and Mary worked—up early to get things started, late to leave the kitchen spotless for the night? Would she mind being so far out in the country, away from her family?

I warned Jo. "The work's hard," I said. "She'll be a long way from her girlfriends."

"Don't worry about that," said Jo. "Bobbi's tough."

Bobbi was tough, all right. She began shaping me up almost immediately.

"You don't miter your sheets?" she said, as we made the first bed together.

"My aunt Marg showed me," I began, apologetically, "but I didn't get the hang of it."

"You do it this way," said Bobbi firmly. Then, after we'd made the bed, she said, "That wasn't so hard, was it?"

It wasn't. It made a lot of sense.

A walk of steppingstones between the houses made sense too. What didn't make sense was Bobbi's building the walk, by herself, evening after evening, when she'd already done a full day's work.

"I want to," she said. "Just see how nice it looks."

All those girls worked long and cheerfully. All of them were funny and silly and a joy to have around. I still don't know how I could have been so lucky.

Without exception the people who came to us from the *Saturday Review* were pleasant to have around, some of them such fun to talk to that I had to discipline myself to stop chatting and get on with my work. They liked to walk, and they liked to see what was going on at the ranch. Levi took some with him to check on the cattle, on horseback or in the pickup. They learned a bit about fence fixing, and they asked a million questions. They went with us on errands and were delighted with the easy neighborliness of a town where you could get a check cashed at the bank without standing in line or showing identification. All the cashier said was, "Oh, you're with Polly and Levi? Pretty out that way, isn't it?"

Some people rented cars and drove around sightseeing. I drove some of them to the museums, Fort Robinson, Sowbelly Canyon, Agate Springs Ranch and the fossil beds, and the Pine Ridge Indian reservation.

We barbecued and had picnics up in the canyons. Most of our guests liked a drink or two—Levi and I liked a drink or two—and everyone looked forward to the time toward evening when we sat on the big stone porch and watched the sunset or before the fireplace in the living room when it was cool enough to have a fire. Some guests played the piano. One middle-aged couple, who had been dance instructors, performed a spectacular tango in our big living room.

There were writers; business people; secretaries; painters; photographers; a ballet teacher; an editor for the *Encyclopedia Britannica;* a naturalized German woman who'd become a police detective in Dade County, Florida; an eminent heart surgeon with his wife and grandchildren; a black police officer from Kansas City at a time when there weren't many black police officers in America; and a teenager who rode his motorcycle out from Omaha.

They came from New York, Connecticut, Pennsylvania, Minnesota, California, Montana, Colorado, and Nebraska. Some came from Canada and England. Many of them returned to us again and again. The shortest stay was ten days, the longest eight weeks, a stay that stretched well into October and made me begin to think about the possibilities of having Christmas and New Year's guests.

The hunters showed up dependably, as I'd been sure they would, spring and autumn, turkey and deer seasons. At first the hunting seasons were for Nebraska residents only. As the game increased, they were opened to out-of-state hunters, and there were license applications from Georgia, Ohio, Illinois, Texas, Kentucky, Iowa, almost all the states. Some of the hunters were prosperous businessmen, some had good jobs in large corporations, and some were construction workers and small-town storekeepers.

My mind rejects the idea of categorizing people. As time went on, however, my gut put guests into four general classifications: one, the boarding guests who came to us through my ads in the *Saturday Review;* two, the housekeeping guests from the same source; three, the housekeeping guests from other advertising; and four, the hunters. I guess the hunters got their place at the bottom of the list because they seemed unable to relax in a group. Even with all the drinking and heartiness and joshing, they put a lot of effort, and tension, into competing. Money was important, of course, but among that group the emphasis was on showing the crudest kind of toughness and contempt for those they considered inferior—women, blacks, Mexicans. There was a sort of brutish innocence about it—I've killed more animals than anybody here; I've traveled farther to hunt them; I can handle the biggest goddamned rig Detroit ever built.

The hunters would converse with the womenfolk only when one of them had to come into the kitchen to use the telephone and perhaps wait for the party line to be free. Then Robyn and I found them mostly likable, well-intentioned people. In a group, however, their good intentions were obscured by the jockeying for position.

Chris was drunk nearly the whole time he stayed with us. He was with a party of five or six others who drank only after they came in from hunting. Chris reeked of whiskey when he came to breakfast; he put his highball beside his plate at lunch; he carried a flask in his hip pocket; and by late afternoon, when everybody came in from the hills and canyons, he was bombed. He'd come into the kitchen and engage me in conversation while he made a fresh drink or reinforced the one he had. He told me how much money he made with his automobile dealership and his construction company. "Mama," he said, "could wipe me out if she ever divorced me. She'd come out of a divorce with a quarter of a million dollars, just like that!" He told me he tried to keep Mama happy—buying her a Cadillac and a mink coat and a diamond bracelet—and, to show me how lucky Mama was, he put his arm around me and tried to fondle my breast.

There was mildly bawdy talk at the table. I don't mind bawdy talk and four-letter words; I use them myself with appreciation of their color and vigor. But I broke in when there were racist stories and racist epithets. One comment that *nigger* and *kike* were filthy words to me was enough to stop them from being used around me, except for one old fellow, the very caricature of a retired army colonel. He just didn't get the point and finally had to be phased out.

CHAPTER FORTY-ONE

People in the area were beginning to get interested in the possibilities for earning tourist dollars. The Raums, who lived near Twin Buttes out north, came to talk to me about the guest business. I showed them what I'd done and told them what I'd learned, what the costs were, what I was charging, and what I hoped to realize from it when the notes were paid off. We kept in touch, and soon I learned they'd borrowed and started developing their beautiful Rimrock Ranch for guests. They worked night and day, as I had done; they built comfortable housekeeping cabins, they got together a string of manageable saddle horses, and they laid in a stock of staples that guests could buy. When we went to visit them, we found them building roads and furnishing the cabins, and I felt a sort of proprietary pride in what they'd accomplished.

Ellis Hale, as nice a guy as you'd ever want to meet, had a program of country and western records on the local radio station. He'd grown up on the tableland, and everyone liked him; local merchants advertised on his program. He began to call himself Peabody—it may have been his middle name—and to dress as country pop performers dress, not rhinestones and satin but galluses and a string tie. He acquired a cornpone accent, and his fans loved it.

Ellis also wanted to help promote the tourist business, and he had an idea he thought would add to Crawford's charm. He gathered up all the old wagon wheels he could find and painted them in various colors—pink, blue, green, yellow, purple—and embedded them in boxes filled with dirt near the curbing all along Main Street. It was a tremendous amount of work. Then he got some people to help him, and they suspended a sign across the street reading "WAGON WHEEL ROAD."

I didn't agree with Ellis at all. I didn't think old Main Street, where Big Annie and her girls had welcomed the white trail drivers and Tish and her girls had sported with the black cowboys and troops, needed its name changed, especially to something as cute as "Wagon Wheel Road."

By this time I was writing a column for the weekly newspaper, and I did a series on the beauty of our area and the folly of hoking up a good thing. What we had, I said, couldn't be duplicated anywhere—Las Vegas, Miami Beach, Disneyland—with any number of millions of dollars and public relations people. Tawdry and phony offerings would drive out the good and real and honest, I argued, and we'd never be able to get it back. Our only chance, I said, was to get the kind of people who'd like us because of our remoteness and quiet, our history and natural beauty and our laid-back, cow country atmosphere—people who'd be put off by fake quaintness.

Plenty of people could participate and make money from tourists, I maintained, by providing board and lodging or by driving people around to points of interest. I suggested that a substantial cottage industry in real western crafts could be developed, with the beautiful things people, white and Indian, made and sold in their homes or shops—quilts, wrought-iron, furniture, and all sorts of handiwork.

I criticized the Game and Parks Commission for encouraging hokey promotion of travel in Nebraska, and I criticized it for setting up a sportsman's award and naming it for Buffalo Bill Cody. In eighteen months Cody slaughtered 4,280 buffalo for the Kansas Pacific Railroad under conditions about as sporting as shooting fish in a rain barrel.

I urged that we continue our good western way of relaxed, genuine hospitality. I derided the proposal that business people and store clerks dressed up in fake western clothes with plastic fringe would improve sales. I suggested that we continue to speak as we'd always spoken; the western accent falls pleasantly on the ear, but the "Haowdy Podner" routine doesn't fool anybody. I asserted that the wagon wheel, beautiful in itself and symbolic of the great movement West, would be cheapened by being painted up and overused as a display.

My articles infuriated many people. Letters came to the editor, almost incoherent in their rage. Who did I think I was, anyway, using "high-sounding words never found in the cowboy's dictionary or the sheepherder's bible and certainly not western or everyday words"? Another reader asked, "Why does she want to tear our fair city to bits?"

"At least the people who put forth the time and effort to honor Main Street as Wagon Wheel Road were trying to do something for the town and not against it."

"The ornaments on Wagon Wheel Road were put there only for those who love and enjoy them, not for those who criticize."

"Senile and confused . . ."

"Taking in loot from hunters and tourists and then turning around and being critical . . ."

"If she doesn't like northwest Nebraska, why doesn't she go live somewhere else?"

Some signed their names; most didn't. All the people who supported my views on Northwest Nebraska and its possibilities for visitors signed their names. Some were local people, some were people who had lived in the area years before and moved away, and some had been our guests. All loved the natural, remote beauty of the Pine Ridge, and all hoped to preserve the hospitality that gave the area and its people their unique character.

As to the views of people who'd been paying guests at Richardson Hereford Ranch, letters came in denouncing them as brainwashed—by me, I guess—and, while supporting efforts to bring tourists to the area, angrily demanding why the good citizens of Crawford should pay attention to the opinions of a bunch of outsiders.

It took a while for the hubbub to die down. No polls were taken, no public relations experts were consulted, no professional advice was sought, but finally Ellis stopped setting up new colors of wagon wheels. Northwest Nebraska continued to be itself, and visitors continued to find that quite enough.

For six years my guests came to Richardson Hereford Ranch. I worked hard, my mind seething with plans, I paid off all the bills and some of the loans, and I made part of the Big Dream come true. And, when I saw that the dream was as far away as ever, I chucked it all and went to live in Los Angeles, where I paid off the last $2,500 loan with money I earned working as a cook-housekeeper.

The end of the Big Dream, when it came, was abrupt. I found myself looking down on the lights of Los Angeles in mild astonishment, realizing that I'd finally given up on the last of the little dreams I'd used to prop up the big one, that I could look back at it, knowing that it was gone, without pain. All my life I've heard that regret is vain, useless, a waste of time, and I believe it. Yet here I was, fifty-six years old, and I'd hung on to the rotting carcass of a marriage for twenty years after it had died. Mostly, I'm a bridge burner. I'll never know why it took so long for that bridge to catch fire.

CHAPTER FORTY-TWO

I learned shorthand and typing in 1928 from Mrs. Hazel Duckett, whose college roommate had been a girl named Lucille LeSueur. Lucille LeSueur later took the name Joan Crawford and became a big movie star. The glamour of that circumstance soon wore off, but the things we learned, as Mrs. Duckett held us at practice on those old manual Remingtons and Underwoods, never has. I became a very good typist, and at shorthand I was sensational. In 1970 I could still take shorthand at 135 wpm, after forty years of using it for nothing more than taking down a recipe from the radio and writing my Christmas list so my family couldn't read it.

I'd worked in an office when I got out of high school in 1930, but those jobs had been in rural Nebraska, and the last of them had been thirty-seven years ago. Could I make it in a big city office? Could my typing and shorthand skills be recovered? I wasn't sure.

I knew, however, that I could cook and clean, so the ad I put in the *Los Angeles Times* was a double-barreled one, reading: "Mature woman; skilled shorthand/typing, cooking/housekeeping. Expensive." If I could get the pay I had in mind as a live-in cook-housekeeper, not paying rent or buying food, I could pay off faster the money I still owed in Nebraska for guest ranch promotion. The *expensive* was to weed out the people who wanted a drudge to work seventy hours a week for minimum wage.

I got a lot of inquiries. One of my first interviews was with a handicapped man who lived in a beautiful penthouse apartment in Westwood. I liked him at once; he was intelligent and charming and, best of all, perfectly matter-of-fact about spending his life in a wheelchair. "I'm not a sick man," Mr. Morewell said. "I don't need a nurse; I take care of all my personal needs." He was a Christian Scientist, he added, and he'd learned to live a good life by ignoring his limitations.

And by having money, I thought; that must help.

We had a long talk, and the more we talked, the more I liked him. He didn't feel sorry for himself and didn't expect anyone else to. His needs and wishes were simple, he told me. He worked at his investments in his office at home a couple of hours a day, he liked reading, and he liked having his friends visit him and take him out for drives.

Mr. Morewell was a lonely man; I could see that. And he said it would be wonderful to have someone he could talk to and listen to. He was fortunate in having good friends, but to have a cultivated woman running his home and being his friend—well, there were no words for how much it would mean to him.

I'd have my own private quarters, Mr. Morewell said; unfortunately, he couldn't show them to me until the present housekeeper had gone, but in any case I was to feel free to use the whole apartment as if it were my own. "I take up very little room myself," Mr. Morewell said, smiling. "The apartment practically takes care of itself. And whatever you want to order from Gelson's will be delivered."

He offered me the job on the spot. He didn't demur at the $650 a month I was asking plus expenses. Of course not, I thought; money is not a consideration for a rich man.

I couldn't give him an answer just then, I said; I had appointments for other interviews. I'd promised those people, and I'd have to keep those appointments.

"Of course," said Mr. Morewell. "I quite understand. Before you go, though, I want to make just one request. Whether you come to live here and run my house or not, you will be my friend, won't you?"

"Of course I will," I promised wholeheartedly.

What a fine man! I'd be proud to be his friend.

A few days later I called to tell Mr. Morewell I'd take the job. There had been one other offer that had appealed to me hugely, as housekeeper to a beautiful, vibrant woman who wrote "Days of Our Lives," a highly successful soap opera. I'd been torn between the two.

Mr. Morewell was delighted that I would be moving in. I'd have a parking space under the building, he said. Everything was set: I'd arrive the next day about ten.

Joe, the parking attendant in Mr. Morewell's building, was pleasant. He got someone to cover for him while he helped me take my luggage to the penthouse.

Mr. Morewell greeted me warmly and told Joe to take my bags to my room. It was smaller than I'd expected, not much larger than a walk-in closet. "Oh well", I thought, "the place is huge, and, with having the run of it, this would do nicely." I was unpacking when the bell summoned me to Mr. Morewell's office.

He said cheerfully, "I've invited a few friends for dinner this evening. Seven people—with me that's eight—just right for the dining room. What do you think you'd like to cook? If you get your order in to Gelson's within, say, an hour, it will be delivered by 1:30."

I went to the kitchen to check out supplies and equipment and to make some quick plans. Lists, that's the only way to go, and I began at once to get organized. What should I serve? Good Nebraska food, of course; that's what I'm good at, and everybody likes it. I'd order yeast and flour and see if there would be time to make rolls.

It was 4:30 when I got everything located, the table set, the roast in the oven, the vegetables washed, the rolls and dessert made. With dinner scheduled for 7:00, that gave me only time for a quick shower, a flop on the bed for twenty minutes with my eyes closed, and a look for clothes that I could wear without pressing.

I was busy in the kitchen when Mr. Morewell's friends arrived. They were mostly young, and they were all Christian Scientists. Mr. Morewell introduced me as a jewel, and they all first-named me. I told myself not to be stuffy; that's probably what people do in California.

I hadn't run across the bar supplies; I guessed somebody would take care of cocktails. I could do with a drink myself, and I hoped that, when a bartender arrived, he would know that Mr. Morewell's jewel would like a drink.

But, in going in and out of the dining room and catching a few words here and there from the living room, I began to realize there weren't going to be any drinks. Apparently, being a Christian Scientist precluded drinking anything of a spirituous nature. It didn't preclude being pleased with oneself, though; then and throughout dinner I heard the waves of self-satisfaction and thanksgiving that through the grace of Mary Baker Eddy they were not like other people but were indeed as people should be.

The dinner went well. My food was praised, and I was praised. But I was getting tired. It had been a long day, and I wanted to go to bed. When the guests finally left the table and I could finish up, I fell into bed like a rock. Thank God that was over.

I woke early, feeling rested, and started unpacking where I'd left off. It was funny, now that I had time to think of it. A company dinner for eight when I'd barely arrived. How like a man!

Mr. Morewell's bell rang, and I went to his room. He was in bed. "The dinner was nice," he said briefly. "But you did go on to bed and leave me to shift for myself. Fortunately my friends were still here, and they did what was necessary. They're such wonderful people." He glanced up at me. "Well, pull the covers back! You've seen a naked man before."

I agreed that I had and hastened to pull the covers back and to follow all the other directions Mr. Morewell gave me as I helped him into his wheelchair, to the bathroom, the toilet and the shower, and into his clothes and back into the wheelchair and into his office.

"I'll have my orange juice and coffee in here," he said. "Later I'll have a couple of scrambled eggs and toast. I'll let you know when."

When I returned with the orange juice and coffee, Mr. Morewell had a list. He said, "Take the slacks and jacket I wore yesterday and press them. I like my clothes kept up day by day. About the laundry," he went on, "You'll send my shirts out; I'm rather particular about them. My sheets too. There's no ironer. Everything else we do here. The laundry room is on level A. One of the other maids will tell you how to run the machines, or you can go to the maintenance office for assistance. The houseplants should be watered twice a week, and I like the leaves clean and shiny. You'll find all that sort of thing in the pantry."

"For dinner this evening I think something a little different," Mr. Morewell said. "Are you familiar with Julia Childs's *French Chef Cookbook?*"

I wasn't, but Mr. Morewell pointed out recipes for the dishes he'd selected, and the directions were clear.

"Just six this evening," he said. "Better vacuum the living room and the dining room and polish the table; they weren't quite up to standard last night. We'll use the same place mats as last evening. You can do them when you do the rest of the laundry." As I started to leave, he said, "Oh yes, do keep the kitchen door closed during dinner; it isn't pleasant for the guests to see into the kitchen."

I made lists as I drank my coffee. I called my order in to Gelson's and went to clean Mr. Morewell's room, turning things over in my mind as I worked. What in hell had the man meant when he'd told me he took care of his personal needs? I didn't know how to lift a grown person, and I didn't want to learn. And what was this crap about "we" do all the rest of the laundry?

I found a big hamper full of towels. I told Mr. Morewell I'd be in the laundry room.

"After my breakfast, please," he said. "Two eggs scrambled very gently, two slices of whole wheat toast lightly buttered, and a bit of the English marmalade, in the stone jar, you know."

When I got to the laundry room, a couple of maids were chatting as the machines hummed. We introduced ourselves—their names were May and Jessica—and they showed me how to work the machines.

"I'm working for Mr. Morewell," I said.

"Hmm, yeah," May said. "You like workin' for him?"

"So far so good," I said. "I just started yesterday."

"Hmm, yeah," May said. "Company for dinner yet?"

I was startled.

"Reason I asked," May went on, "My cousin Louisa worked for Mr. Morewell a while. Man can't get out and go, likes to have company every night. Louisa don't like to cook for company every night. You livin' in or out?"

"In," I said. "I don't have to pay rent that way."

"Hmm, yeah," May said. "That's right, don't have to pay no rent. I don't live in, got my own place. I like to go home and turn the key in the lock; don't nobody bother me. I've tried it both ways."

That evening and the ones following were very much like the first one, except that I waited up to help Mr. Morewell into bed.

There were guests for dinner every evening. I brushed and pressed his clothes every day, I cooked breakfast and lunch when Mr. Morewell felt like having them, I took him to the bathroom when he needed to go, I washed and ironed every day, and I responded to the bell.

"I've been sleeping well," he said. "Haven't rung the bell in the night even once, have I?"

I ran into May again, and we talked.

"I been doin' this domestic all my life," she said. "Boy, I've worked for some beauts!" She laughed. "You new to this, ain't you?"

I admitted I was.

"Thought so," she said. "Well, you get all kinds in this business. There's them that works, there's them that don't work no more than the law allows, and then there's them that works the ones that works. All kinds. Mr. Morewell, he's had a lot of help goin' in and out of there. Them other ones, though, they didn't do no housecleanin', no laundry, didn't do nothing but wait on him and cook for that everlasting company. He had a cleaning service come in twice a week, and they sent all the laundry out. Didn't see none of them women down here washin' every day."

A cleaning service, the laundry sent out? I was astonished.

"And a Japanese fella come in twice a week and took care of the houseplants," May continued. "A lot of houseplants, ain't there? "I've seen all different kinds," May went on. "I got some good ones now, nice actin' folks, both out to business every day, eat out a lot. O' course," she added, "they don't pay as well. It's okay, though. There's some that gets more money, but a lot of nastiness goes with it. Don't get much for free in this world."

"Mr. Morewell didn't balk on the money," I said. "And I put it high. I don't mind working, but he said he took care of himself, and he doesn't. And I thought—"

I stopped and was ashamed. I didn't want to tell May about his remark about having a cultivated woman in his house, someone he could talk to, someone he could be friends with. I looked at May, and she looked at me.

"You green, honey," she said softly. "You don't know nothin' about this business. Prob'ly had your own nice home back there where you come from?"

I nodded.

"Done your own work, maybe had somebody in to help once in a while? Treated 'em nice, set 'em down to the table with you?"

Yes, yes, yes.

"It ain't that way out in the world," May said. "In the world it's dog eat dog, and them dogs is awful hungry."

"Mr. Morewell isn't mean," I said. "But all that money . . . and his friends are always talking about how good they are!"

"Hmm, yeah, Louisa told me," May said. "Prob'ly believe it too. If you gettin' high pay, them people don't see nothin' wrong with takin' it out of your hide."

The fourth day Mr. Morewell told me friends were taking him out for lunch. Since there would be only four at dinner that evening I said I thought I'd drive to the beach while he was out. Mr. Morewell was as pleased as if he'd thought of it himself.

"Wonderful!" he said. "Have a great time! My friends will bring me home about 2:30. You'll be back by then?"

Of course. I hadn't been out of the building since I'd arrived, and nothing had been said about time off, but I'd be back by 2:30.

At the garage Joe offered to bring my car up for me.

"You haven't been out much, have you?" he asked.

"I haven't been out at all," I said, rather shortly, and then, because Joe was so nice, "Mr. Morewell keeps me pretty busy."

"Yes," Joe said, "Mr. Morewell keeps people pretty busy. Been a lot of people in and out of there. I thought maybe this would work out. The others, some of them, maybe didn't do things to suit him, but I heard him telling his friends you were just what he needed."

I stopped at the first liquor store I came to and bought a six-pack of cold beer and a fifth of Kessler's bourbon. I sat on the sand in silence and thought about my job and about what May had said and what Joe had said.

The next morning I told Mr. Morewell I was not going to be able to continue. He was genuinely shocked.

"You don't like it? Is anything wrong?" he asked.

I told him lifting him was too much for me, that the work was too much for me, and, because it was still rankling, I told him I was offended by being first-named by people I'd never met before.

"But they're *friendly* people," he said.

"I like friendliness," I said. "I don't like familiarity. I didn't first-name them."

"But you could have," Mr. Morewell said. "You could have. They wouldn't have thought a thing of it."

"I wouldn't first-name people I'd just met," I said. "I'd consider it rude."

I was enjoying this. I'd heard so much self-satisfaction, self-congratulation, and self-righteousness that I really enjoyed sticking in a few pins. The only thing was that Mr. Morewell seemed truly puzzled.

Finally, he said, "I guess I have a lot to learn."

"I guess you have," I said.

He sighed. "I don't know . . . Could I ask you a favor? Would you stay on just until I can get someone else?"

Of course I would. I wouldn't leave him with nobody to cook for him or get him to the toilet or get him in or out of bed.

I called the woman I'd turned down to take this job, the writer of "Days of Our Lives." If she still wanted me, I said, I'd be there as soon as Mr. Morewell could get someone else. She was pleased, and we laughed together. I told her I was eager to make the change, but I felt bound to stick it out until Mr. Morewell found somebody. I hoped it wouldn't take long.

The bell rang. Mr. Morewell wanted another cup of coffee. When I brought it, I set the cup down awkwardly; coffee sloshed over the cup into the saucer.

"Oh dear, I guess I got it too full," I said.

Mr. Morewell said angrily, "Do you think you could manage to be a little more careful?"

Suddenly, without knowing how it happened, I was the Dowager Duchess of Dawes County, Nebraska.

In tones so icy and measured I couldn't recognize them as my own, I said, "Mr. Morewell, I will not be addressed in that tone, now or in the future. Is that quite clear?"

I was in the kitchen with a cup of coffee when the doorbell rang. It was a young woman who had been a guest at dinner the first evening. "Mr. Morewell would like your social security number," she said timidly. "I'll bring your check to you." I was out of the place in forty minutes.

Joe came up to help me with my luggage. As we got into the elevator, I said, "I'm not sure this thing will work. I'm so lighthearted and lightheaded, it may just shoot up through the top of the building when I push the down button."

We ran into May in the garage, and I told her I was leaving.

"I ain't surprised, honey," she said. "Didn't see how you was goin' to keep it up; you looked so tired every time I saw you. Want to tell you something," she went on. "You out of here now. You get you a little place of your own. When your day is over, you just shut the door and turn the key. Makes all the difference, I can tell you."

I told her I would, knowing that I lied through my teeth. I got my bottle of Kessler's out of the suitcase, and we drank to my deliverance.

"Just like the children of Israel," Joe said, laughing. "Still a few Pharaohs around, but you're gettin' away."

"Lots of luck, honey," said May. "We be thinkin' of you. Lots of luck!"

The year with Pat Fleischmann went faster than the four days with Mr. Morewell. I'd be with her yet if she'd been able to afford me.

Everything about Pat was extravagant: her beauty, her personality, her tastes, her skill at writing a soap opera that enthralled hundreds of thousands of fans five days a week.

I'd never watched a soap opera before. I'd heard bits of "Stella Dallas" and "Helen Trent" on the radio, but those characters seemed ludicrous, wooden, and two-dimensional.

Pat's characters were complex, crafty, and malevolent. They were torn between yearning for true goodness and manipulating others ruthlessly. In these contemporary morality plays they retreated or advanced or sent messages not with a fan or a flower but with a glance, a gesture. To a newcomer, lost in the intricacies of plot and personality, the meaning was esoteric, but the regular audience understood it perfectly. It was composed of housewives and other workers in Boise, Idaho; Rochester, New York; and Crystal Springs, Mississippi. Viewers in Detroit, Chicago, farms in North Dakota, and everywhere else understood these complexities. Pat designed the show, almost before our eyes, to be understood by every one of them. Subtleties that were lost on me were clear to all the steady viewers and to Berta, who typed the scripts.

Sometimes it was like foreplay: a touch of romance, a suggestion of ineffable pleasure, and the certainty that presently one would be transported. At such times the suspense became nearly unbearable, and at exactly the right moment there was a great crashing release, a crisis of yearning achieved, or almost achieved, which, like any good orgasm, simply intensified the eagerness to begin again.

Pat was smart and inventive, but there was more to it than that. She had an instinct for what matters to people: sex, money, power, and love. Also, Pat knew that the deepest yearning people have is for intimacy. Five days a week people who couldn't or wouldn't or had never had a chance to give themselves up to caring for another human being sat in their houses or apartments or factory lunchrooms and felt close to people they had learned to care about. They loved and hated the characters, and they wrote letters to them full of comments and warnings.

My God, I thought, all these years moviemakers have talked about escape, when what people want is involvement. TV comes into the familiar places where people live and work and feel comfortable. Daily, people could see and believe in someone only a bit different from themselves. They could live in a dimension their imaginations couldn't have created. They could be with people they cared about, knowing they'd see them again tomorrow. There was a sense of continuity, a steadiness, to it: I'll be here, and they'll be there, and we'll take up where we left off. And all threat-free for the people who fear intimacy more than anything in the world.

Pat was larger than life. She could do anything and had done almost everything. She said she could cook and clean and run a house, and it was true.

"I can wash and iron and hang wallpaper," she said. "I learned working for my room and board. I was eleven when my sister got me my first job. Our parents were both dead, and Gretchen was only nineteen herself. She sure couldn't do everything for me. She knew this woman, and it seemed like a good chance for me to get a job. It was too; I learned to work, and I learned some other things."

"The woman was nice," she said. "But her husband—one day I was at the sink washing dishes, and that old guy walked up behind me and put his hand right up my crotch.

"It must have been instinct. I'd never even heard of karate, and there weren't any courses then in women's self-defense. But I whirled around and brought my knee up, hard, right into his groin. Just blind dumb luck. He screamed till you could have heard him in Azusa!"

The big party Pat gave was extravagant too, of course. I'd supervised the kitchen remodeling, the cleaning crew, ordered the flowers, dealt with the caterer, taken care of innumerable details, but on the night of the party I was, on Pat's orders, to be a guest.

An enormous swan, carved in ice with arched neck and lifted wings, appeared on the buffet table in the tent. Whole fruits were heaped on the cloth, and waiters brought chilled platters of bright melon balls. There was a whole turkey, a whole roast goose with lace pantaloons, and a whole piglet with an apple in its mouth.

There were crisp raw vegetables and salads, breads, and cheeses. A bartender manned a fully stocked bar, and waiters in cummerbunds skillfully opened wine. Smart maids with frilly aprons circulated with canapés and drinks. The weather was heavenly. A little combo played show tunes.

I walked around talking to people, enjoying myself, happy that everything I'd done had turned out well, delighted to be at a California party talking to people in the entertainment business. I had a distinct impression, even while doing it, that I was drinking rather more than was good for me, and the suspicion was borne out when I rose late the following day with a horrid taste in my mouth. I didn't care.

Early on February 9, 1971, the earth heaved and woke me up. I lurched through the kitchen hearing the spookiest sound of my life so far—the slosh, slosh, slosh, of the water surging from one end of the pool to the other.

"Only an earthquake," Pat said, when I ran into her bedroom. "California has earthquakes."

One day as I was watching the butcher cut lamb chops for our dinner, he asked me if I knew when Mrs. Fleischmann would be able to give him a little something on the bill.

I said I'd mention it to her. "There've been a lot of bills, with the remodeling and the party. She's probably just overlooked it."

I was sure this wasn't true and suspected the butcher knew it as well. My paycheck was mailed from the accountant's office twice a month, and I was pretty sure all the bills were paid in the same way.

I told Pat what the butcher had said, and she asked me, "What did you tell him?"

I told her, and she said, sharply, "Don't ever give anyone we deal with the impression that we're pinched! It's nobody's business what my expenses are. He knows perfectly well he'll get his money!"

Startled, I said, "Of course," and went to the kitchen.

Berta explained it. "The whole thing in show business is to give the impression of success."

"I know, I know," I said. "But the butcher does know about the remodeling—I heard Pat tell him—and he knows about the party. None of it was a secret. Is it any disgrace to run a little short?"

"Not to you and not to me," Berta said. "But in this business it is, or they think it is. It's one of the most competitive businesses in the world, and everything's based on impressions. It isn't how you're doing; it's how people *think* you're doing. You try to give the impression that you're turning down offers because everybody's after you to do this, do that; you have more money than you can spend, and you've got no sags or wrinkles or doubts. You've met some of these people. You've heard them talk. Hollywood ain't called Tinsel Town for nothing."

"But Pat has made it the hard way—an orphan working for her room and board when she was eleven; she doesn't make any bones about being poor and doing hard work."

"Sure," Berta said. "It's rags-to-riches, and she's proud of it. But there are never enough riches in this business. She's Pat Fleishmann, successful writer of a successful show. Money coming out her ears, partner in a production company, looking like a million bucks at openings, big wheel in the Screen Actors Guild—she wants it all. She's got to put up that big front, without a single hairline crack in it."

I was still thinking about it. How could a woman be so matter-of-fact, so ready to do whatever needed doing, so open, and so caring? When I'd been down a day or two with the flu, Pat had cooked the meals and brought me a tray with a camellia on it!

Berta told me, "Pat's smart and successful and gorgeous. Maybe," she continued, "just maybe because it was so damned tough getting where she is that it's all got to be made to seem easy now."

In May the roof fell in on me; I lost my job.

It wasn't wholly unexpected. The Broadway, where Pat had sent me to buy a copper crepe pan, had confiscated her credit card. I hated to tell her about it, but she dismissed the whole thing; it wasn't worth worrying about.

I didn't really worry, but I wondered. How was it possible for a person who earned $1,500 a week to be in debt to everyone? Really I knew how it was possible; my observations had given me the answer. But how, why, when disaster loomed?

I knew my own pay was high; with $650 a month and no expense for rent and food, I'd been able to pay off the last of my notes in Nebraska. I was worth the salary; Pat had told me I was. She loved having her house well run; she loved my adaptability: I could fill in anywhere I was needed, from typing a script to cleaning the garage to making a perfect soufflé to being a fourth at bridge.

When she told me I was laid off, she described the cutback as a technical matter between herself and Harold, her accountant. "He has everything pinned down to percentages," she said. "His calculations indicate I'm paying

too much for household help. He may be right," she added. "I can get a
Mexican girl for $40 a week."

I knew that was true; most of Pat's friends had Mexican maids. All of
them were devoted, hard workers; they had to be, with the Immigration
Service breathing down their necks and a dozen replacements eager for a
job.

I'd known, really, that something would have to change; I just hadn't
realized I'd be the first to go.

Pat told me to stay as long as I liked, to consider her home my home.
She gave me a generous bonus—I wondered what Harold had said about
that—and promised she'd give a glowing recommendation about me to
anyone who asked.

I told her I was going to try for a nine-to-five job in an office; I was
sure now that I could handle it. I'd stay with my son Bill and his wife in
Pasadena until I found an apartment.

A year and a half later, when Pat gave a baby shower for Berta, she invited
me. I was pretty sure the refreshments wouldn't be ice cream and cake. Sure
enough, there was a combo playing show tunes and the buffet set up under
an awning near the pool. Caterers served hot canapés, quiche, smoking
brioches, spinach and mushroom salad, baked Alaska, and champagne. I
wasn't really surprised; however, I think Berta's aunts and her grandmother,
babushkas all, were somewhat startled by the opulence.

CHAPTER FORTY-THREE

I picked the employment agency out of the yellow pages; it was sheer
luck that I got Helen Scott as my employment counselor. That meant
Helen interviewed, evaluated, and tested me and finally got me hired by
an employer for a job she thought I could handle.

Helen and I liked each other. She was a round, pretty little redhead with
an easy manner and a firm way of testing. I wondered what was wrong
when she looked at me after the shorthand and typing tests and said, "How
long did you say it had been since you worked in an office?"

"Thirty-seven years," I said. "Why?"

"It just seems so unlikely," she said thoughtfully. "I have to tell you
that you've tested the highest of anybody we've ever had in shorthand and
vocabulary and right at the top in typing. I've shown your test results
to Elaine—she's the boss, you know—and she's skeptical." She paused a

moment and said, "I kind of hate to ask this, but would you mind if Elaine tested you again?"

I didn't mind, and I did the tests again for Elaine. They came out slightly higher than they had the first time: 137 wpm in shorthand and 82 wpm in typing. Elaine went into her office and checked everything again, then called Helen and me in.

"If you could see some of the klutzes we get in here!" she said, and Helen nodded. "Type about 35 wpm, never heard of shorthand or even speed-writing, vocabulary of a backward seven-year-old—and we're supposed to get 'em a job! We do too, sometimes. Work with them, talk to them, train them, think you've got it through their poor heads, encourage them, send them out, and then you get a call from the employer—one candidate didn't even show up after the first day. Or they lose messages, insult customers, God knows what. When that happens, we don't get paid and probably lose the business for good. And now . . . well, Helen, what are we going to do?"

They both looked at me critically.

"She could probably get away with forty-seven or -eight," said Helen, "But we could run into problems. I don't know . . ."

"Probably wouldn't be worth it," said Elaine.

"Wait a minute," I said. "The way you two are looking at me makes me wonder if my nose is running or what."

They laughed, and Elaine said, "What we're talking about is the law that says employers can't discriminate against people on account of their age. We know the law, they know the law, but they do it all the time anyway. Would you believe we got one guy said he wanted somebody under twenty-two and he wanted her blonde, pretty, and slim but with big boobs. I told him he could get into trouble with the Fair Employment Commission demanding specifications like that, and he said, 'You don't think I'd put it in writing, do you? And if you or anybody else accused me of it, I'd deny it, and just see how far you'd get.' I had that conversation, sitting right here at this phone," she said, "Knew his name and his law firm and everything, and I knew damned well he wasn't kidding. There wasn't a thing we could do about it except tell him we didn't want his business—and you don't do that in this line of work. You equivocate. It's all you can do."

"There's only one smart way to handle this," said Helen. "Just be very careful where we send Polly, promote her on the basis of her test scores, and let the interview do the rest. I'll bet she'll do one hell of an interview."

Helen was right about that. I loved being interviewed. Here I was, a fifty-seven-year-old ranch housewife, a woman who hadn't worked in an office for more than thirty-seven years, and I felt poised and confident, God knows why. I felt none of the nervousness people talked about. I didn't feel defensive about my age or my newness to the business world. I answered questions matter-of-factly, saw that things were going well, and ended each interview myself before it became tedious for either party.

"This is great," I told Helen. "I love driving around L.A., seeing the city, going into all those offices, meeting all those people. How about finding me a job just looking for a job? This is the field you ought to get me into. If you were any good as a counselor . . ."

"There you go being a smart-ass again," Helen said. "I'm getting good reports on you. The banker in Westchester wants to make you an offer. How would you feel about working for her?"

I didn't want to work for that woman. I did think it would be great having a job near the beach, but that was all I liked about the Westchester setup. First of all, I thought banking wouldn't be my best field, since I can't balance my own checkbook; second, the job required working Saturday mornings; and, third, I simply didn't like her. She was Mrs. Middle America personified, with a full list of the fears and prejudices that turned me off. When I said I'd like to live at the beach, she warned me about living so near "hippies." She asked my political affiliation, and I told her, politely, that I thought it was none of her business. A year or so before I left Nebraska, I'd changed my party affiliation from Republican to Democrat. This change had bothered Rosie, the Dawes County clerk, but from her I didn't mind. She'd said, "It's your right, of course, Polly, but *why?*" and had seemed startled when I said that, if Nixon and Agnew and Mitchell represented Republicanism, I didn't want to be a Republican. I felt sure this woman's bank was Nixon country, and I knew myself well enough to know I'd be unable to conceal my distaste for old Richard Milhous. It simply wouldn't work out.

Turning down the job with the banker in Westchester wasn't a mistake. What I did next was.

I saw an ad in the *Los Angeles Times:* secretary to the circulation manager of the *Times* itself. I took the job.

I felt bad about bypassing Helen; she'd worked so hard for me. Still, I explained to her, working in a newspaper seemed right for me since I'd grown up in a newspaper environment. I liked the office, I liked the pay, and I thought I liked the man I was to work for. "It's okay," Helen said. "You have to do what's best for you."

I found a furnished apartment in an old building called the Engstrum, right across from the big library and within easy walking distance of the *Times*. It was none too clean. "You like to clean things," I told myself. "Here's your chance to have a lot of fun." Conversation was impossible unless you closed the French doors onto the balconies on Fifth Street, to lessen the traffic noise a little. I'd never seen many cockroaches before, but at the Engstrum I battled them ceaselessly. Still, at the Engstrum I was living in the middle of a big beautiful city I'd come to love, and from my two small balconies I had a view that was simply spectacular.

The problem was my new boss, Paul Kleckner, was a maniac. He was topnotch in his job but impossible to work for. In a few days I learned he'd had fourteen secretaries in the last year and a half, and every one of them had quit. I made up my mind I wouldn't quit.

"He didn't used to be so bad," one of the women told me. "But something's happened to him. I wanted to tell you the day you came in for your interview, but you know what would have happened to me if he found out I'd warned you off."

Every evening I went home and poured myself a stiff shot of bourbon as soon as I got my shoes off. Every morning I woke up with a leaden feeling in my belly; every day with him made me feel that way. What a fool I'd been to take the job!

Helen called me one evening. I could have wept for joy. She asked me how my job was going, and I told her.

"I'd have called you except that I was ashamed to," I said.

"Never mind that," Helen said. "I'll be keeping my eyes open for you."

I didn't hear from Helen, and I didn't call her. My days were nightmarish. I got drunk as soon as I got home. Weekends I went to Pasadena to see my kids and grandkids, and I got drunk there too.

The day I'd completed one full month with the *Times*, Paul Kleckner called me to his office and fired me. I could see the other people in the office knew what had happened; if I wouldn't quit, he'd told the others, and save the company the unemployment penalty, he'd damned well fire me. All I felt was overwhelming relief.

"That call on hold is for you, Polly," Margaret said, as I got back to my desk.

It was Helen. "You get off at four, don't you?"

"Yes," I said. "But I'm leaving as soon as I get my things together. I just got fired."

"Oh my God, what luck!" Helen said, and I agreed with her. "Can you get over to the State Mutual Building in half an hour?"

Yes, I could, and yes, I did. I tested well, I interviewed well, and I took the job she'd found for me.

I started my new job on Monday, having not missed a day of work.

CHAPTER FORTY-FOUR

I went to work as secretary to the regional head of Eastman, Dillon, and Union Securities, a brokerage and investment banking firm. I liked the man I worked for, and this time I was right about him. His name was Baum; as I grew to know him, I thought it should be spelled *Balm*.

I'd been through a nightmare. Mr. Baum, in an attempt to replace his longtime competent secretary, had gotten a couple of klutzes of the sort Helen and Elaine had told me about. His most recent attempt had good skills, but after the first day, people told me, she'd shown up at work looking like a bag lady. And, when J.C. (Jesus Christ, some said) Cleary, the company's big boss, visiting from New York, asked her to type up an envelope for him, she'd told him she was too busy!

I knew rather less about the brokerage business than a pig knows about Sunday, and I made a couple of monumental gaffes the first week or two. Mr. Baum was nice about it, and I learned from my mistakes and never made them again—not the same ones anyway. I organized my desk as I'd organized my kitchen at the ranch and at Pat's. I learned that I *could* do things I'd have sworn were impossible.

When I was forty I had a lousy memory; at fifty-seven I developed a phenomenal memory. I put hundreds of telephone numbers into my head and pulled them out on cue. I'm sure there's a trick to it, but I still don't know what it is. I learned to remember scores of addresses, complete with zip codes; appointments for Mr. Baum and me; names and functions of people in the company and other companies; organizational structures; and, most of all, how to pace myself to meet my deadlines. I learned to be efficient. I learned to make it in a difficult, demanding job.

And I loved it. Politically, socially, instinctually, the corporate environment and the stock market had no appeal for me. Yet I loved working in the very midst of it.

Mostly it was because of the people I worked with. David Pearson, a senior broker, said, "Now remember, I'm very interruptible. Anything I can answer for you . . ." and he meant it, every word of it. Cathy and Cheryl, secretaries to Mr. Baum's chief assistants, covered for me when I goofed, dropped whatever they were doing to help when I needed a hand, and guided me through scores of spots that were tricky for me simply because I didn't know what I was doing. I was the ultimate greenhorn; they made it possible for me to cope.

I loved the jargon, the in feeling you get when you speak in terms laypeople don't use. Everything was exhilarating—the pounding urgency, people rushing around, phones ringing, intercoms squawking, rumors flying, market going up, falling back, going up again, people caring what the market did, planning their lives by what it did. I learned, and I learned fast. I kept track of hundreds of details, mailed out reports, covered four phones, made Mr. Baum's days run smoothly, kept annoyances away, took and transcribed a voluminous correspondence, and answered questions from everywhere.

No dusty frontier office, this. I was in the heart of the financial district in one of the world's great cities. I was secretary to the regional head of one of the ten biggest brokerage and investment banking firms in the United States. I dressed smartly, and I was brisk and efficient. I'd achieved what I'd dreamed of from the first days in Hazel Duckett's commercial classes in Franklin, Nebraska, in 1928. I was really something.

In fact, I was a nincompoop, a rube who'd just fallen off the turnip truck. I was so innocent it was pitiful.

Helen Scott had done the salary negotiating with Dick Parker, head of operations at Eastman Dillon, and Mr. Baum had confirmed it to me. My starting pay was low, Dick told Helen, because of the horrendous struggles he'd had in getting somebody who could handle this very heavy desk; New York was still complaining about the personnel problems. What we need to satisfy New York, he said, is somebody who can prove herself—then the possibilities were enormous. There'd be an automatic fifty-dollar raise every three months until my pay reached the correct level for secretaries to heads of regions. For such an important executive as Mr. Baum, Dick said, who knew where it might go from there? The whole key was performance.

My performance wasn't just good; it was excellent. When Helen called Dick to find out how I was doing, the reports were glowing. The first raises came on schedule, and the company gladly paid the fee to Helen's agency. When Helen and I got together for a drink to celebrate, she kissed me, and we promised to keep in touch.

"You're really making me look good, baby," Dick told me. "Bill Baum thinks I'm a genius for finding you. It's worth a lot to him to know things will be taken care of when he's gone so much. I owe you lunch."

Coming into the company at fifty-seven meant I was too old to be eligible for the pension or profit-sharing plans. Dick and I talked about that too.

"It's a company rule," he said. "Nothing we can do about it. But Bill understands the problem. You won't lose by it. Everybody says it's nice to hear him laughing so much. I don't think he's ever had anybody working with him before who made him laugh so much."

We did have some laughs. Mr. Baum liked to twit me about being a women's libber; I called him a male chauvinist pig. He offered me tickets to Republican dinner dances; I urged him to support the American Civil Liberties Union. He professed to be shocked that I boycotted lettuce and grapes to help Cesar Chavez's campesinos; I jeered at Spiro Agnew's pomposities. He bought a good electric typewriter at a police auction and carried it to my door at the grubby old Engstrum building as a gift. I'd found my niche. I had it made, I told myself.

Then I saw a memo from New York saying pay increases were frozen. But because my pay was still well below standard for my job, I was sure it didn't apply to me. But, when the date for my automatic increase passed with no more money in my paycheck, I asked Mr. Baum about it.

"Oh, didn't you see the memo?" he asked, not quite looking at me. "You must have; you put it on my desk."

I could see he hadn't thought I'd bring it up. Secretaries didn't.

"The raise was to be automatic," I said, "until I reached standard pay for this job. That is, if my performance was satisfactory."

"Oh, it's satisfactory, Polly," he said, "more than satisfactory. You know that. I'll see what I can do when I'm in New York next week," he added. He turned quickly and picked up the phone.

The answer, when he returned, was no. He said he hadn't been able to swing it for me. I looked at him and didn't believe him. He knew and I knew that he hadn't tried. This man, a member of the board of directors, a wheel in the company, a man with a huge personal fortune, had not gone to bat to get me a lousy fifty dollar a month raise.

After digesting the shock overnight, I went to Bob Bothner, a man I liked, respected, and fully trusted.

Bob at least looked me in the eye. "It's a directive from New York," he said. "The company's hurting, and raises had to be frozen."

"But Bob," I said, "I came in at well below scale for an executive secretary, and Dick promised, Mr. Baum promised, that if my work was satisfactory . . ."

"Oh, your work's satisfactory," Bob said. "Bill thinks you're the greatest. It's just that economic conditions . . ."

"Economic conditions to me are my paycheck, Bob," I said. "That paycheck decides if I can get a couple of new tires for my car and if I can take my grandkids on a camping trip. Can I send my Aunt Marg ten bucks so she can go downtown in a taxi instead of the bus? I have to pay bills, and I need to make plans. How can I plan if the company goes back on its promise?"

"I really am sorry," Bob said, and I knew he was. "It's not your fault, it's not the company's fault, and it's not Bill's fault. I know he likes your work."

Yeah, I thought. Sure, he likes my work, and he likes the way I run his office. Sure, he likes the way I organize the promotion luncheons and handle his appointments and greet his callers. He likes me, and I like him. But this is money we're talking about. It's what he lives for, but he doesn't seem to know it's what clerks and secretaries live *by*.

I asked Dick, someone else I considered a friend. The answer was the same.

"How about the people in the cage—they don't get their raises either?" I asked. "I know they were promised."

Dick admitted those employees would not get their raises, at least for now. He told me the company's position would improve and we'd all be taken care of. "The company's hurting," he said, "The company . . ."

"Those prize trips to Hawaii for the brokers who sell the most," I said. "If the company's hurting so much, how can they . . ."

"That's incentive," Dick said. "Gets the guys really breaking their necks to produce. When conditions get better, selling stocks is what will have made them better."

I couldn't believe it. I'd seen a lot in the corporate scene that shocked me, but this was my first personal experience of the fact that corporations regard employees as fodder—no, nothing so valuable as fodder—as straw, to be used as bedding for bosses to walk on, lie on, and as insulation to shelter the companies from cold or heat. If the employees become a nuisance, they can be thrown away.

I quit my job.

It was a reckless thing to do, and it marked the beginning of a really difficult time. There were two or three years that seem, even in retrospect, to have been unrelieved torture. They weren't, of course. I had friends and fun and, of course, my periods of irrational, idiotic euphoria, but, taken as a whole, those were hard times.

CHAPTER FORTY-FIVE

Born in almost the exact center of the United States, I'd never seen a sea or ocean until, at nearly thirty, I saw the Gulf of Mexico. Yet at my first sight of it—the edgeless expanse of blue water and mist and whitecaps—I felt for the first time what I always feel at the edge of the sea: a sense of coming back to where I belonged.

I felt the great presence of the ocean all the time I lived in Venice, California, on the Pacific Ocean; that's why I moved there. On long summer days I walked to the beach after work.

I liked the social atmosphere of Venice too. I liked its benign disregard, its offhand pride in its resident crazies, and the sense of community fostered by the colony of elderly Jews who'd retired there for the climate and the low rent. I liked helping with the bake sales and picketing Safeway for the campesinos.

Now that I live in the very heart of the big, dirty, beautiful city called Los Angeles, I go to the beach less often but always with the same feeling when I do. I like to watch the little sailboats from the marina bobbing and tacking until dusk, and I like to talk to people.

Looking back, there really isn't much I'd be willing to change, not if it meant missing anything else. I could have been smarter, of course, but it's too late to worry about that now.

Each time everything has seemed just right, each time I thought I'd found it all—the work, the love, and the ideal way to live—something brought change to me. Mostly, I didn't seek it; like a leaf floating downstream, I bumped up against things, a rock or a twig. Or like a minnow, darting here and there as others darted, something always set me on a new course. I had to make the moves I made, and I don't regret many of them.

But I chose life, all the way, and that choice, the choice to live, was the hard one. It was the one that meant wrenching out the most deeply embedded forces in me, the inertia that would have kept me from living.

I've begun to sort out the ideas that matter to me, the ones that stay the same through every shaft of light and shift in perspective.

Love is the answer, of course. That's not going to change, no matter what happens to any of us. If humankind lasts, love will last, all the kinds of love there are.

There is a passage—I think it was written by Sister Mary Corita Kent—which sums up what I've tried to do with my life.

Choose life—
Only that
And always
And at whatever risk.

To let life leak out
To let it wear away
By the mere passage of time
To withhold giving it and spreading it
Is to choose nothing.

—30—

Afterword

by Karl Spence Richardson

After finishing her memoir, my mother continued working in Los Angeles, living in the heart of downtown L.A. Polly loved big cities as much as she loved the buttes and vistas of northwestern Nebraska.

In 1996 my mother underwent a medical episode—never satisfactorily diagnosed—which left her mentally unimpaired but unable to take care of herself. Given my mother's strong preference for living alone, I was surprised when she agreed to move back to Nebraska, to the Ponderosa Villa, an assisted living facility in Crawford, where she would have a roommate.

The move to Crawford was an unqualified success. My mother's roommate was Juanita Phipps, a woman who had lived all her life in Sioux County, west of Dawes County, where most of my mother's memoir takes place. Juanita was a terrific person, interested in everything. My mother and Juanita hit it off immediately and grew fonder of each other as the months went by. My mother told me she considered Juanita the sister she never had.

After living at the Ponderosa for almost exactly one year, my mother died on May 1, 1998, shortly after her eighty-fourth birthday. The days from the beginning of her decline until her death were few, something any son or daughter with an aged parent can appreciate and be grateful for. My mother had never been very interested in organized religion, but she asked that a passage from John 15:12 be read at her memorial service and printed on her remembrance: "This is my commandment, that ye love one another, as I have loved you." She also asked that her ashes be scattered on Crow Butte. My brother, wife, and I went to the top of Crow Butte and threw her ashes into the wind. I take comfort from knowing her ashes are there. I hope she can see the ranch the way she saw Crow Butte thousands and thousands of times during her life. I feel as she felt after her father died. "Wait till I tell Mom," I've thought hundreds of times. "She'll get a kick out of this."

A couple of people at the University of Nebraska Press asked how my mother could write so well. After all, she was not an author. She had only a high school education, having been forced to withdraw from the University of Nebraska by her family's lack of money before completing even one year. Polly wrote so well because she loved the English language and loved to read. An unabridged Merriam-Webster dictionary occupied a place on her kitchen counter where one might have expected to find kitchen utensils or cookbooks. She had a sensational vocabulary and loved Double-Crostics, incredibly difficult word puzzles that were published in the *Saturday Review of Literature*. She loved to argue about the meanings of words. She worked hard on this book. She wanted to leave a legacy for her family and friends, and writing the book no doubt was cathartic for her.

Politically, Polly was an unabashed liberal. She felt that the government has an obligation to correct the injustices in America. Polly could not abide racial epithets. Sadly, some Crawford residents assumed the inferiority of African Americans, Hispanics, or Native Americans, even though they knew few if any people from among these groups. When I was in high school, more than once my mother rode the train to Omaha—then one of the most segregated cities in the country—to join protest marches organized by the Urban League against housing discrimination in Nebraska's largest city. If someone had told her, "Discrimination in a city four hundred miles away doesn't affect you," she would have said, "The hell it doesn't. It affects you too."

My mother cared about money less than anybody I've ever known. She appreciated expensive and elegant things as much as anyone, but she thought that working hard for the sake of accumulating money was misguided. Unlike many people who grew up in the Depression, my mother felt money was for spending, not saving. As my father said, "Polly gets money back in circulation." She lent money to acquaintances, some of whom, it was clear, would never repay it. Before she died, I, as the executor of her estate, asked her if she wanted me to try to recover these debts and distribute them to her grandchildren, the only beneficiaries of her will. "What debts?" she asked. When I reminded her, she said, "I'd forgotten all about them," and so she had.

My mother was an emotional woman. The deaths of her father, her brother, and especially her youngest son, Charley, devastated her. She could not speak about those losses without weeping, even decades after they happened. She loved and admired her father and brother, and their deaths caused her to focus more intensely on her husband and sons. When Charley died, she was totally bereft.

My mother was not a saint. Polly could, and did, hold grudges. She could be quick to anger and slow to forgive. She had a mercurial personality and made little attempt to hide her contempt for small-mindedness, ignorance, and prejudice.

Although I am hardly unbiased, I believe my mother's book makes a special contribution on three levels. First, it is an account of a time and place that few young Americans know much about. Although our family never considered itself poor, until I was about ten years old we did not have indoor plumbing or electricity. Having one's children go to a one-room country schoolhouse is not something most Americans can easily imagine today.

Second, the book gives a picture of rural and small-town America that was capable of generosity and broad-mindedness and which worked hard to improve itself. Yet, at the same time, these communities harbored such organizations of hatred as the Ku Klux Klan and judged people by the color of their skin or their religion.

Finally, the book is a valuable portrait for Polly's friends, family, and those interested in her life. After reading my mother's memoir, my friend Larry Skogen wrote to me, "I feel I know your mother better than I know my own."

The book is something I will give to my children and grandchildren, and I hope they will pass it along to their offspring. Polly was a unique and fascinating person; I'm glad this book will give those who never met her a chance to know her.